CONFESSIONS OF A MINOR POET

Also by Phil Brown

Plastic Parables: selected poems (Metro Community Press 1991)

An Accident in the Evening (Interactive Press 2001)

Travels with My Angst (UQP 2004)

Any Guru Will Do: a modern man's search for meaning (UQP 2006)

The Kowloon Kid: A Hong Kong childhood (Transit Lounge 2019)

CONFESSIONS OF A MINOR POET

PHIL BROWN

MELBOURNE, AUSTRALIA
www.transitlounge.com.au

First published 2025
Transit Lounge Publishing

Cover design: Peter Lo
Author image: Jade Ferguson@VisualPoetsSociety
Typeset in 12/17pt Adobe Garamond Pro by Cannon Typesetting

Printed in Australia by McPherson's Printing Group

A cataloguing-entry is available from the
National Library of Australia
ISBN: 978-1-923023-41-3

For Sandra and Hamish
and in loving memory
of our beloved Sarge

CHAPTER 1

HOW TO READ A DISGUISED WATERMELON

A SURFER should have a nickname. You don't give yourself one, it is bestowed upon you. Rabbit, Minnie, Doris, Nail, Sharkbait … and so it goes.

You just hope the nickname assigned to you is a good one.

Let me take a step back. There I was one day, walking to the water's edge – or trotting, really, as surfers tend to with a sense of excitement – with my new surfboard under my arm. I was feeling pretty good about having the sleek new shooter tucked into my armpit and as I paused to let the water run over my feet, to acclimatize to the coolness, someone called out to me … using the nickname I was stuck with.

'Hey Browneye!'

That's what you get when your surname happens to be Brown. Not ideal, admittedly. If you are a Brown you are doomed to end up Browneye. I must point out, though, that I have never mooned anyone knowingly. I had to cop it sweet, being Browneye, and it has never quite worn off. I recall returning to the beach a decade after leaving the Gold Coast and, pulling up, I was greeted with: 'Hey Browneye, how's it hanging?' Time stands still at the beach.

On this sunny day long ago, with a blue cloud-flecked sky above and a foamy shore break below, I turned to see the grommet who had hailed me. He came closer.

'What's that writing on your board?' he asked.

'A poem,' I said.

'A poem? A fucking poem?' He thought about it for a few seconds then added … 'That's cool. A bit gay … but cool.'

In the Seventies it was common to have illustrative adornments on surfboards, airbrushed waves or sunsets, idyllic hippie scenes with the occasional palm tree. I once had a board with a rainbow spraypainted onto the undercarriage. It was soon obliterated by dings, but never mind.

Having a poem on the bottom of your board was something of a novelty and that first time I turned up with it I got a bit of attention. Pam, a girl who rode a surf mat, was one of the few females (to be honest, we called them chicks back then) to venture into the line-up at First Avenue, Broadbeach. She said she liked it but she wore a lot of cheesecloth so she would, wouldn't she.

Looking back, I now regard that poem as my first published work. It just happened to be on the bottom of the board shaped for me by my mate Peter Kelleher, who created it in a haze of smoke at a shaping shed somewhere in the Currumbin Valley. He was making a few boards at the time and had come up with a name for his label – Disguised Watermelons. Like I said, it was shaped in a haze of smoke, possibly while listening to Pink Floyd's *The Dark Side of the Moon*. Everyone was listening to that album back then: it was the theme album for stoners.

Pete and I were close friends in Grade 12. He lived in a flash riverside home on Monaco Street just inland from Broadbeach. His dad, Jack, was a former cop and successful bookie; his mum, Naomi, a former model. Naomi was a cool mum who let us smoke dope when Pete's dad was away at the races. We would sit in his room, looking out at the river, stoned, listening to Frank Zappa's *Over-Nite Sensation* on Pete's quadraphonic stereo. Pete was a gregarious guy; I was a bit shy and kind of glided along in his slipstream. In today's terms you might call me his wingman.

He knew I was writing poetry and had made this surfboard for my 18th. It was his idea to glass a poem into the bottom of the board, so I transcribed one onto rice paper and then in the process of finishing off the board he embedded the poem, sealing it into the undercarriage with resin. It was a sleek board with a blue deck and a single translucent green fin.

The poem was slight, to say the least. I mean, I was just starting out.

> *All alone again under friendly sun / Quiet moment. / All undone again under friendly sky / Sad time. / All quiet again under heaven / Beautiful feeling.*

More a soppy thought bubble than a poem.

I guess that's the kind of stuff you write when you don't know much about poetry and you're a naïve teenage Gold Coast surfie. In Grade 12 I was a year older than many of my classmates, including Pete, because I had repeated Grade 10 due to misbehaviour and an obsession with surfing that had resulted in failure the first time around.

My misbehaviour took many forms – from insubordination to a stubborn refusal to hand in any homework to classroom antics to impress my mates. On one occasion I received a severe caning (six of the best) from the psychotic deputy headmaster. My crime? Removing the brain from a demonstration torso and placing it on the teacher's desk wearing my glasses. When the teacher turned around from writing on the blackboard she had what my mother would have called a conniption and I was sent to the office immediately. In retrospect I regret taunting her because we found out later that she was alcoholic and a bit of a sad case. And she had a moustache, which didn't help.

Repeating Grade 10 – could anything be more hellish? It was Nietzsche's theory of eternal recurrence in practice. If there is a hell I've been there: Grade 10 at Miami State High School, twice. Having to experience it a second time was cruel and unusual punishment.

My father, Ted (Edward John Brown, but Ted to everyone), had threatened to chop up my surfboard the first time I failed but he never went through with it. He decided to take a different tack – offering me a $500 cash bonus (a lot of money in 1972) and a surfing holiday in New Zealand (where we had friends) if I passed the second time. Which I did.

Regardless of my loathing for school (this school in particular), I was always bookish and had been since my Hong Kong childhood when I had read voraciously. When I lobbed at Miami State High, I discovered that in literary terms they were at least three years behind King George V School, the British international school I'd attended in the then British colony before my life was disrupted with our abrupt return to Australia after seven years abroad.

That changed my world irrevocably. I was transplanted from a school like the one in *Goodbye, Mr. Chips* to one more akin to *Lord of the Flies*. But while my outward life tended to be surfing, partying and reading *Tracks* magazine, I retained a rather bookish inner life. I was a Hemingway buff, regularly read C.S. Lewis and Tolkien, and in Grade 11 I don't think anyone else in my circle was burying his head in the latest Patrick White.

Even stranger, I thought I understood it.

Half the students at Miami State High were probably too stoned to read, although actually, if they had read White, they might just have been high enough to understand him too.

The dope smoking wasn't confined to after hours, it was so integrated into our school day as to be almost part of the curriculum. At recess and lunchtime, you would see little groups of students ducking into the bush for a joint. The school backed onto a bushy hill capped, rather appropriately, with a tourist attraction known as Magic Mountain. This castle aloft was at the top of Nobby's Hill with the school below. It was accessed by a chairlift and I remember one day the mechanism broke down, leaving the passengers stuck with legs dangling in mid-air for hours while the student body taunted them from below.

The bushy slopes of Nobby's Hill gave the school's dope smokers the cover and privacy they needed.

I was never that keen on marijuana and didn't start on the evil weed until late in Grade 11. Even then, I was pretty abstemious. I was never really what you could call a pothead. Actually, the dope smoking and the poetry probably started around the same time in 1973, not that the two were necessarily related.

I started reading poetry only after I started writing it, which may have been the wrong way around.

So how the hell does a teenage surfie on the Gold Coast come to be writing poetry anyway? Well, it all started, as it sometimes does, with a girl. A girl by the name of Colleen.

I knew of Colleen because her brother was part of the surfing crew at First Avenue, Broadbeach. I had become part of this crew in early 1973, by invitation. Prior to that I had surfed a more unfashionable break just north of the Kurrawa Surf Club where we were often hounded out of the flagged area by the surf lifesavers, the hated clubbies. In those days there was a low-level war between surfers, who were a tad rebellious, and lifesavers, who symbolized regulated authority.

Kurrawa, at the southern end of Broadbeach, was my home break for a couple of years. But when I became friends with Pete he invited me to move up the beach to join the First Avenue crew. It was a cooler spot. Surfing on the Gold Coast was very tribal then and probably still is. I had found my new tribe and was settling in there when I properly met Colleen.

This occurred at the school dance. Something happened. Our eyes met across the crowded room, as they say, and that was that. Shortly afterwards I started writing poems for her. I'm not even sure how I got the idea to do this but I recall scratching them out on foolscap pads – a practice I follow to this day – and I'm sure they were silly and mawkish, so thankfully none of them are in my archive to remind me how bad they were.

Colleen left school not long after that dance and was living at home just a block from the beach with her mum and brother Tom. I would visit her there, and I think I gave her some of these poems. I recall reading one to her. Not sure what her mother, who was a bit eccentric, thought of this.

I had no real experience with girls and was, as I've said, quite shy, unlike my mate Pete who could charm the birds out of the trees.

My crush on Colleen never went any further. I can't even recall us going on a date. There was just this fleeting, imagined romance that never actually eventuated. Unrequited love, they call it. But it did start me writing poetry, something I'd never had a yen to write up to that moment.

The only book of verse I owned at that stage was *When We Were Very Young* by A.A. Milne, which my grandparents had given me. It includes that famous poem about Christopher Robin attending the changing of the guard at Buckingham Palace with his nanny, Alice.

I had done a poetry recitation for the Hong Kong Schools Music Festival in 1968, reading excerpts from a humorous poem by E.V. Rieu entitled *Sir Smasham Uppe*. According to the judges I had good diction but was 'too hesitant'. (I still have their report in my desk drawer.)

I didn't read poetry either but, now that I think of it, I was gorging myself on pop music throughout childhood and teenage years so I guess you could regard song lyrics as poetry. Some don't, but Bob Dylan did win the Nobel Prize in Literature after all. I think there's plenty of poetry in The Beatles, and I was a Beatles tragic. The Doors' songs were often poetic too, and my favourite album of theirs as a boy was *Strange Days* which includes a poem recited – or rather shouted – by Jim Morrison who becomes more and more strident with each succeeding stanza. Called *Horse Latitudes*, it's a bizarre maritime poem that talks about the sea's *sullen and aborted currents* breeding tiny monsters. Morrison, who virtually shouts the lyric, wrote it as a teenager.

I had absolutely no literary pretensions after arriving on the Gold Coast. I was too busy trying to survive at a tough surfie school where the schoolyard was akin to a prison exercise yard. Being a bespectacled lad from Hong Kong with a British accent, short hair and no suntan made me a target for bullying and ridicule.

I knew there was only one thing to do, try to be like everyone else. So, I spent my first few years there learning to surf, and surfing as much as I could so my hair would be streaked with sun bleaching like the other surfie kids at school. They were cool and I noticed they were never picked on.

My only poetic memory from my early years at Miami State High was of studying a work by the Queensland poet James Devaney. It was entitled *Winter Westerlies* and was significant mainly because it was about the offshore wind required to create perfect waves on the beach breaks of the northern Gold Coast where I was serving my apprenticeship as a surf rat.

By the time I got to Grade 11 (after those two torturous years of Grade 10) I was established and had enough blond streaks in my hair to be acceptable. Things got easier, and falling in with Pete and his crew at school (we were the G Block Boys) and at the beach helped.

And that's around the time I met Colleen. But, as I said, the relationship never progressed: in fact you couldn't really call it a relationship.

Whatever it was, it came to a dramatic halt one night during a party at her beachside home.

I went to this party unaware of the one thing that ruled out any chance of Colleen and me getting together. On the few occasions when I visited her at home her mum was usually there, which made it awkward. Her mother knew that whatever was going on between us was doomed – but I didn't.

I rocked up blissfully unaware of what everyone else seemed to know. I was a fool.

So when, after a few drinks, we ended up in the kitchen snogging in plain sight of the entire party (it was a small house), I had no idea what would happen next. It was just a spontaneous thing and we took no notice of the fact that everyone could see us.

That included her boyfriend, Brian. Yes, she had a boyfriend. Who knew? Apparently everyone. Except me.

When Brian saw his girlfriend sucking face with me in the kitchen, all hell broke loose. There was shouting and drama with people trying to placate him, bottles being knocked over and broken, and joints being quickly stubbed out in ashtrays as he reeled around the lounge room. People were holding him back as I stood there in inebriated shock.

'I think you'd better go,' one of Colleen's friends said to me, so I left the party and the maelstrom in my wake. It was like a nightmare scene straight out of *Puberty Blues*.

I behaved quite decently, I thought. Had I been a different person I would have stayed and fought him. Maybe knights of old would have done that for the sake of honour and chivalry but instead I just got the hell out of there.

And that was that. There would be no more poems for Colleen, no more house calls, particularly in light of what followed.

There was a swell running at the time and we all got up early the next morning and drove to the southern end of the coast to surf the point breaks there. By then I had my licence and my mum had given me her old car, a black Isuzu Bellett. It became famous in the surfing scene as The Black Bellett and was often stuffed to the gills with long-haired teenage surfies.

That next morning we drove south in The Black Bellett and pulled into the car park at Greenmount Beach to see a pleasing corrugation of waves marching in from the horizon. We walked around the point and paddled out at Rainbow Bay, surfing right through to Greenmount Point on perfect peeling waves.

At one point I was sitting out the back scanning the horizon, waiting for my next wave, when Brian's twin brother, Peter, paddled up to me.

I knew who these guys were and that they were twins but being a newcomer to First Avenue I had completely missed the fact that Brian was Colleen's boyfriend. I thought it was odd that the brother would be paddling over to say hello to me after what had happened the night before.

It turned out he wasn't paddling over to say hello at all. When he got close to me, he kept it simple.

'Keep away from Colleen,' he growled. 'Or we'll bash you.'

I was too dumbfounded to reply. He had turned and paddled away pretty quickly. But I got the message!

And I never really had anything to do with her again. It's weird when you're young. Things like this happen, you go your separate ways and that's it, forever. We never spoke again. We never met again. I wouldn't even know that she'd had breast cancer if I hadn't run into a friend of hers in, of all places, Hobart, a few years ago. Her friend contacted me a couple of years later to tell me Colleen had died. That made me feel so sad.

Out of that fleeting and somewhat disastrous love affair that never was, I had started writing poetry. And, call me crazy, I intended to go on with it.

I received some encouragement from my mum, Janet, the literary half of my parents. My father never read a book, as far as I know. I'm not kidding. Not one. When he was sick in bed, he would read those *Commando* comics or the newspaper but that was it. Dad was a self-made man who had left school at 15, was in the army by 17 and landing on the beach at Balikpapan, Borneo, under fire, at 18. He was a very successful businessman, a civil engineering contractor whose preferred reading texts, if I may put it that way, were building specifications.

My mum, on the other hand, had been brought up in a bookish family and loved reading. She seemed pleased that I was writing poetry while I think my dad thought it was a tad effeminate. Anyway, she bought me a book of poems, supposedly to inspire me.

It was by Rod McKuen, the American singer and poet who was so popular in the Sixties and Seventies. I found his poetry a tad excruciating. It was awful. I can only recall one all these years later and it stands out in my memory for all the wrong reasons. It was called *Rome Itself.*

He wrote about carrying Rome *down between my legs* and

followed that with other clunky allusions to sex. Enough with Rome already! Even as a teenager my critical sense baulked at that.

The next book I acquired was more promising: *The Spice-Box of Earth* by Leonard Cohen, another singer. I happened to like his songs, depressing as they sometimes were, and his poetry too. I could understand it. That always helps.

So I started writing poems about subjects other than Colleen, although most of my juvenilia were still emotionally inspired. Wordsworth says somewhere that poetry is 'powerful feelings … recollected in tranquillity' and that sounds about right. I wrote slight, lyrical poems such as *Islands.*

> *Islands seem to / Come in dreams, / Emeralds green, / Or so they seem / With fresh and rushing slopes / With silvery veins of streams / Cleansing all my hopes.*

I was thinking of the rugged islands of Hong Kong.

I started keeping a journal in which I would write little scraps of poems and copy things from books that inspired me. I wrote at the desk in my room, a room wallpapered with surfing photos torn out of magazines. Every morning, the first thing I saw upon waking was Gerry Lopez standing in a huge Pipeline barrel.

My desk window looked out over the Nerang River. We lived on the river a few kilometres inland from Broadbeach in what was really the country then. When the surf wasn't running, I spent quite a bit of time ranging across local heathland, canoeing down local creeks, fishing and birdwatching.

A bit of a nature boy, I wrote poems about the water and sky and moon. Quite a bit about the moon. *Halo moon / Cool of night / Thinking it out / Can't work it right.* My poems were very short, probably due to oriental influences.

I had got hold of a little book of Chinese poetry which I liked – *Li Po and Tu Fu: Poems Selected and Translated with an Introduction and Notes* by Arthur Cooper, with Chinese calligraphy by Shui Chien-Tung. Who can resist a book that begins with a poem entitled … *On Visiting a Taoist Master in the Tai-T'ien Mountains and Not Finding Him*? The pages are yellowing now and this little Penguin Classic is a bit battered but is still a prized part of my library. My Hong Kong upbringing made an orientalist of me, even as a teenager.

Poetry was probably therapy for me then because our home life was a bit fraught. We had moved back to Australia for a new start. One of the reasons behind the move was the desire to curb my father's alcoholism. He'd always liked a drink but it had developed into a problem.

You wouldn't really move to Australia to escape alcoholism, though, would you? That doesn't make sense.

And, of course, it hadn't worked. It is distressing to watch someone you love slowly drinking themselves to death in front of you. At least I could retreat upstairs and lose myself in my books and jottings. That seemed to help.

My literary leanings were encouraged at school by my English teacher, Peter Kunkel, a wild, Rabelaisian character with long black hair and a flowing beard. He looked like Rasputin. He decided that one of the poems we would study in senior class was The Beatles' song *She's Leaving Home*. This was cool, and a revelation. So The Beatles wrote poetry after all? I loved that.

Aware that I was an aspiring writer, Mr Kunkel was quite supportive of that notion. I remember he asked us to write a short story with the title *I Was Happy Here* and I wrote this romantic Robinson Crusoe-style tale about a young man marooned on an island with a perfect surf break that he could ride day in day out, by himself. It was the kind of Paradise I yearned for as things got more complicated in my life.

As the character in the story is paddling out, at one point he is slapped in the face by a breaking wave, 'a watery gauntlet' as I described it. Mr Kunkel liked that and I was pleased. I got top marks for that story. It was a seminal moment.

With one of my surfing friends, Glenn Puster, I ended up working for Mr Kunkel on Saturdays for a time. He had put an ad up on the blackboard one day asking if anyone would like to earn a bit of money landscaping for him. We put our hands up and each Saturday morning for a month or so we would turn up at his place and toil away in his backyard while he watched us from the verandah, sweating and drinking Coke – to assuage his hangover, we assumed.

In the torrid heat of summer we worked like slaves in *Spartacus* while he only lifted a finger to point out another spot where we were to dig.

We were building some kind of raised garden, out of soil reinforced with timber. All I can remember is how bloody hot it was and how uninterested he actually seemed because I think the whole project may have been his wife's idea. I also remember clearly how brusque she was. Her name was Sue and she completely ignored us.

After each session Mr Kunkel would bring us into the kitchen to get a drink and would reintroduce us to her anew each time. She would look at us (or through us) with disdain, as if the hired help shouldn't be allowed inside. She would never say a word or acknowledge us. We would smile and gulp down our drinks, then get the hell out of there and drive straight to the beach to surf it off.

Mr Kunkel may not have been that interested in our gardening, beyond the fact that he was happy he didn't have to do it. But he did encourage my writing, and I know he wrote a bit himself.

Recently, looking through old editions of literary journals I have published in, I was chuffed to see his name in one, in the same issue I had a poem in. For some reason I had never noticed that before.

So, by the end of Grade 12, and buoyed by a degree of encouragement, I was rather audaciously beginning to think that maybe I could actually be a writer. I was already starting to regard myself as a poet – regardless of whether I was any good or not. I wrote poetry, *ergo* I was a poet. And then I had my first little poem published … on the bottom of that surfboard.

Sadly, the surfboard didn't last long. Late that summer I snapped it in half at Kirra Beach during a cyclone swell. A wave had washed me onto the rocks, picking me up and dumping me. When the water receded, there I was, bruised and bloodied with a surfboard in two parts.

I remember walking up the beach with half the board (and therefore half the poem) under one arm, the other half of the board (and therefore the other half of the poem) under the other, with blood pouring down my chest from a gash where the board had ripped my flesh as it was torn asunder.

With my first poetic offering and Disguised Watermelon both sundered in twain, it was an ending of sorts … a beginning too.

CHAPTER 2

MY KEROUAC YEAR

THERE's something impressive about beards. In a mature man a beard suggests wisdom, a sense of sagacity.

John McLaren had a beard that was part Abraham Lincoln, part Thomas Keneally, with a touch of Walt Whitman thrown in for good luck. Sitting across from him one morning in early 1975, I could feel he exuded a calmness, warmth and intelligence that was, to me, comforting.

McLaren was head of the School of Arts at the Darling Downs Institute of Advanced Education (DDIAE) in Toowoomba and I was attending my enrolment interview. He didn't behave like a headmaster, thankfully, or even an assistant headmaster, for that matter. I still had a touch of PTSD from time served at that open-air penitentiary they called Miami State High School where, you may recall, I was once savagely attacked by the assistant headmaster. He called it caning me but it was really a brutal assault.

I'm not sure if John McLaren had had the power to veto my application or whether the whole thing was just a formality. I'd received a letter saying there was a place for me at this college.

I hadn't made the cut for the major universities due to a patchy academic record at Miami State High. Eventually, though, I matriculated with reasonable marks – not great marks but acceptable.

In the absence of any real ambition, I had decided I wanted to be a writer, and journalism sounded like an entrée to that world. It isn't always, though, and newsrooms are full of writers who never wrote their books because they were too busy writing about politics, finance, food or any number of other irrelevancies. Never mind, journalism seemed my only option and DDIAE had the reputation of having an excellent journalism course.

John McLaren, an esteemed figure in Australian letters (I had no idea quite how esteemed at the time), seemed interested in my literary aspirations and in retrospect I can understand why. He smiled, a smile that suggested the wisdom of Solomon to me.

'You want to be a writer,' he repeated after me. 'Well, that's admirable.'

'I'm not sure what kind of writer, though,' I said. 'I'm writing poetry now.'

'Well, that's good,' he said. 'You'll enjoy Bruce Dawe's lectures.'

I intended to do a literature stream as well, which turned out to be so much more interesting than my journalism studies.

I didn't know much about Bruce Dawe at that stage, but he was already one of the nation's pre-eminent poets. He had moved to Toowoomba as a schoolteacher and then joined McLaren's staff. Bruce had actually visited Miami State High once to give a talk. It was before I got interested in poetry but I do remember his visit. He addressed the roiling student body gathered in the school's Great Hall, which became a popular venue on the Gold Coast. Hiring it out made the school a lot of money. I recall seeing Aunty Jack on tour there in the mid-1970s. Talk about culture.

When Bruce Dawe graced the stage of the Great Hall, he delivered a short lecture followed by a poetry reading that went down like a lead balloon.

A boy who had his hand up high in the front row was chosen to lead the questions after the reading and Bruce pointed to him. His question was: 'What the hell are you doing here?' That caused general hilarity and was a fair question in the circumstances, one that Bruce Dawe probably asked himself after the event. Talk about casting pearls before swine.

John McLaren was a man of letters and a respected educator. He played a significant part at several literary magazines over the years, was associate editor of *Overland* from 1966, becoming full-blown editor in the early 1990s, and was founding editor of the second series of *Australian Book Review*.

He went on to become Professor in Humanities at the Victoria University of Technology.

Strange to find such a talented Melburnian in Toowoomba. He had come to the capital of the Darling Downs in 1972. Wife Shirley abhorred the joint and had apparently considered leaving him over his acceptance of a job there, and she must surely have influenced his relatively early departure in late 1975.

My meeting with him had been at the start of '75 when I explained that I was going to take a gap year and defer my degree until 1976. He looked puzzled about that but said it would be fine, as long as I was sure. I was.

So by the time I actually began my degree he was gone.

In retrospect he wasn't that complimentary about Toowoomba. 'The town embodied the worst of the Australian legend,' he once observed. 'It was like the men in Henry Lawson's stories, hiding the sense of its own failure behind a vision of virginal innocence that could only be corrupted by contact with the evil world.

'Most of my time there was spent during the great days of the Whitlam government, when the townspeople thought they were living in the first days of Stalin.'

McLaren wore a tie mostly while he was there so the locals would respect him in the same way they did the local medicos who were top of the local social pecking order.

I had driven up from the Gold Coast in my HD Holden station wagon for the interview with Mr McLaren, my hair still salty from the surf, wearing a T-shirt and jeans while he was dressed professorially, and now I know why.

DDIAE – it sounds like a pesticide, doesn't it – was known colloquially as 'The Institute', which always makes me think of the Mel Brooks movie *High Anxiety* in which he's confined to the Psycho-Neurotic Institute for the Very, Very Nervous, a wacky sanatorium for the mentally unstable. That seems to fit, now that I think of it.

The Institute was a rather bizarre addition to Toowoomba, a conservative Queensland garden city perched on the edge of the Great Dividing Range. It's an historic provincial city which has some beautiful heritage homes and buildings, but DDIAE was not one of them. It was set away from all the historic architecture on a flat, windy site on the southern edge of the town. Brick-venereal suburbs were spreading in that direction and beyond them the Darling Downs swept away to the horizon. The landscape reflected a certain monotony.

The Institute's location was bleak, uninviting and dead as a doornail the day I arrived for my interview with McLaren. Still, the year hadn't started.

'It will get busy soon,' he promised. I guess he gave his imprimatur because my enrolment to do a Bachelor of Arts majoring in journalism was confirmed soon after my visit.

But it would be 1976 before I would find out what it was like. Taking a year off was, in retrospect, probably not such a great idea. Better to just keep going with education rather than press pause: get it all over and done with.

However, I had this romantic notion that a writer should experience life, and that was the plan, one worthy of any Beat poet.

Mind you, I wasn't really a writer at that stage, not in any formal sense. Unless you count the poetic scribblings, those short, wistful poems.

Tall sad wooden men / Up so late alone again / Wind blowing and you can't bend.

Or this:

It's hard to feel very large / When walking in the night / And looking up to see the stars / A world in every light.

(Not astronomically accurate but never mind.) Another went:

So many things half done / Part cloud, part sun / Cast your eye, choose one.

These little bits of verse were the epitome of my juvenilia and I have them still gathered in a folder entitled *Little Flowers: Tiny Poems.*

I guess they do point to a poetic sensibility developing. I hadn't written much prose but I also aspired to be a short story writer, not a novelist. I have always loved short fiction and my literary heroes at that time were W. Somerset Maugham and Ernest Hemingway, particularly Hemingway.

In my senior years at high school it was Hemingway, Hemingway and more Hemingway; I had copied a Hemingway quote and stuck it on my bedroom cupboard among my surfing pictures. 'A man can be destroyed but not defeated.'

Hemingway got me kicked out of maths in Grade 11. I hated maths and, despite being tutored by an older teacher, a man in a cardigan who always smelt like stew, I made no progress. I simply refused to engage and during my final maths exam (I didn't know it *was* my final until afterwards) I basically just sat there reading *Islands in the Stream* – by Ernest you know who.

I have a letter that the deputy headmaster sent home to my father and which I treasure. 'Enclosed is Phillip's latest attempt at a mathematics C test,' he wrote. 'It would rate barely any marks at all.

'Further, after spending a minimum of time "working" on this paper, he opened another book, *Islands in the Stream,* and commenced to read it, making no further efforts to improve his answers. Miss Conway took the book from him and I am now holding it.'

Which was silly, really, because it was a school library book anyway, not mine. My parents were asked to come to the school the following Monday and it was decided that I would not do any more mathematics that year or the next, which suited me. I had to spend my maths period in the library studying. How scary.

I keep the letter, now yellowing like some ancient parchment, in the top drawer of the desk where I sit writing this. It makes me feel so proud.

Along with Hemingway, Maugham, Morris West, Nevil Shute and other authors, I was reading more poetry. But I wasn't writing much even though I wanted to be a writer. Wanting to be a writer is, of course, much easier than being one. I spent my whole gap year wanting to be a writer without actually writing. It was bliss.

The idea was that I would concentrate on experiencing life first: not so much in the vein of *Down and Out in Paris and London* (I lacked the Orwellian commitment to suffering). I hankered for more of a Beat experience.

Next year, '76, I would study to become a journalist and that would be a pathway to becoming a writer, but I didn't have to worry about that until after my gap year.

I was encouraged by the idea that Hemingway had been a journalist. Graham Greene also; Dickens too; and Mark Twain.

Maybe I was aiming a bit high thinking of them. But I was in Jack Kerouac mode for my gap year and while I wasn't about to ride the rattlers into the hobo jungle, I did aim to try out different jobs for life experience.

I started by organizing a trip to Sydney to spend a couple of months living with my dad's younger brother Cyril, who was in business with another uncle, John Wheeler. They built and renovated houses, and I was going to be a labourer and general roustabout for them for a few months. Cyril lived in Belrose, Uncle John virtually next door at Davidson.

I drove south in my trusty station wagon, which was fuming by the time I arrived at my uncle's place in Peacock Parade, Belrose. A cousin's husband, who was a mechanic, was summoned to look at the car. After examining it and removing the dipstick, he asked me: 'When did you last put oil in this car?'

'I knew I had forgotten something,' I said, at which he just shook his head.

I set to work the next day and was doing odd jobs at first, helping clean up sites. One day not long into my tenure I was dropped off by my uncle's foreman on a hilltop near Mona Vale to dig a trench for some concrete footings. It was marked out clearly for me with stringlines.

Wearing my King Gee shorts and a blue singlet (I wanted to look the part), I toiled away until early afternoon when Uncle Cyril turned up with the foreman.

I stopped digging and looked up to see them both standing there with frowns on their faces. My uncle, who was scratching his head to indicate how confounded he was, was not one for mincing words. 'You bloody idiot!' he said.

'What?'

'It's crooked!'

'What's crooked?'

'The bloody trench.'

And yes, on reflection, from their vantage point, I guess it was. It became known, in the folklore of the firm, as 'Phil's banana trench'.

It was then decided that I needed supervision, so I was assigned to a brickie called Carlo, an escapee from East Germany who had married one of my Aunty Ruth's sisters. (My Aunty Ruth was also German.)

That created a happier situation with relatively straightforward work as a brickie's labourer, mixing mud and toting bricks to supply Carlo as he laid them. We generally worked around the Northern Beaches area and finished around 3pm every day after an early start, and that meant I got to go surfing most afternoons at Manly, Dee Why, Long Reef, Curl Curl and sometimes Mona Vale. I may not have been writing anything at this time but I was experiencing life and collecting raw material. Or so I told myself.

I have a lot of cousins in Sydney and one of them, Susan Reeves, had married a North Narrabeen surfer named Michael. Being a young surfer, they thought Michael might take me under his wing.

It was arranged that I would have a night out with him and his best mate, Dave West, another North Narrabeen local, who sported a shark's-tooth earring.

This pair took me to their local pub, the Royal Antler Hotel, which was the hangout for the North Narrabeen crew, a pretty heavy local outfit – not quite the Bra Boys, but close. These two blokes filled me full of beer and forced some girls to dance with me. I felt as awkward as the shambolic British comedian Norman Wisdom, who starred in a string of comedy films in the 1950s and early 1960s.

Never a good drinker, I got intoxicated fairly quickly, and then they took me with them to another popular haunt, Millers Manly Vale pub, a rock venue and drinking trough. There I proceeded to get drunker and drunker until I blacked out. I woke up in the wee hours in some bushes near the venue.

I was woken and ejected by a security guard who foolishly let me drive my car home. It was the only car in the car park at that stage. Thankfully, it wasn't that far to Belrose.

Michael and Dave had obviously abandoned me. I never saw either of them again. So much for taking me under their wing. Thanks, guys.

After my stint in Sydney, I went back home to the Gold Coast and spent a few weeks basically doing nothing but surfing off First Avenue, Broadbeach.

Idyllic as it might sound to do nothing but surf, I found it less satisfying now. It was even a bit bleak on weekdays with no one much around besides a few locals on the dole who were just surfing and smoking dope and collecting their cheques. On Broadbeach Sands I could connect nothing with nothing … with apologies to T.S. Eliot.

One day I ran into S, one of the local crew, who seemed surprised that I was just bumming around. 'I thought you were one of the guys who would make something of himself,' he said. Nice that he thought so but sad that he was disappointed, so I set him straight.

I explained that I was taking a gap year before uni and that *seemed* to satisfy him, but I think he still had his doubts.

S was a good-looking rooster who did modelling work as well as surfing. He was even in some ads on TV at the time, including one for a popular deodorant, so he was kind of famous.

But S had other business interests. He was a drug dealer. I know this because I went to his house one day with some mates to score some marijuana. It was an ordinary suburban home in Florida Gardens, one of those faux American suburbs the Gold Coast sprouted back then. It was quite a scene, he and his brother sitting at a big table with bags of dope piled up in front of them and loose leaves being sorted on a cutting board.

There was a bong going round, and half a dozen others there, with people constantly coming and going. It was a family home. I'm not sure where their parents were or what the neighbours thought. What happened to him and his brother I have no idea because I lost touch with the Broadbeach crew after my gap year.

Which still had a way to go.

My next job was working in a bottle department at The Grand Hotel in Southport. I wangled that one because my old man knew the publican. He knew a lot of publicans.

I worked with a South American bloke who was not exactly a barrel of laughs. It was pretty depressing, actually, because I was on the day shift and the sort of customers who came in to buy grog in the morning were often people with problems, alcoholics desperately trying not to seem like alcoholics, although some didn't care at all what we thought.

Others were more tentative, even a little ashamed, and made little excuses about why they were there. It wasn't much fun but I was a few weeks into that gig when Fate intervened, as it tends to from time to time.

One morning at home my mum called up to me around breakfast time that I wouldn't have to go to work that day.

'Why not?' I asked.

'Because the hotel burnt down last night.' True story. So that sorted that.

My next move was a strange one. A very strange one. And I'm not sure whose idea it was.

Since I was going to be a journalist – well, that was the plan – I wanted to learn touch typing and shorthand, and there was pretty well only one place I could do that on the Gold Coast: Christine Percival's Business Girls' Academy at Southport.

They accepted me as a student despite my gender and I was the only bloke in the class at Mrs Percival's rooms upstairs on the corner of Nerang Street and the Gold Coast Highway. The lady herself was a kind of June Dally-Watkins of the secretarial world: prim and proper, dressed beautifully, enunciating every syllable with a plummy accent. She was firm but kind.

Mrs Percival was preparing young ladies for secretarial work and there I was, a confused young aspiring writer and surfie tapping way in the middle of them.

I think it was actually quite brave of me to do that – or mad – and proved that I was up for a bit of adventure. It wasn't really a struggle spending a month or two in a room full of young women, some of whom thought I was a bit odd.

I managed to learn shorthand, though, which I had completely forgotten by the time I finally entered journalism. And my touch typing went by the wayside fairly quickly too. I soon reverted to two-finger typing and am now one of the fastest two-finger typists around. In full flight I swear you will see smoke coming off my keyboard.

After completing the course I went on with my gap year, surfing some more and spending countless hours mooching around at home. In the evenings I often spent time at my desk scribbling out snippets of poems – again they were still very short at this stage – and writing in my journal. I had decided to keep a journal after reading Somerset Maugham's *A Writer's Notebook* and I wrote observations and copied out quotes from various sources, whether it be something from Muggeridge or C.S. Lewis, or even Alan Watts. I was interested in comparative religion and had recently read *The Wisdom of Insecurity*, Watts' timeless classic drawing on the wisdom of Buddhism and other Eastern religions and philosophies.

Despite this esoteric tendency I was also behaving like an 18-year-old (soon to be 19) surfie – smoking pot, listening to Lou Reed and David Bowie, and wasting time at Surfers Paradise nightspots or at The Patch, a notorious surfie hangout at Coolangatta.

I had a couple of other jobs that year and the more menial work I did the more determined I was to become a journalist. In my mid-teens I had already done hard yakka at my father's blue metal quarry, a semi-retirement project after all his years in construction in Hong Kong and elsewhere. The blokes I worked with at the quarry weren't wrong when they suggested I was allergic to hard work because I would only ever put in two-thirds of a day, after which I would scarper to go surfing. Being the boss's son I was allowed to do that. 'You won't work, ya bastard!' they'd say as I disappeared from view.

One of the other gap year jobs my old man got me was on roadworks at a new Gold Coast Housing estate. These estates were popping up like mushrooms after rain in the mid-1970s as the 'white shoe brigade' held sway, devastating the local environment to construct new suburbs for certain pesky interstaters who saw the Gold Coast as the ultimate escape from their miserable lives down south.

So, for a few weeks, I worked with a team of guys on this housing estate, a development which was being overseen by an engineer who was a mate of my dad's. My job during these few weeks was essentially holding one end of a piece of string. I can't tell you how mind-numbing that was but that's not going to stop me making the attempt.

I worked in a team – three other blokes and me. These guys were the most uninspiring, unfriendly, soulless bastards I have ever met. They barely said a word to me all day, which was embarrassing, humiliating and excruciating.

The work itself was deadening enough. We were flattening out stretches of road and checking it was flat enough using a spirit level and a stringline, with me on one end.

If anyone ever asks me 'How long is a piece of string?' I say to them, 'I'll tell you how fucking long a piece of fucking string is! *Too* fucking long!' It was boring, soul-destroying work in the baking heat and there was almost no relief. One day I had to drive a truck round the site after a driver called in sick, and that was heaven compared to toiling alongside three blokes who might as well have been deaf mutes.

The sad thing is that I tried to befriend them. I even found out where they socialized. One of them, Darryl, spent his evening playing darts at a Surfers Paradise bar. I turned up there one night to have a drink with him and he completely ignored me even though I wasn't too bad at darts. To him I was non-existent. He looked straight through me.

After one game of darts, he sat drinking beer, smoking a cigarette and staring straight ahead as I tried to engage him in conversation, which was utterly pointless.

Another evening I adjourned to The Paradise Room at the Surfers Paradise Hotel, a venue I was familiar with (The Parasite Room, we used to call it), where I knew the other two slightly younger blokes hung out practically every night.

I turned up there and tried to have a drink with them too, but just like Darryl they both ignored me. Had they made a pact of some sort? To convince me I didn't exist? That would have been positively diabolical.

Next day I was back on the end of my piece of string wishing the ground would open up and swallow me. I couldn't take it anymore, and a few days later worked up enough gumption to quit.

But my father had more torture in store for me on my languorous gap year.

I already had form as a powder monkey's assistant from my days working at the quarry. Basically, I just helped the bloke who blew shit up – rock faces, in more formal language – to extract stuff, mostly blue metal for crushing and occasionally a rogue boulder or two.

My father had sold the quarry but kept the air-track drill and compressor unit used by the powder monkey. The powder monkey at this particular quarry was a man called Neil Frank, a taciturn fellow who wore a German World War Two helmet at work. That always drew comments. I never found out why he wore it. He hardly ever spoke either.

My dad retained the services of another powder monkey after he sold his quarry, hiring him and the unit out. After my failure on the roads, I was appointed powder monkey's assistant yet again.

This time I was assigned to work with Don, a diminutive Yorkshireman who had been a coal miner and served in British submarines during World War Two.

He was a small man but had a huge capacity for alcohol.

At that time we were working at a small council pit outside of Yatala, a little piece of nowheresville halfway between the Gold Coast and Brisbane. Its main claims to fame were, and still are, a pie shop and drive-in.

We toiled away at this small dusty council pit which I guess supplied rock for roads, like my old man's quarry. The work was straightforward enough: we would drill holes in the ground, stuff them full of petrol-soaked nitro, add sticks of gelignite and then … from a distance, press a small button on a box that would blow the designated patch of ground sky-high. It was like training to be a terrorist.

The work wasn't exactly stimulating and the dust got into every orifice.

At this stage of my life, I had the beginning of tummy troubles. I've always had a wonky gut but Don had the cure. Sherry.

Each day for lunch we went to a nearby pub, The Gem, where he would sink numerous glasses of beer while I sipped sherry followed by stout, a combination that he insisted would fix my tummy. It didn't.

The astounding thing is that afterwards, when we would go back to work drilling and blasting, we'd be half cut. Don would take a six pack of stubbies back on site which he would put on the blind side of the compressor to drink during the afternoon as we went about our ostensibly dangerous work with explosives.

Not a lot of occupational health and safety was being observed. How my mother, who was a nervous type, felt about me engaging in this work I will never know. How I ever agreed to doing it is also beyond me.

My father considered it amusing enough, though, and Don thought it was a hoot. He would regale me with war stories as he sipped his stubbies while the drill powered away. I guess someone from the local council must have been overseeing the project but I don't recall anyone ever coming to check up on us.

When we finished, Don would head back to the pub to get a six-pack to take home for dinner, and the next day he would do it all over again. Thankfully, that job lasted only a month and a half: I managed to live through it.

With an inebriated powder monkey and a powder monkey's assistant who was tiddly too, it all could have ended rather badly. But I survived.

This is how I suffered for my art, the life I was enduring for my writing, writing that was not happening. In some ways it was a lost year, and thinking of it now I have a picture of myself standing on the shore at Broadbeach and looking out at the sea feeling quite lost.

Or not so much lost as in suspense between school and further studies, with that vague idea of being a writer but nothing to show for it beyond my wistful, naïve little poems.

I had experienced enough manual labour to eschew any more in favour of exerting the mind and hopefully the following year I would get started on that. I was kind of marking time, postponing the inevitable.

I was in limbo. One good thing was I hadn't blown myself up. I was still there, hanging in.

The wind blows / Leaves fall / I stay on / Through it all / Knowing little / Feeling less / I stay on / What a mess.

I was ready to forsake the beach for The Institute, that copse of nondescript buildings on a bleak expanse at the windblown arse-end of a small-minded Queensland provincial city which was hot in summer and freezing in winter. It was not quite a university, but it was all I had. I was like a patient longing to be admitted to … The Institute.

God help me.

CHAPTER 3

A MAN CALLED BRUCE

WE WERE sitting there in awe, but awe quickly turned to concern as we watched one of Australia's greatest poets choking. On a peppermint.

Bruce Dawe had a packet of Steam Rollers on his desk, and he popped one into his mouth in mid-sentence, paused, then gagged. I guess if any of us had had command of the Heimlich manoeuvre, we would have tried to help.

But Bruce quickly regained his composure as the peppermint finally went down. 'Sorry about that,' he said. 'I've given up smoking.' And taken to popping peppermints to stave off the cravings, obviously.

Bruce Dawe has been described as the man with the 'map of Australia' profile. In a certain light he reminded me of one of the Easter Island statues, those silent sentinels gazing out across the South Pacific.

Bruce was craggy, certainly, with dark eyes and a five o'clock shadow … at midday. He didn't look like a poet (however poets are supposed to look). I certainly never saw him wearing a beret or a silk scarf. He was a balding middle-aged man who dressed like a public servant.

It was rather special having him as my tutor and lecturer in literature, the strand of studies I found so much more interesting than journalism. In my time at DDIAE (the dreaded 'Institute') it was literature, history and film that sparked my enthusiasm, not journalism.

Our journalism lectures were dry to the point of desiccation. One day I had a rather public spat with one of the lecturers. I had used F-bombs in writing up an interview with the student union president and was told I couldn't do that. 'But it's the truth,' I said.

'What is truth?' he replied, echoing Pontius Pilate.

Bugger journalism, literature with Bruce Dawe was a revelation. So was history with Ron Frazer, another import (from Canberra, I think), a turtleneck-wearing Marxist with dishevelled Ted Hughes hair.

We studied film, too, and I remember – not long after arriving in Toowoomba – cramming into a theatrette with the new cohort of arts students (journalism students were in the Arts faculty also) to watch Jean Cocteau's film *Orphée*, which was like being stoned without having smoked a joint. Now that was a revelation. I wasn't in Kansas anymore!

I went up to Toowoomba (I say *up* not to suggest a connection to Oxford but rather because road trips from the 'Downs' to a city sitting 700m above sea level can only be ascents) with appropriately high hopes. This was my first time living away from home, discounting that sojourn in Sydney with my uncle and aunty.

I moved into a share house on Tor Street, opposite a spacious park in the suburb of Wilsonton. That thoroughfare is the main highway out of town so it was busy with trucks night and day.

Being a long slow downhill grade it was perfect for skateboarding, so me and my old surfing buddy Glenn Puster, one of the people I was sharing with, took to surfing down the road late at night when there was little traffic besides the occasional semi-trailer. The drivers would sit on their horns going past in a bid to clear us long-haired surfie vermin from the road.

We lived in a typical student house, that is to say … it was a decaying dump backing onto a small paddock containing a couple of cows. My abiding memory of the place is of lying in the bath one day playing the Rolling Stones album *December's Children (and Everybody's)* while each song was punctuated by mooing.

It had a fireplace, as any Toowoomba house should, but it was boarded up, and on our first night there Glenn and I cut up surfing magazines to create a collage over the plywood covering that hearth. Glenn was studying art, after all.

I lived there for the first few months, and it was uncomfortable and freezing as winter approached.

Completely unprepared for life away from home, I didn't eat properly, I smoked and drank booze when I should have been eating, stayed up late and rose whenever I achieved consciousness again.

At one stage I took long walks at night and meandered around the large park across the road. I was having a sort of spiritual crisis (one that has never actually ended), wondering the usual things young people sometimes wonder about – does God, or any god, exist? What about evil? That sort of thing …

On my midnight strolls I would challenge the evil one to show himself that I might denounce him. I was reading the gospels at the time and was thinking about Jesus and his confrontation with Satan in the desert, where he was tempted but resisted.

I'm not sure anyone else in the house realized what was going on with me. And I'm not sure how much my spiritual quandary was affected by my lifestyle. Maybe it was just malnutrition or low blood sugar that was making me loopy.

Ultimately, the share house didn't work out and I moved into digs on campus, Davis College, named after Arthur Hoey Davis, the Queensland writer born at Drayton, near DDIAE. He was better known by his *nom de plume*, Steele Rudd, creator of the much-loved fictional father-and-son farming duo Dad and Dave, of book and radio renown.

But the regimentation of life at Davis College didn't suit me either and during my brief stint there I never once managed to wake up in time for breakfast.

Anyway, I heard that there was a room going at a house in town. This formerly grand, now ramshackle, old Federation-style mansion at 128 James Street was within easy staggering distance of a pub. Perfect.

The girls who lived there were studying to be teachers and seemed to like me. They showed me round this rather beautiful but unloved old house, and on a wall in the lounge room was an old movie poster of the actress Jean Harlow, which looked so cool and retro I thought, *This is the place for me*.

It also fed my poetic illusions (or delusions, call them what you will) because I was reading Michael Dransfield at the time (another doomed poet!) and this place made me think of Courland Penders, his mythical ancestral home somewhere in rural Australia, a ghostly stately pile symbolic of past glories. Courland Penders had seen better days and so, for that matter, had 128 James Street.

The house dated back to 1894 and rumour had it that it was once home to the mayor of this leafy city, but I'm not sure that was true. I had numerous housemates in the time I lived there, one of whom reported coming home late one night to find a ghostly party in full swing with people dressed to the nines ... in the sort of clothing that people wore at the turn of the 20th century.

It was gracious, albeit, as I say, fairly dilapidated but the grand old house has since been renovated and heritage-listed.

Clearly enough, the landlord back then wasn't too fussed about its condition as a residence. We were just blow-ins from out of town, drug-crazed, pot-smoking bohemian students, probably Communists too.

I wasn't smoking much pot at that stage (it always made me too paranoid) but I had a roommate for a little while – it was a big room – known as Brunt (Rob was his actual name) and he used to puff a reefer each night before going to sleep. He would sit up in bed immersed in sci-fi, toking away while I read Richard Brautigan or jotted away in my corner.

When he moved out, I shifted a little desk in so I could set up my typewriter to tap out poems and study in the room properly, although studying wasn't exactly my strong suit.

Neither was attending lectures because I still had great difficulty waking up in the morning. My life had no routine: nights were often spent in Rabelaisian mayhem, and I was also something of an insomniac, often typing up poems all night, which my housemates did not appreciate.

At first I shared with the teachers but after the summer holidays, in early 1977, the personnel changed and there was a high turnover. Eventually four or five of us were living there, our numbers usually swelled by a small crowd of attendant friends and hangers-on.

It became a bit of a party house and apparently that disturbed the neighbours, particularly the old biddy who lived next door and whom I immortalized in one of my poems. I wrote it after a conversation with her over the back fence one day.

The steel winter dusk made conversation no easier / And from the outset my main aim was escape … I couldn't concentrate on farms / Or ailments / And even less on her brother-in-law's cremation … I just fixed my eyes on the faraway rusty red gate / And offered Hmmms.

From our conversation I gleaned that she had suspicions we were running the contemporary version of an opium den so when, one night, we were raided by the local police, I assumed she'd been the one who had given them the tip-off.

Two burly Queensland cops arrived, and they were scary because these were the bad old days of the Bjelke-Petersen regime when the boys in blue ruled and the notorious Special Branch kept an eye on subversives.

These cops just swanned in unannounced and looked around, sniffing, expecting to get a whiff of *Cannabis sativa*, no doubt.

They went into the kitchen where we all gathered with them as they started going through the pantry. We were too polite to ask if they had a search warrant and, frankly, we didn't want to get bashed. We were taken aback by this abrupt turn of events but tried to be accommodating.

Rifling through the pantry they hit paydirt – or so they thought. One of them pulled out a plastic bag with green plant material inside it and, with a slightly triumphant smirk, asked:

'What's all this then?'

'It's peppermint tea,' said one of the girls. They sniffed it and seemed annoyed that, yes, it definitely was peppermint tea and not the dreaded weed they had hoped to find.

To them I must have looked drug-addled because they asked which room was mine and I led them down the hall. Once in my domain they insisted on going through my desk drawers and inside one they found a pipe. I happened to smoke a pipe when I was young.

This was an aha! moment for our sleuths. One of them picked up the pipe, looked at me knowingly, and asked: 'So what do you smoke in this?' He was sure he had me.

'Amphora,' I replied. 'My favourite tobacco.' They looked angry. Foiled again!

Back in those days you wouldn't have been surprised if they'd actually planted some dope in the house just to get a bust, but these two must have decided we weren't worth the trouble or the paperwork so they left, warning us that we had better behave or they would be back.

I guess the DDIAE students kept them on their toes because there were legions of us. The town had been invaded by an unruly bohemian horde that had disrupted a century of cultural stagnation. We were everywhere: in flats, in gracious if crumbling old mansions, in farmhouses peppering the surrounding countryside and in various other hovels unfit for human habitation … long-haired louts, braless girls in hippie dresses. What was the place coming to!?

Locals craved their status quo back. As Bruce Dawe wrote in his poem *Provincial City*:

> *This is a city which is all present … It moves, but oh so slowly / You would have to sleep years / Waking suddenly once in a decade / To surprise it in the act of change.*

But change had come to Toowoomba since what was originally the Queensland Institute of Technology (Darling Downs) opened in 1967. The name was later changed to DDIAE and in 1990 it became the University of Southern Queensland.

It became a destination for students from all over Queensland, and Australia for that matter. Tertiary education was free then, so any deranged young person could enrol.

When I was living at 128 James Street, I had a bike (my HD station wagon had recently kicked the bucket) and I used to ride it out to classes sometimes. I also rode it around town late at night when in the throes of insomnia. There was no traffic at all then, besides the occasional truck passing through, so it was quite freewheeling.

I was still having waves of religious and philosophical wonderment and recall one night circumnavigating the CBD as I sang, out loud, George Harrison's *My Sweet Lord* over and over until I finally exhausted myself enough to sleep.

My room at James Street had a window looking out onto the street, a street which Bruce had also described in *Provincial City:*

> *Down James Street the semis hurtle / nightly, brutalizing through the quiet / civilized dark like the Eumenides, / or conscience, or history.*

Both houses I lived in as a student were on a main thoroughfare through town and it is hard to sleep when a truck is grinding its gears outside at 2am.

I wrote a poem about my room there. It's just called *Room*, a rather intense quasi-religious piece in which I compared that room to, of all things, Calvary.

> *Forgive me if the nails rend your flesh / When I remove the old Christ / To crucify a more contemporary messiah upon your wall.*

This because I was putting a poster up!

I mean you no harm, room / That has hovered above me / Like a departing soul / While I lay crucified in sleep / With sordid dreams my crown of thorns.

That last bit is a line directly attributable to studying T.S. Eliot's *Preludes.*

You tossed a blanket from the bed, / You lay upon your back, and waited; / You dozed and watched the night revealing / The thousand sordid images / Of which your soul was constituted.

Well, if you're going to be derivative, why not be derivative of the very best?

The subject matter may have been Eliot but the form was pure D.H. Lawrence. Another poem in the Lawrentian shape, if not style, was simply called *Sun* – and it was me railing against it.

You fancy yourself, I'm sure / Pagan with the sunbeam lash … bastard! / I wish you gone today, / I have no joy for you to illuminate.

Oh yes, I was a fun guy.

I guess you could say I was confused, trying to make sense of the world, but it would probably be more accurate to say I was just depressed.

It probably had a lot to do with the way I was living, not looking after myself, drinking and smoking and eating meals of peanut butter on a spoon straight from the jar. I was on a self-destructive bent that suited my poetic aspirations. And the undercurrent to all this was, I'm sure, worrying about my dad and the situation at home.

My poetic life was punctuated by a sort of chronic sadness about that. It wasn't doing my health any good and my *laissez-faire* attitude to my own health was reflected in an inability to properly concentrate on my studies.

Missing tutorials and lectures was a problem, but somehow I managed never to miss Bruce's.

Studying literature with Bruce Dawe was eye-opening for someone who was still very much a literary ingénue. But little by little Bruce was laying the foundations of deeper knowledge and understanding. He was teaching me, in his own way, how to live the literary life, how to think like a writer. I think, therefore I am … a writer?

Our poetry primer was a book in the Longman English Series: *Poetry 1900 to 1965*, edited by George MacBeth. I still have this tattered volume and it is sitting on my desk as I write – a talisman, if you like. Dipping into it, I see that I have jotted notes all the way through.

The poets I really warmed to were Dylan Thomas, W.H. Auden (we dug into his classic *Musée des Beaux Arts*), T.S. Eliot, D.H. Lawrence (I prefer his poetry to his fiction, actually), Sylvia Plath, of course, and Ted Hughes (I mean, you had to study both Plath and Hughes together). Also Philip Larkin, who I have always loved and admired for his unabashed curmudgeonly ways and his clarity.

I couldn't warm to Yeats, for some reason, and William Empson's neck beard was just too weird!

Studying under Bruce Dawe opened up the Universe of verse to me. He taught us how to read good literature, to go deeper and deeper. He brought poetry alive for us, popping peppermints as he went.

A few of us were more attentive than others because we were young aspiring bards, and there is no more desperate breed.

My partner in poetry, I guess you could call him, was Rod Warrener, a lanky Toowoomba lad.

We were both intense, as you are at that age, about expressing our innermost feelings and world-views in our poetry. We shared poems with each other and at one point Rod wrote a kind of manifesto and critique of my poetry and short fiction, because I was also writing short (very short) stories. I still have that document – three yellowing pages of foolscap written on a dodgy typewriter with occasional jumbled letters, all held together by staples that are now rusting.

'Phil, you are now a bonified *[sic]* member of the anti-materialist society of North Borneo. My personal belief is that if we are subtle enough about our writing, we will establish ourselves in time as good writers. If you piss off don't neglect your writing. Because you have stacks of ability.'

After that it got a bit withering about some of my work, but never mind. I was still only a baby writer.

After a couple of months as a student of Bruce's I summoned up the courage to put some poems together in a manila folder to present to him, to ask if he would mind having a look at them. Bruce was only too happy to do this and came back to me reasonably quickly, urging me to contribute some poems to the campus literary journal.

One he particularly liked was published soon after, and I guess that may have been my second published poem, counting that Disguised Watermelons publication on the bottom of my surfboard as the first.

Entitled *Gunfight (A Hemingway Vignette)*, it's about two gunfighters facing off in a dusty high street. I have no idea what actually spawned this work besides the fact that I liked westerns. My brother Stephen (Steve) and I used to watch them with Dad on weekends and I know Bruce enjoyed movies like this too. He even mentions Gary Cooper, star of *High Noon*, in one piece of poetry.

My poem was influenced by a love of Hemingway's plain-talking style.

The dust hung wearily around / as he stepped out into the merciless sun. / It hit him. He felt good. / Then he remembered the fear inside / And his guts were numb with it.

Spoiler alert: it finishes with the protagonist getting shot because he isn't quick enough on the draw.

But he was too late. / He was hot. / And then he was gone.

I don't know, I think it still flies. Bruce liked it and that was enough for me. It was a lot.

He was always very encouraging. I guess he liked the fact that Rod and I were serious about our poetry. A few others on campus were also writing some, including a young guy called Jeremy Rorke who I met whilst urinating outside a small rural School of Arts hall one night on the outskirts of Toowoomba.

We were there to see a local punk band called Brian. As we pissed, steam coming off it in the cool Toowoomba night, he said he was glad to meet another poet and afterwards we talked about poetry and our horribly romantic ideas. Serious young insects we were.

Rod and I attempted to stir up some interest in a poetry reading to be held at 128 James Street. We put posters up on campus but in the end only two girls showed up and we had the reading around the kitchen table.

Rod and I were thrilled when Bruce invited us to his house one weekend for afternoon tea. It was like the master inviting his disciples. We were both nervous when we arrived, as any followers visiting their guru would be.

It was a familiarly domestic scene that greeted us … Bruce on a ladder down the side of the house in Cumming Street. He was wearing stubbies and a flannelette shirt, doing a spot of painting, if I recall, and his wife, Gloria, was in the backyard pottering in her vegie garden.

It was refreshingly suburban, and that's not unexpected if you know Bruce's poetry because it is full of ordinariness made extraordinary.

Bruce came down off his ladder, invited us inside, and we sat around chatting and drinking tea and eating Saos topped with Vegemite, cheese and tomato. The television was on and Bruce glanced at it from time to time as there was an Australian Rules game being broadcast. From Geelong himself, Dawe was a mad Cats fan and Aussie Rules references abound in many of his poems.

It's not a game I have ever warmed to, but I understand the passion some have. I'm more interested in cricket.

It was the very prosaic nature of the scene that impressed us most.

I had started reading more of his poetry. There's no doubt many of his works are of national and historical importance, even though he is becoming somewhat neglected these days. His anti-Vietnam War philippic *Homecoming* reflects that era perfectly and at that point the war was still fresh in the public's mind. His conscience and yen for social justice shine through in so many poems.

As fellow poet John Kinsella once wrote: 'Always behind Dawe's seemingly playful banter with us, his readers and public, [are] his commitment to sympathy and connection with the less empowered, the disenfranchised, downtrodden, neglected and exploited.'

His protest poem on the hanging of Ronald Ryan, *A Victorian Hangman Tells His Love*, is as horrifying as it is beautiful.

There are lines of Bruce's that come back to me regularly. Among my favourites are these: *Happiness is the art of being broken / With least sound.* That's positively Zen.

And I have always found the opening lines of another poem quite moving and beautiful:

> *I am always here leaning against the fog / Saying, is that you? … Melbourne is like a distant war / In which I lost my life and gained some ghostly wounds / That ache when the weather's raw.*

The other thing I have always loved about Bruce's poetry is that you can understand it.

When I was his student, I was, at his suggestion, sending off contributions to literary magazines that were full of poetry I couldn't understand. I was being rejected by all of them, I might add. When Robert Adamson was editor of *New Poetry* (what was wrong with the old poetry?) he rejected me on several occasions, so I should feel proud, I guess, to have been rejected by the best.

Bruce was remarkably realistic about the poetry scene which was, in the 1980s, a tad radical. He was socially progressive but conservative in other ways. He once suggested to me that poets occupied the lowest rung of the literary world. He pointed out that writers of longer forms had to really sit down and work every day while poets could just toss off a new work now and then to call themselves poets. The rewards of poetry were so inadequate, he suggested, it was like seagulls fighting over a chip.

He and Les Murray were outliers who didn't partake in the salons of the south. Bruce was geographically remote from all that and dedicated to teaching. He inspired a generation.

I was, however, still a bit in love with the bohemian idea of poetry and was, foolishly, influenced by the whole tragic poet myth. I was, after all, reading Sylvia Plath, D.H. Lawrence and Michael Dransfield, for God's sake, and all died young, although I guess D.H. Lawrence couldn't help it, having consumption (it killed Keats too, among many others) while Dransfield and Plath both perished as the result of their own misadventures.

I suppose it's no surprise that one of my favourite musicians at that time was Nick Drake. I had recently discovered him and he, too, died tragically young. That his music was deliciously melancholy suited me to a T.

I was enamoured of the idea of being a poet, and living in that grand old dilapidated mansion in James Street suited my poetic pretensions. I recall only snippets of that house now, vignettes if you like.

In one I am home alone, which hardly ever occurred, smoking a cigarette and typing away with the house in near darkness and Lou Reed's *Coney Island Baby* on the record player. In another, a party is in full swing and we are getting drunk to the sounds of Captain Matchbox Whoopee Band who were big at the time. They came to Toowoomba to do a gig while I was a student there, and I remember lead singer Mic Conway being so stoned they had to carry him off stage at the campus refectory.

One abiding memory that I play back in my head sometimes, like a reel of grainy old family film, is a scene starring me sitting on the front steps of that house in James Street on a coolish morning reading an interview with Swiss-French poet Blaise Cendrars in an issue of *The Paris Review*. The article was accompanied by a photo of Cendrars, whose visage was described by Ernest Hemingway, who ran into him in Paris, as a 'broken boxer's face'.

I recently wrote a poem about that experience – *Good Morning Blaise Cendrars* – which was published in the online literary journal *Meniscus*.

In it I write of:

bathing in the insipid morning sunshine after being up all night / all the long freezing fucking night, hammering away on an old Remington. / Living the dream with a cigarette hanging off my lower lip / a little too much like Cendrars, actually, or Kerouac, or someone else / labouring over poems that seldom came out right.

That was at a time which I guess I could describe as the end of the beginning, or the beginning of the end, or something like that, with apologies to Winston Churchill.

Because the whole experience of being at DDIAE was turning me into someone who might well qualify for admission to some place called The Institute. For a start I was physically ill with what turned out to be the beginnings of a duodenal ulcer.

My lifestyle of cigarettes and stout and peanut butter from the jar was taking its toll.

My physical state affected my mental state, and my affinity for doomed poets also didn't help. I was getting sicker and sicker, living on bottles of antacid and trying not to drink, as well as trying (unsuccessfully) not to smoke, something I wrote about at the time in a poem entitled *Report*.

I have, of course lit / Another cigarette. / Where? When? Why? / For those reporters among you / It's somewhere past one AM / On a farm near Toowoomba / Where the wild wind wanders. / Lighting this thing / Was the last course of action / I had in my furry mind / But light it I did / For one needs company / In this spongy darkness.

As I say, I was trying to stay off the booze too. I remember sitting there in my room trying to write poetry one night, swearing I was off the grog and just half an hour later I found myself at the bar of the pub across the road knocking back a Scotch.

I was making it to fewer and fewer lectures, too, although I kept up my literature class attendance until the bitter end of my year and a half in Toowoomba. I had done well in my literature exam the first year even though it had been a last-minute cram. My Greek friend Cratis and I decided that we could attack the exam by doing one Herculean evening of study beforehand.

Wearing old army greatcoats against the bitter cold, we stayed up most of the night sitting at my desk testing each other and writing things out to remember them. That may be why my poetry book is so full of written comments in the margins.

Around 4am we both collapsed, fully clothed and still in our coats, and woke up just in time to get to the campus for the exam, which we both passed with flying colours.

But ultimately I had to relinquish my studies with Bruce because I just wasn't coping. I deferred my degree and retreated home to the Gold Coast. It felt like defeat and still feels like defeat, and it's something I have always regretted.

I guess I could say I have half a Bachelor of Arts because I passed everything right up until my downfall. Before I left, we had started a campus publication entitled *DDT* (*Darling Downs Times*), inspired by the pesticide-like acronym of DDIAE, and we raised funds to publish it by holding a dance at the refectory.

After publishing one issue I left and, with the blessing of my colleagues, took away some of the funds raised that night. Is that embezzlement? I guess so.

After leaving, I kept in touch with Bruce. In fact, I wrote regularly and he always wrote back with extensive critiques of my work. Our correspondence over the ensuing decades, and our friendship, were the subject of a piece I wrote for *Meanjin* in 2010, commissioned by then editor Sophie Cunningham, entitled *Memories of a Mentor: Bruce Dawe.* And I have only recently discovered that fourteen of my letters to him are kept in the Fryer Library's Bruce Dawe collection at the University of Queensland.

When a book about Bruce's work was launched at UQ many years ago, I went along to support him. One of his daughters greeted me warmly and told me how, as children, they always knew when a letter from me had arrived for their father because I signed the back of the envelopes with a smiling crescent moon, part of my signature at the time.

The moon was inspired by Michael Leunig, whom I came to know through his work in *Nation Review* and whose own sad loss was reported soon after I wrote the first draft of this chapter. His cartoons often had crescent moons, a symbol of wistfulness or melancholy. My crescent moon was smiling and that made the Dawe kids smile too, apparently. How lovely.

The correspondence with Bruce, and his encouragement, sustained me over the years, including during some dark times. He was generous enough to write the introduction to my first slim (very slim, even) volume of poetry, *Plastic Parables*, published in 1991, and when he was poetry editor of *The Courier-Mail* (the newspaper where I would end up serving as Arts Editor many years later) he published a poem of mine entitled *The Serial Killer*.

When Bruce died in 2020 at the age of 90, I was honoured to write his obituary for that newspaper.

'RIP Bruce Dawe: Poet of ordinary Australia dies' read the headline. He would have liked that; ordinary Australia was his thing. I can still see him now up that ladder down the side of his house in Cumming Street, and now and then I hear his voice in my head, an encouraging voice: 'Good on you, tiger.'

CHAPTER 4

THE HOSPITAL BY THE SEA

I WAS THINKING about the opening line of Bruce Dawe's first published poem, *Enter Without So Much As Knocking*, when I awoke on my first morning at Glen Pacific Private Hospital.

Blink, blink. HOSPITAL. SILENCE.

The poem follows a person's life from birth to death in Bruce's inimitable vernacular style, a style I would seek to emulate from time to time.

And I blinked but it wasn't quite silence in this hospital. I could hear muted voices echoing in the spacious corridor outside.

Soon a woman wearing a shower cap came in with breakfast on a tray. The toast was cold and a bit limp, the sort you get served in bad motels … but the tea was hot and strong. I sat up and added three teaspoons of sugar. Eating my toast, spread thinly with jam from the single sachet provided, and sipping my tea, I thought how nice it was to have brekkie brought to you. I felt like some ailing English aristocrat. Soon they'd bring the mail in on a silver salver.

Here I was in an airy room bathed in soft morning light, banged up in an old seaside hospital that, if it had survived the Gold Coast development boom, would have been a retro treasure by now, a boutique hotel like the Hydro Majestic in the Blue Mountains.

Sitting up in bed between crisp, clean sheets (there was, perhaps, a tad too much starch), I had my books on the bedside table and a notebook for jotting down ideas for poems should they arise. Bliss.

It felt a little like a holiday but I was forgetting, for a moment, that I had been admitted to hospital due to what could be loosely called a nervous breakdown. *Poets have them*, I figured, *so maybe that's okay*. I mean, it goes with the territory, doesn't it? I read once that poets are among the most likely classes of people to suffer depression. Think of poor old John Clare: *I am! yet what I am none cares or knows*. Things weren't at that low ebb just yet, though.

I was a bit groggy from the pills they had given me the night before when I was deposited by my mum at this hospital by the sea.

My student days in Toowoomba had come to an end with the sort of whimper T.S. Eliot wrote about in *The Hollow Men*.

After a year and a half as a student in Toowoomba burning the candle at both ends – not to mention the middle – my constitution had finally given out on me. It was a combination of things: that developing duodenal ulcer; exhaustion from partying compounded by too much drinking and smoking; and, last but by no means least, staying up all night at times banging out doggerel on my trusty portable Remington.

How long can you live on sugar sandwiches and peanut butter straight from the jar? It seems I wasn't equipped, at that stage of my life, to look after myself.

The official line was, however, that I had deferred my studies but, despite good intentions, I never went back to them. Which qualified me to emulate that gentleman from Calcutta (in the joke) who tried to impress a prospective employer by mentioning that he had at least attended university.

He had a card printed, so it goes, that read: 'BA Calcutta (Failed)'. Perhaps I could write 'BA Toowoomba (Half Done)' on my business cards because I hadn't failed. Years later I met Brisbane socialite and newspaper columnist Brian Sweeney who had a card with 'Poet (Failed)' printed on it. At least he tried!

Anyway, I had gone home to the big house on the Nerang River with my tail between my legs, donning a white moustache from the antacid I was chugging down daily at that stage. Eighteen months earlier I had set off with high hopes but had crashed and burned like some sad second-rate rock star, and here I was in my very own version of *One Flew Over the Cuckoo's Nest*.

Home should be a haven, and it was, but only to a certain degree. Because my father's drinking continued unabated.

I'm not entirely sure how my brother and sister dealt with this, but my coping mechanism was to internalize my anger, sorrow and confusion. Living with active alcoholism, survivors experience a sort of PTSD, I think. It's hard to be in a house where this is happening yet you are powerless to stop it.

Life was never ordinary at our place, which is not to suggest we didn't have good times. But I found it difficult, to say the least, watching my dad, an amazing man, slide into abject alcoholism. He had done so much in his life, which began in working-class London – Catford, to be exact.

The family moved to Shanghai in the 1930s and then to Canton (the city today known as Guangzhou) and on to Hong Kong, and during World War Two my dad and some of the family were evacuated to Australia as the Japanese headed south. He fought in the Australian Army (the illustrious 2/14th Battalion) and went on afterwards to a hugely successful business career as a civil engineering contractor in Australia and then back in Hong Kong.

He was a self-made man and in the 1960s had his own company in Hong Kong where we lived the high life in what was then a British colony. But, since returning to Australia at the end of 1969 on a promise that he would curtail his drinking, things had got worse and seven years later his health was suffering – and we were all suffering with him, in our own ways. It must have been terribly difficult for my mum.

So I'd decided to become ill as my strategy for coping.

Since my last year in high school, I had been on and off pills for my supposed nervous disposition. When I was 18, I went to see a doctor at Broadbeach who, after asking me if I was in love ('Not as such,' I told him), prescribed me Mogadon. I went home, took a tab and walked around the house like a drunken sailor, bouncing off the walls. I was nicely numb.

As a student in Toowoomba, I had been prescribed benzodiazepines for my 'condition' (a rather nebulous one) and they certainly helped because they put you in a mild vegetative state where nothing really matters much. What did they used to call them? Mother's little helpers? Okay. They help, but there's a catch. You swap pain for addiction. The opioid crisis in the US demonstrates this rather tragically.

I wasn't quite hooked yet. Waking that morning at Glen Pacific Private Hospital I was, as I said, just a bit groggy but, strangely, happy enough. Should one be happy after being admitted to hospital following a nervous breakdown at the tender age of 20?

It's strange to me that my memories of that brief confinement are overwhelmingly positive, as if these were somehow my salad days, even if the tomatoes weren't ripe and the lettuce was wilted.

It did, as I said, feel a little like being on holiday in this funky old hospital at Main Beach, a retro pile, long since demolished (there's a block of nondescript apartments there now). Originally it was the Hotel Sans Souci, opened in 1938 at the tail-end of the Art Deco period. During World War Two it served as an officers' club for the Americans based in Queensland. There were thousands of Yanks in Queensland then: 'oversexed, overpaid and over here' was how they were seen.

I remember my first afternoon there sitting on the verandah overlooking the sea amid a small group of largely elderly patients, not all of whom were fully conscious.

It was another scene from some movie adapted from a book … *A Farewell to Arms*, the story of a wounded soldier escaping the rigours of the front in World War One and recuperating in a hospital by the sea. In my imagination I was Hemingway's protagonist, a cipher for himself, Frederic Henry (Rock Hudson in the famous 1957 film), and I might soon meet a nurse to fall in love with as Frederic did with Catherine Barkley, who was played by Jennifer Jones on screen. And there is something about a woman in a crisp white uniform. As Jerry Seinfeld says when asked why he's attracted to a uniformed chambermaid:

'Well, it's a woman in your room.' Exactly.

This was also the year Mel Brooks' *High Anxiety* – which I name-checked earlier – came out, so in my mind I was still in 'The Institute', not the DDIAE but the Psycho-Neurotic Institute for the Very, Very Nervous. There was more than a hint of the sanatorium about Glen Pacific Private Hospital. Strangely, none of this worried me in the least. I was revelling in the respite.

Our family doctor, Emmanuel Cominos, had helped with my admission. He was a very nice man although, according to my father, something of a hypochondriac, which was ironic. Then again, I guess if you're a medico you know exactly how sick one can get.

I recall my dad telling us the story of how he went to see the doctor once and told him, as a parting shot, that he didn't look at all well. My father did have a hell of a sense of humour. As he left the rooms, he saw Dr Cominos examining himself in the mirror, sticking his tongue out, obviously concerned by what my old man had said. My dad's sense of humour remained intact when he was sober enough to still be funny.

I'm not sure there was an actual diagnosis for my malaise at the time of my admission. It was a combination of things, and I'm not sure anybody ever actually defined it as a nervous breakdown. I refer to it as 'my first crack-up' (with apologies to F. Scott Fitzgerald) and I can never recall it without thinking of that Rolling Stones song *19th Nervous Breakdown*. Hopefully, I wouldn't emulate that.

Looking back, I think of it more as an existential crisis than anything else. It was my mind and my soul that were really the problem. It was all very Nietzschean and I thought of the novel *Iron in the Soul*. Maybe I was afflicted by iron in my soul?

My inner turmoil was being reflected outwardly in the physical body, that's my non-professional diagnosis of what was happening to me. Of course, I have no qualifications for such a diagnosis and in those days there was no Dr Google.

I like to think of it as a kind of 'existentialitis'. After my hospital stay I was referred to a psychiatrist, a stylish bloke by the name of Dr Bianchi who had rooms in Surfers Paradise and was probably kept pretty busy. There have always been a lot of nuts on the Gold Coast.

Anyway, I was, as I said, strangely happy in my hospital by the sea where I spent the first couple of days lounging around, reading and jotting a few lines here and there.

Mind you, maybe *The Bell Jar* by Sylvia Plath wasn't the ideal reading material but I guess the choice of that book reflected my state of mind, and having studied her poetry in Toowoomba I was a fan although I was inevitably aware of her sad ending. I also had a book of D.H. Lawrence's poetry with me which I was still a little bit in love with at the time. There was a freedom in his verse that I loved, and the image of the consumptive poet and author in his pyjamas in his poem *Snake* appealed to me. (Staying at Taormina in Sicily at the time, he says he was wearing them for the heat.)

I wasn't consumptive but there are so many cases of poets and writers dying young from tuberculosis that it seemed almost fashionable, in a literary sense. I'm not saying I wanted to be consumptive, but I was kind of living the consumptive lifestyle banged up at Glen Pacific Private Hospital and taking the evening air on the balcony overlooking the ocean, whereas others sat around me with rugs over their knees.

As well as reading *The Bell Jar*, a novel inspired by Plath's own mental issues, I was reading *Death and Eternal Life*, a jolly little volume by John Hick. This subject was fascinating to me at the time, even though I think it was more death as an abstract notion than anything.

A poem of mine from around this time is simply called *Death*. Mum, who sometimes used to look over my verses, was not happy to see her 20-year-old son writing about death as something to be welcomed. I can imagine how worried she was about me. As if she didn't have enough concerns with my father. He was drinking himself to death while I was at risk of thinking myself to death.

My *Death* ends:

When we saw him coming / Why did we not rejoice / In his pleasant, endless dreamer's tales / And his lovely, lulling voice?

The other book that was my constant companion at this time was *The Intellectual Life* by P.G. Hamerton, which had been published in 1873. I had an early-20th-century edition that was given to me by my mother's aunty, Lois. Aunty Lo, as she was known, was in her eighties at the time and still rattling around an historic home on Gregory Terrace, Brisbane, in which she had lived with her late husband, Dr Karl Brunnich, a medico who had his rooms at the house as doctors used to do.

The house, still there, is called Lokarlton, and not many people know it is called that as a hybrid of their names (Lois and Karl).

Karl was a very literary man with an extensive library and nobody to pass it on to, as he and his wife had no children. As far as Aunty Lo was concerned, the relatives extant at the time were philistines and she did not want to cast pearls before swine. So she took to drip-feeding me her late husband's books. I made several visits and came away with boxes of antiquarian titles, including the twenty-volume *Masterpiece Library of Short Stories* and a ten-volume leather-bound collection of the works of Guy de Maupassant who I'd learnt about from Somerset Maugham, himself a big fan of that French writer.

The Intellectual Life was among the treasure trove of books I thus inherited.

It's a wonderful investigation of the creative life in an epistolary style. In his preface, Hamerton writes: 'I propose, in the following pages, to consider a satisfactory intellectual life under various conditions of ordinary human existence. It will form a part of my plan to take into account favourable and unfavourable influences of many kinds; and my chief purpose, as far as any effect upon others may be hoped for, will be to guard some who may read the book against the loss of time caused by unnecessary discouragement, and the waste of effort which is the consequence of misdirected energies.' It's delicious stuff and a fascinating read. I mean, who knew that Kant couldn't sleep unless he was wrapped tightly in a sheet?

When I opened the book, I found a pressed flower between the pages which led me to write a poem entitled *A Flower (for Lois).* My mum loved this poem. In her later years she had it framed and hung it in her bedroom.

Reading it with slow reverence / One silent midnight / The last pages fell open / To reveal a flower / Pressed.
God knows whose hands, / Young and soft in the sunlight, / Placed it so.
Do older hands still recall / The gentle act?

I wrote that just before my admission and some new poems while ensconced in the hospital by the sea. One that I cherish in particular is called *Lady by the Sea*. It's about an elderly lady I chatted to a few times on the front verandah. She couldn't quite work out why I was there.

She had the air of an aged, faded screen starlet (there was a touch of the Gloria Swanson about her) and I watched her one day as she sat near me overlooking the ocean. As she dozed off I wrote:

Alone she sits, nodding into the breeze, / Stranded by relatives long gone / Whose desertion cut her old heart / Like a secret knife.

The poem ends:

Her ancient ignorance of all around / Seems bitter-sweet to me, / Younger, stronger, lover of the sea / Which is slowly draining / Like the colour from her leaven cheek.

Ah, but all good things come to an end, and soon I left my hospital by the sea, never to return. It was an enforced life of leisure for a little while, but I was soon back home with no prospects and facing a Shakespearean dilemma. To be or not to be? And that is as pertinent a question as they come.

I found some solace in religion at the time. I converted to Catholicism, which seemed odd to some people and shocking to others, I think. The Catholic Church was certainly surprised. I say that because I had done a correspondence course on Catholicism due to my interest in the faith, and on being received into the Church I got a letter from the priest who ran the correspondence course and he was ecstatic. It was like, *Wow, we got one!*

I have always had Christian beliefs and, unlike a former Brisbane Catholic priest I heard on the radio once, I do believe that Jesus existed. We weren't brought up in a religious household though. Mum was Presbyterian, and my siblings and I were all baptised in her Church due to my father's lapsed Catholicism.

He was from a big Catholic family. I had shopped around various churches, including the evangelical ones on the Gold Coast, but just couldn't come at that sort of religion, and the sound of 'Christian rock' is anathema to me.

The fact that Bruce Dawe and Les Murray were practising Catholics impressed me and there are other literary models including, of course, Graham Greene, who has always been a favourite of mine. I grew up reading short stories by him, Hemingway and Maugham. Greene's conflicted Catholicism demonstrated that you could be a Catholic and imperfect. Very imperfect in his case, and mine too, I guess.

I enjoyed the formalism of the Catholic Mass and was accepted into the Church at St Vincent's in Surfers Paradise by Fr Paul Molony, who was a bit of a celebrity priest of that time. He could be seen in the morning jogging along Surfers Paradise beach.

I know that eventually he left the Church and imagine that being based on the Gold Coast didn't help. He became a teacher.

At home I was just reading and writing and sponging off my parents who weren't quite sure what to do with me. God knows what my brother and sister thought was going on.

A couple of years earlier I had been a tearaway surf rat and now I was an aspiring poet with depression tapping away on a typewriter set up in the spare bedroom next to mine as I emulated certain deceased literary figures.

I was taking various potions for my ulcer and trying a bland diet to deal with it. I read that the herb comfrey could actually heal ulcers so I started a little comfrey garden down the side of the house. I tended it daily and got quite a little patch of the green stuff growing there, although I did get some funny looks from the neighbours, country folk who had retired to the Gold Coast. I think they suspected I was cultivating something altogether different.

I also took to drinking various herbal teas, including basil and borage, because I read that the knights of old used to drink it to fortify themselves for battle.

Living by the river as we did was in some ways quite idyllic. Our house, at 8 River Crescent, Cypress Gardens, was virtually in the country when we first moved there. Suburban sprawl was only beginning to encroach but nearby farms largely sustained its rural character.

As a teenager I spent a lot of time ranging round the countryside there. I was a keen birdwatcher and had a copy of Neville W. Cayley's classic *What Bird Is That?* which was my ornithological bible at the time. I had a canoe and used to paddle up the nearby creek into the wilder part of the local landscape. It's a lost world reflected in a poem entitled *A Little Idyll*, which uses a sort of nonsense language to extol the virtues of the natural world.

I won't bore you with the whole thing but here's the first stanza:

I wandered down by the Stygian creek / Just so I could use the word, / When all of a sudden the sun came out / Illuminating a small, azure bird / Twitching its tail in a thicket. / The air was cool as a wet towel. / I felt the magic deep in my bowels / And was happy as a Greek.

In the evenings at home at River Crescent I would walk round our little suburb by the river. I would set out after dinner with my walking cane and sometimes my pipe. My mother had bought me that pipe when she realized I was smoking. She thought a pipe was better than cigarettes, though I still smoked them too, on occasion.

In fact, I'd had a packet smuggled into the hospital when I was there and, late in the evening, would steal into the adjacent car park and puff away in the cool seaside evening air.

Walking along River Crescent, I might have seemed a tad eccentric. All I lacked was a deerstalker hat and you could have called me Sherlock. No affectation involved, of course.

In C.S. Lewis's *Mere Christianity*, which I was reading at the time, I had seen photos of Lewis smoking a pipe. I'm not saying I thought I *was* C.S. Lewis. I didn't know who I was. One minute I was D.H. Lawrence, next minute Dylan Thomas, sometimes maybe C.S. Lewis and, very occasionally, Somerset Maugham.

I was writing short stories at the time, too, although I think they were inspired more by John O'Hara, a writer Bruce Dawe had introduced me to. Walking at night was good for composition, I felt. I had read a biography of P.G. Wodehouse, who loved to walk and received inspiration for his novels on his long strolls. I walked to get inspiration too, as well as to get out of the house. Walking at night gave me a few poems, including one from this period (my blue period?) entitled *Night's Estate*, which is a tad wintry and dour.

Midnight and the suburban wastes / Spread beneath a brittle sky.
I wander the dark street floes / Weaving past houses that lie /
Pristine, still / Like butterflies pinned under the glass of the hour.

It ends with a bit of religious imagery.

Once, on a white morning I heard a voice calling from a distance,
faintly / … 'All is love.'
But all is quiet.
Only the autumn's song of woe / Is remembered by the sky /
And silently the white moon mouths / Its ghostly lullaby.

I liked that poem, but poetry editors didn't. I was submitting it to various journals at the time and rejection slips were coming back thick and fast. In those days you would send your poems out with a stamped self-addressed envelope so that they could be returned to you, rejected or accepted.

I was getting a lot of rejection. I remember getting a 'Dear Phil' letter from the poet Kris Hemensley, who was editor of *Meanjin* at the time. He pointed out that my writing was narrative poetry and that wasn't fashionable.

'I am not able to consider the poems for publication because what I'm seeking is a poetry that's more than a simple story,' he wrote. 'And written in language a bit more demanding than simple rhyme.'

He suggested I seek publication elsewhere and finished with the rather unnecessary line: 'What is poison for one might well be life's elixir for another.' Ouch.

I was a bit too square for *Meanjin* and the poet Judith Rodriguez wrote me a number of nicer rejections in later years when she was poetry editor.

It is amazing to me that poets continue writing, considering the amount of rejection dished out – and I have had decades of it. I mean, in some ways I was fairly fragile in 1977 yet, despite the knockbacks, I kept scribbling and submitting. I guess that shows a certain doggedness and determination, and maybe a will to persist rather than cease to exist.

Poetry is such a subjective business, though. Poems that have been dismissed as piffle by one editor can be embraced by another.

Poets are funny creatures and some editors make sweeping statements about poetry that are patent nonsense. One has to remember that it is just their opinion, no matter how dogmatic they are or how right they claim to be. Even Les Murray could be wrong.

You can't take it personally (although we do!) and you just have to fire your arrows into the air and hope they land somewhere and that, eventually, one of them will find a target.

I have written a few pieces about resilience, focusing on that virtue in sport, namely junior cricket. I watched my son Hamish learn resilience on the cricket field week in, week out, with moments of agony and ecstasy. Cricket requires patience and teamwork: it forges resilience.

But I reckon nothing builds resilience more than being a poet. The amount of rejection poets get is staggering and yet we persevere, putting ourselves out there, setting ourselves up for failure time after time. We're just asking for it, really.

And the rejection doesn't stop even when you have made it as a poet. I remember Bruce Dawe telling me once how, when his reputation had already been made and he was regarded as part of the pantheon of Australian poetry, some bloke starting a new literary journal in Melbourne had solicited some verses for their first edition, to help get them going.

Bruce, being Bruce, had obliged only to have his poems rejected. He thought that was funny. I didn't necessarily think rejection was funny but kept at it. Crazy, huh?

I was certainly something of an anomaly in our household. My brother Steve, who is five years younger than me, was more into sport and his burgeoning body-building career. He played Australian Rules football for Broadbeach. I wasn't into sport then and can honestly say I never attended one of his games. My father and mother went, and Dad used to sit and watch Aussie Rules football on telly at the weekend.

My sister, Jane, had a busy social life and a boyfriend, so that kept her busy too. They were out and about while I haunted the house like the ghost of Christmas past, reading, writing or playing my music. I wrote upstairs at my table (you couldn't really call it a desk) overlooking the river.

I would write poems there in longhand and also jot in my journal, every day, every day lines I thought worth revisiting or quotes from books that had inspired me.

I would type my poems up in the spare room after a couple of longhand drafts (I still use the same method today) and then put them into folders.

I didn't have much interaction with other writers. I was still in touch with my poet friend Rod from Toowoomba. He was as confused as I was but still versifying. I had my regular correspondence with Bruce Dawe and that kind of kept me going. I did also, at one point, find a little writers' group which met in a hall at Mermaid Beach and the people there were very kind to me.

The Gold Coast was not exactly a hotbed of literary activity at that time. My social life was limited. I didn't have any actual relationships before getting married in my thirties. Okay, I did have some dalliances that never quite worked out, possibly because I was certifiable. The fact nothing worked out romantically was always good for poetry though.

And I think it was poetry that sustained me at that time in my life. Composing poems can be very cathartic and therapeutic. That does not mean it's always good poetry, but who cares? If it helps, write it, I say.

I have never been very intellectual in my approach to poetry. For me it has always been more about feelings, or a feeling. Wordsworth's previously cited 'spontaneous overflow of powerful feelings … recollected in tranquillity' – a beautiful idea – has it just right. For me, as a young man, poetry was sustenance. It kept me going at a time that was full of risk. When one is young and depressed and taking various medications, it can be a bit dangerous.

I'm always mindful of the deaths of Nick Drake and Heath Ledger, both of whom overdosed on antidepressants and died young. It's too sad. And being a Michael Dransfield admirer I was also keenly aware of the death trap that drug addiction can be. Those last lines of his poem *Fix* are tragic and haunting:

> *Once you have become a drug addict / You will never want to be anything else.*

The illogical logic of drug addiction.

Some of the poetry and music I imbibed was full of such pessimism, whether it was Dransfield or Lou Reed's album *Berlin* or Jim Morrison. Looking back, having survived, I do feel a certain nostalgia for that time, the dawning of my poetic sensibilities, fraught as it all was. And I remember those wilted salad days, banged up with my books and notebooks in that hospital by the sea with *The Bell Jar* by my side.

The Glen Pacific Private Hospital seems like a rather romantic place in retrospect. I can't revisit it since it's not physically there so I preserve it in the aspic of memory. And when I play back scenes from that Glen Pacific time in my mind's eye it's like watching an old movie but it's me starring, not Rock Hudson. Is it weird to think fondly of my time there?

Who looks back on a hospital admission as one of the fondest memories of their youth?

Okay, you can put your hands down now.

CHAPTER 5

RADIO DAZE

THE DOOR SLID open and Maurie the salesman stuck his head in.

'Anyone home?' he asked.

'Welcome to my broom closet,' I said. He edged into the room, if you could call it a room. I was reading a book while waiting for the next ad brief to drop into my in-tray.

'What are you reading?' Maurie asked.

'*The Story of My Experiments with Truth* by Mohandas K. Gandhi,' I said, holding the book up.

'Who?'

'Gandhi,' I said. 'You may know him as the Mahatma.'

'I don't know him from Adam,' said Maurie. 'But as long as you're happy.'

He put the sheet of paper containing the latest ad brief into the tray and rushed out through the other door just over a metre away. Maurie was always in a rush, off to do the next deal. It was a bloody short trip across my office at Gold Coast city radio station 4GG.

That office was just big enough for three or four people at the most to stand up in, as long as none of them were overweight.

In that room under a naked, glaring bar of neon there were two filing cabinets and me sitting behind a poky little desk with an old Olivetti typewriter that looked like it could have once belonged to Sir Keith Murdoch. To the left of it was my in-tray and on the other side, logically enough, my out-tray.

I was the station's copywriter, responsible for churning out 20-second and 30-second ads to be recorded for airplay on a radio station that most of the population of the Glitter Strip slavishly listened to in 1977 when I started work there.

Looking back now I can see it was great training – for poetry and journalism. The discipline of being concise and writing within a template was valuable, even if what I was writing was commercial inanity. I wrote ads for white-goods sales, car yards, new housing estates that were daily eating up the natural habitat of the Gold Coast, boats, takeaway food … you name it, I was writing ads about it.

Like so many things in my life, the job was not something I aspired to but rather something that circumstance had dished out: the fickle finger of Fate, as they used to call it on *Rowan & Martin's Laugh-In.* Somewhere it was written that I would, almost by accident, spend a year-and-a-half toiling away in an office as big as an outdoor toilet writing those annoying ads you sometimes hear on your car radio driving to and from work.

Before I got the job I had largely been lounging at home, depressed, under the care of my new psychiatrist, Dr Julian Boulnois, writing poetry and musing on my future fame as a literary figure. I was on sickness benefits at the time so, technically speaking, my writing was federally funded, but my father thought I should get a job.

It was sometimes hard for me to take his advice because we were at loggerheads much of the time. His drinking had eroded our relationship. I loved him, of course, and I guess he loved me but, as

I have said, it's hard to watch someone slowly drink themselves to death. It's heartbreaking, actually, and tinges your world-view with a mix of anger and sadness. There were good days and bad days in our household but that's just how it rolls sometimes.

To say it was difficult for my mother would be a gross understatement.

Our house had two wings, one for the three kids and one for my parents, and by sticking to my own wing I managed to live in a kind of fog of denial. Everything I wrote, however, was shadowed with melancholy.

Despite our at times rocky relationship, it was my father who got me the job at 4GG, which was really my first proper one. He was always looking out for me. As I said, it was the station everyone listened to and all the stars who were appearing at various venues up and down the Gold Coast were guests on air as they passed through Australia's very own Tinseltown.

As a teen I was glued to 4GG, listening to it religiously for *Mick Carey's Surf & Beach Report*, which was introduced, like most things, with a hokey jingle. Any surfer growing up on the Gold Coast in the 1970s would remember it.

I got the job at 4GG through Dad's friendship with Barry Ferber, the charismatic former Melbourne DJ who ran the station and in September 2024 died in Las Vegas, to which he had long since relocated. Ferber is credited with being the first person to play a Beatles record on air in Australia. My old man had a steam bath a couple of times a week at a gym in Surfers Paradise, a joint owned by a bloke known – God knows why – as Turkey Taylor.

Dad sometimes ran into Ferber in the sauna there. I had first met Barry when I was shanghaied into competing in the Lions Youth of the Year quest in my senior year at Miami State High School. Our headmaster, Bill Callinan, had summoned me, my mate

Pete Kelleher and another schoolboy into his office and enthused: 'Congratulations, lads, you have just entered the Lions Youth of the Year quest.' We just looked at each other and shrugged. He wasn't asking us to enter, he was *telling* us, and you always did what Big Bill told you to do.

I won my local chapter, held at the Broadbeach International Hotel, where I would one day be fired as a waiter working in the Celebrity Room. Just because I threw a bread roll at someone. How unfair.

My Lions Youth of the Year speech was entitled 'Australia – The Lucky Country' (yes, I know), and I delivered it wearing sky blue flares and a body shirt, reeking of Brut.

I got knocked out in the next round held at Southport.

Ferber was one of the judges for my triumph at Broadbeach. So, a few years later, when he was taking a steam with my old man, he asked him what I was doing now and I guess Dad told him I was doing nothing which, despite my literary endeavours, was close to the truth.

Barry told him to send me in to see him. I went reluctantly and Barry told me they had a job going as a copywriter and, as a journalism dropout who wanted to be a writer, I might be just the man for the job. He gave me the outlines of a couple of ads, the sort I would eventually work on, and sent me off to write some of my own as homework. I was to come back and see him the following week, which I did – but I hadn't written a word.

I don't know, if I were in his place that might have been it but, maybe because he knew my dad or because he could see a glimmer of hope for me in the absence of actual evidence, he sent me off to try again.

This time I did sketch out a few advertisements on my Remington at home. I went back to 4GG's offices, which were at

Bundall on the outskirts of Surfers Paradise. He looked my work over and then called in the creative director, a former Kiwi DJ by the name of Paul Lineham. We chatted, seemed to get on okay, and then, to my surprise, I was hired on the spot, somewhat against my will.

I was shown into my office, a cramped little room behind reception. In reality, that job probably saved me. I still wanted to be a journalist but falling into this copywriting lark was a start, the first step of the thousand-mile journey, as the Chinese say, even though I couldn't see that at the time.

So, there I sat behind an old Olivetti all day hammering out an endless stream of what I imagine was excruciating copy.

Every now and then the sliding door to my right would open and Mark, the production guy, would appear. He had a moustache that looked as if a large black caterpillar had died on his upper lip and he would whisk my finished products into the nearby studio where the ads were recorded for airplay sometimes that same day. Some were read out live on air by whichever DJ was on at the time. They were all blokes except for the lady who did the night shift, Bev Francis, who was known as Miss Midnight. No, really, that's what they called her.

There were lulls in the proceedings when I would sit and daydream or read books such as Gandhi's autobiography. I had a lovely cloth-covered edition which I had bought at a little alternative bookshop in Kirra. I was interested in Gandhi not necessarily because he was such a great man (this was before Ben Kingsley immortalized him in Richard Attenborough's classic film) but primarily because my father used to refer to me as Gandhi and that made me curious about him.

I wore round gold-rimmed spectacles like the Mahatma's and often my father would call me by shouting 'Hey Gandhi!', which

I got used to. So, I thought I might as well find out a little bit about the bloke.

My father was built like a brick shithouse and had played rugby (he was a forward) for Hong Kong Football Club in the late 1940s, but I have always been slim, taking, I think, after my mum's side of the family. She had been a GPS sprint champion when she was at Brisbane Girls Grammar School.

I wasn't a sprinter, but I guess I was built like one, and my father had various other terms for me too, such as being built 'like a racing tadpole'.

When not reading Gandhi's autobiography I would be dipping into something by Hermann Hesse, Ken Kesey or Richard Brautigan, or have my nose in a book of poetry. I wrote some of my own stuff at 4GG between jobs, quickly stuffing the poems into the top drawer of the desk when anyone came in. One of my 4GG poems was a lament about being desk-bound. It was entitled, well, *Lament.*

> *No creatures came to my desk today, / To my lonely wooden shore, / Not one small mouse or a butterfly / Or two or three or four; / All I saw were these silent walls / And the ceiling and the floor.*

I had also decided to learn a couple of poems off by heart and did that by writing them in longhand over and over. One was Dylan Thomas's classic villanelle *Do Not Go Gentle into That Good Night* (a poem about his father, which resonated for obvious reasons) and Shakespeare's *Shall I Compare Thee to a Summer's Day?* (Sonnet 18).

The rest of the time I sat in that little room with music piped in through a speaker behind me all day writing turgid advertising copy. The music of that era, like it or not, is stamped indelibly on my consciousness, burnt into my memory by repetition.

I can't tell you how many times I listened to *Reminiscing* by LRB or *Jeans On* by David Dundas, a song about him putting his trousers on, or *Jet Airliner* by the Steve Miller Band, one of my favourites. These songs and many others filled 4GG's airwaves on high rotation.

I was indoctrinated with the soundtrack of the late Seventies. It was like something out of *The IPCRESS File*. Yet at the same time I was imbibing alternative literature, reading, writing or reciting poetry: I learnt poems off by heart while producing those tedious radio ads. But I had a bit of a knack for it, apparently.

4GG was a pretty happening place and, as I suggested, it was celebrity central. I remember during my first week there running into the celebrated and flamboyant Bernard King in the hallway, a figure in a big red hat approaching from the other end of the corridor who, as he approached and saw me, announced with undisguised enthusiasm: 'Oh, a new face!' in response to which I smiled bleakly in passing on my way to the men's room.

Noel Ferrier, Barry Humphries, Noelene Brown, Barry Creyton, it was a cavalcade of Aussie stars through the place, often doing guest stints on air. People like Liberace and Sammy Davis Jr visited 4GG at one time or another. Some years later I was invited back to have lunch in the boardroom with Barry Ferber and Ronnie Corbett, the shorter half of The Two Ronnies.

The atmosphere was cheerful and full of fun. 4GG was a beacon of brightness, supposed to reflect the sunny disposition of the Gold Coast as a tourist haven. There's an apocryphal story about how at one point the announcers were counselled not to mention when it was raining, so as not to put visiting Victorians off.

Things were a little less cheerful in the copywriter's closet where, it was rumoured, a somewhat melancholy young poet laboured away day in, day out.

I couldn't quite get into the spirit of a place so relentlessly sunny. All the salesmen and executives wore white shoes, white trousers and colourful resort-style shirts. They looked like Ricardo Montalbán wannabes or extras from Seventies British TV series *Paradise Island.*

My boss, Paul, didn't wear that clobber as far as I can recall. He was a pretty mellow, rather cool dude who was very good to me and seemed to understand that I was not as others were. Promotions boss Ian Cousins was another who treated me with empathy and understanding and we became friends. Barry Ferber was also on my side even though he was a tad distant, ruling the roost and fraternizing with the stars who frequented his office and the boardroom.

The disc jockeys, who were compulsorily bright and bubbly, were known as Double G Great Guys. They wore T-shirts (or sometimes the colourful station shirts) with 4GG logos on them. I wore my *Nation Review* T-shirt emblazoned with Leunig's famous Ferret.

I became close friends with a DJ named Greg Newman and we are still mates. Greg was a born-again Christian (still is) and we seemed *simpatico*, even though my own Christian beliefs were a tad complicated compared to his. I couldn't quite embrace the happy-clappy kind of church he went to, although on occasion I tried.

The morning announcer was a bloke called Bert Robertson, a bit of a legend on the airwaves. Birdbrain Bert, they called him.

He took a shine to me and I even got on his show once posing as a woman called Phyllis. (This might not be acceptable today.) I burst into the studio in drag, armed with an umbrella and pretended to beat Noel Ferrier, an on-air guest at the time, with it. Strange behaviour, but I guess it proved that I could get into the Pythonesque spirit of the joint when I wanted to.

I also occasionally raided the props department for clown noses or giant plastic elf ears which I would wear at my desk, much to the amusement of the salesmen.

Increasingly, I also wrote myself into some of my ads, inspired by my love of The Goons. So sometimes my advertisement would include a silly voice that only I could do. Nobody else at 4GG seemed able to mimic Bluebottle or Eccles. Clever, wasn't I!

My life in 1977 and '78 revolved around the radio station, my desk at home and the armchair in my bedroom where I did my reading late at night. Surfing had dropped off and social life was patchy, although I did go out at times with friends like my pal Mark Mitchell who had two sisters everyone was in love with. Socializing sometimes involved smoking dope, which I don't think was very good for me, looking back on it now.

My depressive episode had scarred me to a certain degree and, struggling with my ulcer, I lived on a diet designed not to inflame my gut. Of course, the disturbances in my gut probably had more to do with my emotions than my diet but that's easy to say in retrospect.

I was submitting poems regularly and they tended to reflect my general state of being. One I was quite proud of at the time was *Bert*. It was not about Bert Robertson *per se* but, rather, about an old man having a stroke.

> *He was never again the same for her, / That shaky old man with the shell-shock slur.*

I had been corresponding with the poet Les Murray at the behest of Bruce Dawe, and Les had shown interest in my poems. That relationship was soon to bear fruit.

In 1978 while working at 4GG I had my first real poetic breakthrough when I was included in a little anthology, *8 Poets 1978*, published by the North Brisbane College of Advanced Education. My poet mate from Toowoomba days, Rod Warrener, also made the cut and we had both been recommended to the editor, Ken Albion, by Bruce Dawe. I guess that probably got us across the line. My poem *Bert* was, gratifyingly, among the five I had published in that slim volume. I went to Brisbane for the launch and along with me came my mate Cratis Hippocrates, who by then was studying at UQ.

Another of the poets in the anthology was Peter Anderson, a writer and art critic who would later become a friend and who, sadly, is no longer with us.

It was a debut of sorts for several of us, as we discovered years later.

Also departed now is the Dutch-Australian performance poet Cornelis Vleeskens, who had a bit of a profile on the Australian literary scene back then, was included as well. At the launch, where we all read briefly from our work, he chose a poem entitled *The Political Situation in Laos* which included the line:

They're journalists: they know what's going on in Laos.

I liked that because I thought of myself as a journalist then even though I wasn't one. Not yet. I wasn't quite sure what I actually was, or what I wanted to do. A writer? Yes. A journalist? Maybe. Copywriter? Perhaps.

At one point, while still working at 4GG, I decided I wanted to save the world by joining World Vision. I instituted a child sponsorship on behalf of the station and applied for a job as a copywriter at the Melbourne-based charity.

To my great surprise they granted me an interview and even flew me down for it, which was problematic because, due to my high-tensile nervous state, I had developed a fear of flying. I still remember sitting in that plane gritting my teeth all the way south, looking out the window at the earth below and wishing I was on terra firma.

It was the first time I had ever been to Melbourne, and I wore my turtleneck under my op-shop-bought tweed jacket for the trip. I remember arriving in the city and walking along a pavement in a scene that resembled John Brack's famous painting of Collins Street.

I was very much out of place, unsure of which direction I was supposed to be going, and was, apparently, walking on the wrong side of the footpath at peak hour, an antisocial act pointed out to me by a short stocky bloke in a suit who knocked me over.

'Get out of the fucking way,' he said. No 'Welcome to Melbourne' or anything. I ended up in the gutter with my overnight bag on top of me.

But the indignity did not end there.

I had my interview at World Vision shortly afterwards (I eventually found my way to their office) and it was obvious to them and to me that I was not going to save the world at all and in fact was, for so many reasons, unsuitable for employment with their organization. Next morning I flew north and the day after that was back at my desk at 4GG listening to *Reminiscing* for the umpteenth time.

I eked out just over a year at 4GG, which was pretty impressive considering my mental state. That it was a station full of eccentrics helped me survive and, despite my bouts of depression, the experience was enjoyable. In his reference, Paul Lineham cited my sense of humour as a positive. Go figure.

But for some reason I'd decided I needed to move on so I left in September 1978. What I was going to do now was unclear although, having made a start in advertising, I considered going on with it. I mean, a lot of great writers have worked in advertising, have they not?

Peter Carey, Augusten Burroughs, Salman Rushdie, F. Scott Fitzgerald, Brisbane-born Peter Porter … the list goes on. So maybe

I could also pursue a career in that field? Not that I am comparing myself to those writers but you get my point.

With that in mind I had my eye on the Big Smoke, Brisbane, the city we had so derided when I was a teenage surfie. Brisbane was the arsehole of the Universe as far as we were concerned and anyone who emanated from that shithole was to be shunned and hounded out of the water on our home break at First Avenue, Broadbeach. Such was the local myopia of my surfing crew. It was locals only. Brizzos were banned.

But I had softened somewhat regarding Brisbane, and now, having obtained an interview with Clemenger, an ad agency there, was summoned to the city.

Their office was reasonably flash, and it was there I met the creative director, who looked over some of the work I had brought with me in a slim folder. He suggested I meet a few of the writers. It's a loaded term, 'writer', one that can mean different things to different people.

I was taken to a room where several of the agency's 'writers' were sitting looking intently at a small television set which was playing vision from, well, I guess it would have been a videotape back then.

On the screen was a plate of sizzling sausages and these 'writers' were focused so intently on the screen that at first they didn't even notice us come in.

But then their sausage-inspired reverie was momentarily broken as I was introduced around. They then quickly went back to the sausages, and each of them made jottings in a pad balanced on his knees.

I wanted to quip: 'What is this, *Ode to a Sausage*?' but resisted the urge. Don't get me wrong: I like sausages but have never been inspired to write about them. Not so far, at least.

They seemed to be taking the whole thing very seriously. I could have come up with several puns involving the word 'snag' but thought better of it.

We left them to their sausages, went back out into the corridor and embarked on a short tour of the office. We then shook hands and I drove back to the Gold Coast, leaving Brisbane literally (and the sausages metaphorically) in my rear-view mirror.

Maybe a job in advertising wasn't such a good idea after all. I mean, what would I be selling, the sausage or the sizzle?

CHAPTER 6

A BUDDHA IN SUBURBIA

It was late and the passengers were slowly draining from the train's dining car as the official sitting was long over. My ticket was for the second session of the evening so I remained in my little booth.

I topped up my cup from time to time with what was now stewed tea.

A couple of staff – a waitress and a conductor – sat at a nearby table. The waitress kept looking at her watch and then at me, obviously hoping I would get the hint.

I paused and stared out the window, beyond my own reflection, at the bush outside, *rushing rivers* of it as Kenneth Slessor had described just such a scene in his classic poem *The Night-Ride*. Slessor's poem was intrinsic to my love of train travel, and I was thinking about him when the staff figured they'd finally had enough.

'That's it for us and that's it for you too, matey,' the conductor said. 'We have to get some sleep. Time for you to go back to your seat.'

The waitress, in her soiled white uniform, then got up and ushered me out. She had been very friendly earlier in the evening but was now decidedly grumpy. I couldn't know it then, but she would turn up in one of my poems many years later.

I was putting off returning to my seat because that's all I had – a seat. I couldn't afford a sleeper cabin so I would have to spend the night fetching as much shut-eye as I could sitting up, which I had done before. It took me a full day to walk fully upright again after that.

After being ejected from the dining car I walked, with the sort of sailor's gait that is required on a train, back to my allotted seat to continue my pilgrimage.

People make pilgrimages to all sorts of places: Mecca, Rome, Lourdes … the cathedral in Santiago de Compostela via that long trek known as The Camino. I'm thinking not so many make pilgrimages to Chatswood on Sydney's North Shore.

That's where I was bound, ultimately, as the Gold Coast Motorail rattled through the night on its way south. I travelled on this train a few times when I was young. It used to depart from Murwillumbah, just across the border in New South Wales. It was easier to catch a train from there than from Brisbane.

The first hour or two on board was nice, winding through the verdant hippie hills and past Byron Bay, and then you settled into the rattling rhythm as the train ground on through the night.

I had adventures on this train, met some interesting people – including other students heading for Sydney or the various country towns along the way. We would stop at these places with platforms largely deserted save for a few lonely figures.

Train travel was the appropriate mode of travel for a poet, I told myself. And yes, I did have a fear of flying in those days so that may have had something to do with it. I preferred more terrestrial forms, but train travel was certainly literary, I mused on the 'Camino de Chatswood'.

Chatswood may not be a well-known pilgrimage site but it's home to a large Chinese diaspora and, correspondingly, some excellent Chinese restaurants. We would often enjoy yum cha there with our extended family in Sydney.

In January 1979 Chatswood also happened to be home to the great Australian poet Les Murray, The Bard of Bunyah, who sits high in the pantheon of Australian letters. He died in 2019, never winning the Nobel Literature Prize although for many years touted as our greatest hope to do so.

In 1979 he was already revered although he was, and remained, unfashionable in many regards. He was no bohemian, no darling of the avant-garde who tended to think they owned poetry. Les eventually became poetry editor of the conservative journal *Quadrant*, which tells you a bit about his politics and disdain for literary fashion.

I had started a correspondence with him after an introduction from my mentor, Bruce Dawe. Bruce and Les were friendly and fellow Catholics, although their politics differed somewhat. Having recently converted to Catholicism I did feel a certain kinship with Catholic writers.

Les was editor of *Poetry Australia* magazine in the 1970s and I figured if I could get published in that journal I would be really on my way.

I had just left my job at 4GG and was at a loose end. So I booked passage on the train. Les had invited me to visit him if I was ever in Sydney. I'm not sure he realized it would be so soon.

That particular journey south to meet Les stayed with me, became part of my personal mythology and eventually spurred me into writing poetry again after a long layoff. That first flowering of my return to this creative form, composed during the pandemic, is entitled *Long ago on a train* and chronicles the journey in a decidedly

Beat fashion. (Nocturnal rail travel inspired another inclusion in my late-Seventies output, a tercet poem entitled *Scene from a Train; Midnight*, as if proof were needed that the hum of the rails is a tune something deep within me knows how to sing the words to.)

On any train journey I take, Slessor's *The Night-Ride* is always playing in my head, and every small town along the route resembles his fictional Rapptown.

The fact that the Gold Coast Motorail was also a night ride helped and was also the inspiration for my own homage, *Night-Ride Revisited*, a poem that I had written following a previous journey and the one that got Les Murray interested in publishing me.

In fact he had already accepted that poem, which I guess was another reason for my pilgrimage. I mean, I probably wouldn't have been so keen to meet him if he had rejected me, like so many others.

Night-Ride Revisited would appear shortly after my pilgrimage to meet him. It begins:

> *I whistled, swaggish, climbed aboard / Saw Slessor seated in a doze / And yo-ho strode to claim my berth / Somewhere in the theatre rows / Like a wobbly sailor full of mirth / Following a keg with his ruby nose.*

It's odd, isn't it? It appeared on Page 9 in *Poetry Australia*, No. 69, February 1979, and I was in good company. I happen to have my tatty copy of it sitting next to me as I write this and, flipping through it, I see there are some truly significant names in Australian letters in that issue: Peter Porter, David Campbell, Peter Goldsworthy, Geoffrey Lehmann, Chris Wallace-Crabbe, among others. Oh, and me.

Les Murray had kindly worked through that poem with me (it was revised a couple of times, with me following his suggested changes to the letter – I would have painted it purple if he'd asked me to!) and there was a short flurry of correspondence between us regarding it. I still have those letters.

That the man who was ultimately regarded as our greatest poet could be bothered to do this for me is, in retrospect, monumental. It was a watershed in my poetry career, such as it was.

He would later accept two more poems – *Aqua Song* and *The Streets of Surfers Paradise*, both published that same year, before relinquishing his editorial role and thereby ending my *Poetry Australia* winning streak. I was quite fond of *The Streets of Surfers Paradise.*

> *Suntans and concrete. Plastic smiles / Switch on and off like dreary dials. / When the clouds are gone the sun's like ice / On the streets of Surfers Paradise.*

Chuffed with the prospect of seeing my verse in such a respected literary journal, I was on my way to Sydney to meet and pay homage to the great man who had made it all possible.

I would be staying with a different aunt and uncle this time, my mum's sister Meg and her husband, Maurice, in Cecil Street, Gordon, on the North Shore, not that far from Chatswood. Here I stayed in a little back room where my maternal grandfather had spent his last days. This was not exactly the heart of bohemian Sydney but, never mind, it was near the train line, which was handy.

I had with me a couple of folders of my poetry and when I got to Sydney I did a bit of mooching around bookstores – one in The Argyle Centre at The Rocks that I used to frequent and where I bought my copy of *The Autobiography of a Super-Tramp*, a 1908 classic by Welsh poet W.H. Davies. It had a preface by George Bernard Shaw, no less, and was, I reckon, the first Beat book ever published, long before the Beat Generation hit the road.

In a bookstore on George Street I discovered a rare edition of some early writing by Ernest Hemingway, a slim volume comprising twenty-five of his poems. They weren't very good and that pleased me.

Not long after arriving I also purchased a copy of Les Murray's book *Lunch & Counter Lunch*. I thought it would be nice to turn up with one of his books and ask him to sign it.

On arriving in Sydney, I had rung him to make a time to visit. Had he changed his mind or was I still welcome? Yes, I was, apparently.

So, on the appointed day I caught the train to Chatswood and trekked along the main road, then downhill into the street where he lived with his wife and kids. It was quite suburban, much like Bruce Dawe's place in Toowoomba. These guys were not inner-city bards, they were family men and practising Catholics. Ye gods!

At this stage of his life Les was a full-time poet, which is a rarity in Australia. And he worked from home (not from a garret somewhere), long before that became fashionable.

Knocking on the door, I had a severe attack of the butterflies and my mouth was dry from nerves. It was audacious, wasn't it, seeking an audience with a master poet? What the hell did I think I was doing? I was just a young dude from, of all places, the Gold Coast. I must have been mad.

Then Les's wife, Valerie, opened the door with a smile and my nerves evaporated. I was ushered inside and presented to the great man, who was sitting at a little table which he apparently wrote at. He sat there like some sort of immigration official and I almost expected him to ask for my passport.

In front of him was a foolscap tablet with writing in longhand – no typewriter flanked by an ashtray full of cigarette butts. The table seemed a tad small for him because Les was quite a big man.

We shook hands and he then led me into a small sitting room. He sat at first, Buddha-like, on the couch and I perched in a chair opposite, on the other side of a coffee table, making small talk and thanking him profusely for agreeing to publish my poem.

Valerie brought in a cheese platter with a baguette and a plunger full of coffee.

Les sliced pieces off the baguette and carved out chunks of cheese, then reclined somewhat. I was reminded of the actor Charles Laughton, who had played the occasional Roman Emperor in his long film career. Les was certainly Emperor-like and a tad Romanesque.

Our conversation is lost in the recesses of my mind. I cannot for the life of me recall anything we spoke about. There were no smartphones to record with in those days or to get a snap of me and Les together, more's the pity.

I must have been there nearly an hour when I could see Les was getting a bit restless. He had poems to write, and soon it was clear my audience was nearing an end.

I asked him then to sign my copy of *Lunch & Counter Lunch* and he wrote in it the inscription: 'For Phil Brown, This unsteady compass needle (which at least points away from evil, I think) with warm regards from Les 7/1/1979.' I still have it and, of course, treasure it.

In parting I asked him if he was aware of any poetry readings I might attend while I was in Sin City, to which Les nodded and said he knew of one happening that very week. It was being held by the Poets Union, which met in Kings Cross.

'Tell them I sent you,' Les said with a wink. I wasn't quite sure what the wink signified but I would soon find out.

I hadn't actually done much poetry reading at that stage. There was that poorly attended reading at our house when I was a student in Toowoomba, and I had read a few poems at the small-scale writers' group I attended in that little hall at Mermaid Beach back on the Gold Coast. Plus I had read one in Brisbane at the launch of *8 Poets 1978,* my most significant publication to date.

But I was still pretty green in that department.

I thought maybe this Poets Union meeting would be my national debut. And Les had recommended it to me (with that wink) so I had to attend.

A couple of nights later I made my way from sedate Gordon to Kings Cross, a locale that, coincidentally, Slessor had also written about in his poem *William Street* which celebrated its gritty, somewhat sleazy, inner-urban ambience.

While most folk regarded it as grungy and ugly, Slessor assured his readers: *I find it lovely.*

I was propositioned several times while making my way to the reading, a nervous young poet clutching his folders on the crowded footpath. I guess I looked like someone ready to be taken advantage of.

There were the usual spruikers outside the strip clubs and the couple in front of me at one stage were stopped by the bloke framed in the doorway enticing the young woman in with this charming pitch: 'Come on, luv, bring your boyfriend in … turn him on for later on.'

I hurried past, eventually found the address where the Poets Union met and went upstairs.

I was greeted, if I can use that word, by Nigel Roberts, the poet who seemed to be in charge. He was a well-known figure in the Australian poetry scene, originally a Kiwi, who had made Sydney his home. When I say I was greeted by him I'm exaggerating, because it wasn't really what you would call a greeting.

I presented, announcing that I was a poet visiting from Queensland, and as I said this I heard someone snigger. Roberts himself, clad in a leather jacket and looking every bit the inner-city Beat poet, couldn't have been less impressed.

He looked me up and down – me in my corduroy trousers, calico shirt, John Lennon glasses and little cap. I thought I looked like a poet but he didn't look so sure.

After an awkward pause – during which I got the impression he was hoping I might turn and leave – I said, nervously: 'Les Murray sent me.'

'Oh, yes,' intoned Roberts, turning his back and walking away, 'he's always palming people off on us.' I was a bit thrown by this, but I must have been more resilient then than I imagined.

Undeterred, I entered the establishment and sat down at a large table at the far end, away from the other poets, who looked at me as if I had just come in with dog shit on my shoe. I kind of nodded hello: nobody nodded back.

The only other poet there that I can recall from that awful evening was the famous Melbourne bard Pi O, who was visiting. I remember quite clearly that he was wearing a blue singlet, a Jackie Howe (named after the famous gun shearer) or, as was commonly known back then, a wifebeater. I call it a Jackie Howe.

Pi O was small, intense and interesting to listen to.

The air filled with talk and laughter, people read their verses and I sat down the end of the longish table, my folders placed strategically in front of me. I flipped through the pages now and then to try and draw attention to the fact that I was there, ready to recite my work.

But nobody even so much as glanced in my direction. I was, to all intents and purposes, invisible. There were several carafes of very cheap wine on the table. Tastewise, it was nothing more than a kind of vinegar.

As the meeting dragged on ('drag' being the operative word), I began quaffing the stuff; the more they ignored me, the more

I drank. It was depressing and humiliating in equal measure, and eventually I realized they would not be asking me to read anything because, basically, I didn't exist. To this crowd I might as well have been Joh Bjelke-Petersen.

Had the 1980 box-office hit *The Elephant Man* come out a year or two earlier, I could have hurled John Hurt's plaintive cry at the taunting crowd (mine indifferent but nonetheless taunting for all that: 'I am not an animal; I am a human being; I am a man!' Or, if I had been thinking straight, I could have had a bit of fun paraphrasing Shylock's speech from Shakespeare's *The Merchant of Venice:*

> *'Hath not a Queenslander hands, organs, dimensions, senses, affections, passions? Fed with the same food, hurt with the same weapons, subject to the same diseases, healed by the same means, warmed and cooled by the same winter and summer, as a Sydney poet is? If you prick me, do I not bleed?'*

I wonder how that would have gone down. I didn't say anything, of course; just sat there drinking that cheap plonk. Inside me was a torrent of anger and shame. I wanted the earth to open up and swallow me whole while, on the other hand, I yearned to smite my tormentors.

Thinking back, I wonder how I recovered from episodes such as that. There are so many times in life when you could just go under, when you could just give up, stop trying. When you thought that you were nobody and nothing.

Drunk as I was by now, I realized why Les Murray had winked at me when he suggested I attend. Was it a kind of black joke? Did he just have a really sick sense of humour, or maybe he was blooding me, preparing me for the slings and life as a poet (more Shakespeare, less art) and all the rejection that goes with it.

No wonder many of the poets I have known gave up along the way.

I would have resigned from poetry there and then if I'd had any sense.

At the end of the meeting I stood, swaying a bit, snatched up my folders and, swearing under my breath, made for the door. I half turned as I did so, thinking that, despite my fury and indignation, I should say goodbye. But the other poets had broken into small groups and were busy chatting so, unsurprisingly, nobody even noticed me stumble out.

At least it was over.

On the pavement outside, I was ripe for getting rolled and it's a miracle I wasn't as I staggered down William Street thinking once again of Slessor and what he had written about this place.

You find this ugly, I find it lovely.

'Bugger Slessor,' I muttered as I wandered off into the jangled city night.

CHAPTER 7

A POET WITH A LIQUIDITY PROBLEM

It was my first day of work in Monto and I was revelling in the romance of the bush as we tramped through the still dewy forest. My friends Wayne Sanderson and Heather Nancarrow had invited me to come and stay with them in their hometown.

I had never been to Monto before. I had, in all honesty, never even heard of the town until I met Wayne and Heather when I was studying in Toowoomba. Heather was a housemate for a time at 128 James Street.

For the uninitiated, Monto is a small town in Central Queensland, part of the Central and Upper Burnett District, and in early 1979 it had a population of around 1700, town and district. Well, 1701 now that I had arrived to stay for a while. Ostensibly I was there to write poetry, meditate and work with Wayne. It would be good honest work in the bush, hard yakka, cutting railway sleepers.

Wayne was finishing his journalism degree by correspondence at the time, and cutting railway sleepers was financing his future career. We would end up working together some years later when we were both real journos but, right now, I was to be his offsider. Being a fan of the poet John Shaw Neilson, who was once a timber cutter, I saw poetic possibilities in the work and fancied becoming something of a pastoral poet in the process.

I had packed up all my goods and chattels and left the Gold Coast at the insistence of Dr Julian Boulnois. Here was I at 22 already onto my second shrink. Dr Boulnois was an Englishman who would have made a rather good Archbishop of Canterbury, I think, considering his manner and his Christian beliefs.

My previous shrink had passed me on to Dr Boulnois, the junior in his Surfers Paradise practice. Dr Boulnois had just arrived on the Gold Coast via a stint in New Zealand and I was one of his first patients.

We sat, one day in early 1979, in the sort of cushioned cane chairs everyone's parents had in their lounge rooms back then, discussing my fate as the sun streamed in, the burgeoning concrete jungle of Surfers Paradise towering beyond the windows of his rooms.

We discussed my situation at home, and I recollect that Dr Boulnois believed my malaise was as much an existential problem as a clinical one.

After leaving 4GG I was living at home with all the *joie de vivre* of a World War One war poet. My head was full of lines by Wilfred Owen and other doomed bards including D.H. Lawrence and John Keats. I guess it's no coincidence that *Ode to a Nightingale* was one of my favourite compositions at the time. *I have been half in love with easeful Death* had become a bit of a mantra of mine.

Dr Boulnois, a literate fellow with a theological bent, was just the man for me. And his advice was pretty straightforward.

'You have to leave home, dear boy,' he confided. 'It's that simple.'

Not long after that brilliant prognosis (a prognosis that would rob him of a patient) I got the invite from my friends in Monto. It seemed that the fickle finger of Fate had intervened again and was pointing straight at me.

So with some trepidation I packed my books and a vegetable juicer into my Ford XY Falcon 500 and set off for foreign parts – of my own state.

Wayne and Heather occupied a small weatherboard house. I moved into their spare room and after only a day to acclimatize set off with Wayne to start work.

We drove to just north of the town where the undulating landscape (Monto is an Aboriginal word that means 'ridgy plains') became thickly forested. We veered off the main road onto a bush track with Monty Python ringing in my ears. '*I'm a lumberjack and I'm okay ...*'

We soon pulled up and got out, twigs crunching underfoot. Wayne was decked out in his work gear – sturdy boots with ankle covers and khaki workwear that had seen better days. I was wearing my King Gee shorts, a T-shirt and sandshoes that may not have been strictly acceptable but I had promised to buy something more durable once I got established. As it turned out, that would not be necessary.

Let me explain. It so happens that in the business of cutting railway sleepers there comes a time when the sleeper itself has to be carried off by the two silly buggers doing the cutting.

The set-up in the bush was like this ... there was a small tractor for 'snigging' the timber: dragging the logs, that is, once they had been cut. Wayne would first identify an appropriate tree, then cut it down with a chainsaw while I stood well away watching. The tree would fall and it was then fastened with some chains and snigged to a spot where a buzz-saw was set up ready for action.

Then the saw would buzz and whirr in a fashion that Wayne described as 'fanning the breezes through the treezes'. That was a bit poetic.

It was at this point that the log and, later, the sleeper itself would be manhandled by the pair of us into stacks which would later be loaded on a truck and transported to the rail yard in town.

Pretty simple business, really, and one of the noble professions that made this wide brown land with the green bits around the edge what it is today.

But when it came to the crunch there was a problem.

'Okay, Phil, you grab that end and I'll grab this end and lift,' Wayne said. Easier said than done. Much easier said than done.

This was the crucial moment that my future as a railway sleeper cutter depended on.

'Okay, lift,' Wayne commanded, and I did, but nothing happened.

'Lift!' he repeated.

'I am lifting!' I insisted. He paused, pushed his bush hat back on his head and drew his hand across his brow. He seemed a little exasperated.

'I said bloody lift!' I tried again but could barely move the newly cut sleeper.

This was not good. Not good at all.

We struggled on through the morning with Wayne doing most of the work. I enjoyed being in the bush but it was obvious that I was not cut out for this line of work.

On the way back home in the early afternoon came the crushing realization: *I'm not a lumberjack and I'm not okay.*

So I was fired on my first day. Wayne explained that it just wouldn't work out if I couldn't lift the other end of a railway sleeper. Wayne happened to be built like a tree stump while I was weedy and totally inept in the field of railway sleeper cutting. Probably not so bad in the grand scheme of things. As a friend's wife was wont to say, 'What does it matter in the face of eternity?'

There I was marooned in Monto with nothing to do but write poetry and contemplate my navel, which I was quite good at. I meditated daily, spent a lot of time sitting on the front steps watching bees pollinate the vine cascading down the lattice at the front of the house (I got a poem called *Bees Are Working* out of this) and read.

At that time I was reading Colin Wilson's *The Outsider*, which was all the rage then, and was also ploughing through a work called *Survival into the 21st Century*, popular on the outer fringe of the counterculture. On reflection I shouldn't have gone anywhere near such a book. It was full of wacky philosophies – which I was susceptible to – and ways of preparing for the Apocalypse. Would we even get the Apocalypse in Monto?

I was drawn to stuff like this then. Maybe I was, as my father once suggested, 'a crazy mixed-up kid'.

Survival in the 21st Century (*into* became *in* once the old century had made way for the new) remains an eccentric tome full of extreme dietary advice. Wheatgrass could save the world, that was one of its central tenets, and there was a segment about breatharianism, a movement whose devotees were said to be able to survive just on fresh air. No chocolate or anything! I wasn't sure if this was really possible, but it was fascinating to me and I was drawn to this sort of zany stuff in the same way onlookers are attracted to a car accident.

I was on a special diet myself at the time in an effort to get rid of my ulcer, and that diet featured things like millet porridge for breakfast and lots of rice and vegetables.

Every evening I would spend time juicing vegetables for a pre-prandial cocktail. I think having me around the house was getting on Wayne and Heather's nerves and when the juicer started whirring I could see them both recoil, wincing and looking at each other.

They were thinking, no doubt, *How the hell are we going to get rid of this guy?*

But I was happy with my little daily cycle. A Catholic church was just across the road and I would sometimes pop over to the presbytery to chat with the parish priest, a tall rangy bloke by the name of Fr Johnson. I bent his ear at confession a bit.

I felt guilty but my guilt was a little vague so I may have embellished somewhat in the confessional box and, to assuage that guilt, real or imagined, I volunteered to mow the church lawn for him.

I was writing some poems, too, and having my mail forwarded to me from home. Not long after I arrived in Monto, I received a copy of the issue of *Poetry Australia* carrying my first nationally published poem, *Night-Ride Revisited*, the one I had laboured over with the guidance of Les Murray.

To open that journal and see my name was a quasi-religious experience. There I was on the contents page – Phil Brown … Page 9 – and I quickly flipped past the relatively unimportant opening leaves to see my poem following on from one by Chris Wallace-Crabbe entitled *The Old Brigade.*

This was really something, and in August that same year the other two were published … one of them *Aqua Song*, a poem imagining my room as a fish tank.

> *My room's a tank where currents run, / A quiet place where no suns come, / The small fish waver, dart and play / While I rise up and float away … And when each night our swim is done / I find a wreck, my treasure's won / And in the silence of the deep / I doze and bubble into sleep.*

The other one was *The Streets of Surfers Paradise* and Les Murray had published them both unaltered. 'No changes, straight in,' he wrote in the letter of acceptance, which I still have.

Life-changing as this was for an aspiring poet, the fact remained that I had overstayed my friends' welcome and had no visible means of support in a small town where I was a complete stranger. A complete stranger with long hair, John Lennon glasses and that little cap.

One day I walked downtown – it was a short stroll – and along the way two motorbikes pulled over. Local toughs, it turned out. One guy looked me up and down and said: 'What the fuck are you doing in my town, poofter?' I deduced that he wasn't from the local tourist bureau.

He was belligerently shaping up to me as I searched for an answer to that question. That's when my mate Wayne, riding his own motorcycle, just happened to be passing. He did a U-turn, pulled over, got off his bike and could see what was going on. He turned to the fellow accosting me.

'Phil's a mate of mine' was all he said. It was all he had to say to elicit an immediate apology. The two hostile bikers backed up and drove off without a further word being exchanged.

'Plastic bikies,' Wayne said dismissively. 'Don't worry about those dickheads.'

How long could I stay in this funny little town? It was Wayne's hometown, although he had experienced life outside. He had no illusions about the joint and liked to describe Monto as 'not a bad little town, as far as bad little towns go'.

A few days after this incident I was meditating on the seagrass matting late in the afternoon when Wayne came in after a hard day's sleeper cutting. He called out to me, breaking my reverie, and I came out of my room.

'I've just been down the pub, and the editor of the local newspaper is at the bar crying into his beer,' he said. 'He's complaining that nobody likes him and nobody will talk to him. He says he needs to hire a reporter.'

Wayne looked at me and I looked at him.

'You mean me?' He nodded.

'I told him about you and he said he's happy to have a chat.'

As it happened, I had with me my little scrapbook from uni containing bits and pieces of my student journalism. Next morning I went downtown, if you could call it that, to the shed that housed the *Burnett Herald*.

I introduced myself to the editor, Ian Gleeson. He was a small gruff man and his office was the newsroom and compositing room all in one. It was in a kind of shed within a vaster shed that once housed the *Monto Herald*, the precursor publication from Monto's glory days.

He must have been desperate because he hired me on the spot. I went home and broke the news. Wayne and Heather were ecstatic because it signified that I would now have an income and that meant, they explained not too delicately, that I could now move out.

The question was, to where? But they had obviously thought that through too.

My new home, for my new job, was the Monto Caravan and Cabin Park, owned by Brian Bambrick, whose brother Merv was a local councillor I would soon get to know. I'm not sure of their origins but Merv was quite swarthy and I remember once, when covering a council meeting, the local mayor referring to him, in the chamber, as a 'black bastard'. Charming.

The *Burnett Herald* covered the Central and Upper Burnett District which included the towns of Gayndah, Mundubbera, Eidsvold and Monto.

I had very little knowledge of country life or the rural industries that sustained it, but I bit the bullet and took the job. Ian Gleeson was a rather uncommunicative bloke: he seemed troubled and rather gloomy. He'd had some run-ins with the local community over a few issues and had withdrawn into himself to a degree. Untainted by all that, I guess that's why he hired me.

I was now a journalist, accidentally. I immediately joined the union, the Australian Journalists Association (AJA) as it was then.

My cluelessness about rural life was clear from my first assignment, which involved covering an evening meeting of the Monto Lucerne Growers' Association. I turned up to find the meeting full of hulking farmers, some fresh from the shower, others fresh from their tractors. I sat down next to a human side of beef and waited for the meeting to begin.

I thought I would take the opportunity to clear something up at the outset and, turning to this bloke, said: 'Tell me, what is lucerne?'

He looked at me dumbfounded and responded, out of the side of his mouth: 'Hay.'

'Ah,' I said, and jotted that down as the meeting was called to order.

Eccentric and different as I seemed to many of the people in Monto, I found many of the locals friendly and welcoming, unlike the plastic bikies. And so I settled into life as the local cub reporter, happy in my little caravan, writing poems at night and reading *Anna Karenina*.

Not a lot happens in Monto. The big event in those days was the Monto Dairy Festival which that year had as its special guest the actor Michael Caton, the town's most famous son, celebrated for his role in *The Sullivans* and, later, *The Castle*.

Monto has produced a few artists too. The renowned Aboriginal-Anglo-Celtic artist Gordon Bennett was born there; artist Patrick Hockey was from the district (the nearby hamlet of Abercorn); figurative expressionist painter Gil Jamieson was also a local still living in the district. I hadn't met him yet although his wife, Maureen, worked on the paper helping lay it out a couple of evenings a week.

The annual Monto Show was also a big deal and, of course, I had to cover that as part of my beat. It was a kind of organized chaos. As well as all the events involving livestock judging there was all the action in the ring at the local showground. There was a stuntman who set fire to himself and dived off a tower into a pile of mattresses as people came running to put him out. While he was doing that, various motorcycles ridden by local hoons experiencing their moment of glory tore around the perimeter of the ring.

Inside that, circling the showground's inner reaches, was a ute with a bloke standing up in the tray doing rope tricks and whip cracking. This was Hollywood George from Goondiwindi, a tall tanned dude in a cowboy outfit … In another life, 'Hollywood George' was a chancer who liked a plunge on the nags so much that the newspapers down in Sydney habitually described him as a 'colourful racing identity'. Way above all this was a small plane skywriting the name of the town in the heavens.

By the time that was completed, though, the first letter had dissipated, leaving only ONTO inscribed in the sky.

The rest of my reporting life revolved around the likes of bull sales and CWA morning teas at which I gorged on scones and pikelets. In fact, covering the Mulgildie CWA jubilee (Mulgildie is a village just outside Monto) was a highlight of my short career as a reporter for the *Burnett Herald.* I have an abiding memory of sponge cake, lamingtons and the best scones I have ever eaten. The CWA ladies are like 'first responders, with cake' according to the comedian Mandy Nolan.

I was invited out onto stations by some property owners too. People seemed interested in me as an oddity, and I certainly felt like one.

Looking back at the yellowing pages in my poetry folders from that year in Monto I notice a few sonnets. I have always been a fan of sonnets, Shakespearean sonnets in particular, and return to the form from time to time.

During my first few months in Monto, I briefly fell ill and penned a sonnet entitled, in the English fashion, *On Fever,* which ended rather dramatically:

All night I'll burn and dream of fire; / Tonight this bed will be my pyre.

Some later poems mined my Monto experiences too, among them *Morning Ride to Bilo* which featured in my second slim volume, *An Accident in the Evening.*

That poem arose from a day trip to the town of Biloela, north-west of Monto. I had wanted to visit Bilo, as they call it, and my friend Wayne arranged a lift with a bloke called George Kelly who drove the truck delivering cream to all the local households. I had to get up early for a lift and the trip is recalled in *Morning Ride to Bilo* which finishes when we arrive.

He pushed his butchered hat back /Squinted and added, with a sneer, / This is the end of the line, young feller … climbing down from the tatty cabin / I had the feeling he was right.

I had a small circle of friends among other out-of-towners in Monto: a guy who worked in the bank and some schoolteachers, including Helene who, for my sins, asked me to the Monto Show Ball and taught me how to do the Pride of Erin.

And in the street one day I finally got to meet the artist Gil Jamieson – a figure that approached me wearing a bush hat and a kangaroo skin jacket. He had long, black, unruly hair and a bushy beard, and stopped me with: 'Who the hell are you?'

Turns out he knew, since I worked with his wife. He accompanied me to the newspaper office to see the editor. (He was friendly with Gleeson, in his way. For some reason he seemed to enjoy taunting him.)

After some months in the caravan park I met Paul, a bloke who was working as a dental technician at Monto Hospital's dental clinic. Like me he was an outsider and the two of us ended up renting a house together just out of town, at a place called Hurdle Gully.

The house was owned by a family that ran a nearby piggery overlooking a flat plain known as Three Moon and named for the creek running through it. The creek had got its name from an incident where a bushman, or a Chinese miner, depending on who is telling the story, had been getting water for his billy from the creek on a night of the full moon and had seen three moons … one in the sky, one reflected in the surface of the creek and the other reflected in his billy. Or his bucket, depending on which version you prefer.

Gil Jamieson lived nearby at a property that overlooked the Three Moon plain. He invited me over for dinner not long after I moved in and I was amazed by his rich history. He was living back in Monto with his wife, my co-worker Maureen, and kids Matthew and Alicia (Monk and Lizard, he called them) following the pursuit of a promising career in Melbourne where he'd been associated with the Antipodean art movement.

Gil was close mates with the great Fred Williams and exhibited with Tolarno, Bonython and Rudy Komon, all top commercial art galleries in their day.

He had also been mates with Clifton Pugh, Charles Blackman and others, and was part of the Melbourne painting scene for some years but eventually came back to live on the land and paint the life of the land, which he is famous for – but not famous enough, as it happens.

We hit it off immediately. I spent time with him drinking wine and smoking cigars in his studio, a large shed adjacent to the farmhouse he and his family lived in. As we got to know each other he took to calling me Superman but only because Clark Kent, who like me was a reporter, changed into Superman whenever needed.

Gil was more impressed that I was a poet. He thought that was far more important than being a journalist. He loved poetry – painters often do – and was a huge fan of the Bengali mystic versifier Rabindranath Tagore.

And because I was nearly broke at that point in my life, something he regarded as honourable and part of my vocation, Gil also began referring to me as 'a poet with a liquidity problem'. As an artist, that was a plight he was also familiar with. When I went to his house, he sometimes had visitors and would introduce me using that descriptor. I would smile wanly.

He referred to himself as the Cigar Smoking Artist. He encouraged people to send him letters addressed simply to: *Cigar Smoking Artist, Monto*; and insisted that these letters always reached him. I guess there was only one Cigar Smoking Artist in Monto.

Gil could easily outdrink me – that wasn't hard. I was imbibing intermittently at that stage and when I did the results were never good. I never could hold my booze.

One night, after a long philosophical discussion in his studio while listening to Beethoven, consuming copious quantities of red wine and smoking cigars I nearly choked on, I set off across the paddocks to my home on the nearby hill in the dark, tangling with several barbed wire fences along the way.

Arriving home bloodied and battered, I collapsed into bed much to the alarm of my housemate, Paul, a clean-living born-again Christian who was, he assured me, completely against sex before marriage … but not masturbation. Too much information really.

I memorialized Jamieson in a poem entitled *Hunting with Gil on Three Moon Flat*, which is about a fruitless duck hunt we once went on. We didn't get any ducks but that was kind of beside the point really as I make clear in the last stanza:

> *Missing the ducks hadn't really mattered. / It was enough to be out in the crisp air / And to feel, for a while, unfettered. / The stars were coming out everywhere / as we headed home in the last dregs of light.*

The Cigar Smoking Artist and the Poet with a Liquidity Problem became good friends in the years that followed, before the Artist's untimely death from prostate cancer in 1990. And our friendship was forged in the crucible of that studio near my Hurdle Gully home.

I was in Monto for most of 1979, although it seemed longer. After a few months at Hurdle Gully my time in the town was coming to an end.

The editor was, I think, miffed that I had been embraced by the town while he was still a virtual pariah. This may have got the better of him or it may be more complicated than that; or maybe he just didn't want to pay me anymore.

Whatever the reason, one day he fired me based on some trumped-up charge – my supposedly making long-distance calls without permission. Those phone calls were in the course of my duties but that didn't seem to matter.

So there I was at a loose end, marooned in Monto. To keep busy I did some gardening work for an elderly lady in the town, a Mrs O'Connor.

I had recently met her son Gerry and his wife, Anne, who were visiting from Rockhampton. They knew Gil Jamieson and he had introduced me to them. Gerry was news editor at the ABC in Rocky and his father had owned the old *Monto Herald*.

I well remember gardening for Gerry's mum because it gave me a poem that my mum loved, called *In a Thousand Gardens*.

In a thousand gardens, / Beneath a thousand trees, / Hover those eternal hordes / Of butterflies and bees. / Time is obsolete there / And everything is green; / Widows with their verdant thumbs / Toil away unseen.

Sentimental, I know, and the finale is even more so.

In a thousand gardens, / Beneath a thousand trees, / Weep a thousand widows / But no-one ever sees.

The O'Connors invited me to stay with them in Rocky and I thought I might try my luck in the Big Smoke. Or the Medium Smoke, at least: it was too small to qualify as the Big Smoke.

My Monto sojourn had come to an end. I felt as if I had just spent nearly a year in a production of Dylan Thomas's *Under Milk Wood*. Like his native Swansea, Monto was 'an ugly, lovely town'.

That departure is charted in my poem *Memories of Mungo*, Mungo being a thinly veiled version of Monto.

When I eventually left / I remember the water tower / was the last thing I saw in the rear vision mirror / when the rest of Monto was obscured / by the ruined, undulating pastures beyond. / It looked like the last thing standing / after some terrible cataclysm / and I recalled the joke I'd heard / in the pub once: someone thinking up a new slogan / for the local tourist board: 'Die first, see Mungo later.'

CHAPTER 8

VIVA ROCK VEGAS

I SAT IN A SMALL GLASS BOOTH staring into the lens of a camera uncomfortably close to my face. I felt like Odysseus staring down the Cyclops but I was a long way from Serifos. Rockhampton, in fact. You couldn't get much further if you tried.

A disembodied voice came out of the ether like an admonition from beyond.

'Read what is on the paper in front of you and look straight at the camera,' it said in a monotone. It was all a bit Orwellian. I obeyed and began reading some banal rural report. It was like another language to me. I pressed on, though, as instructed, pausing at one point to ask if I was doing it okay. But the emotionless voice, which seemed to be all around me, just said: 'Keep going.'

This was my audition for a job as a newsreader at the regional television station in Rockhampton, beef capital of Australia. The thing is, I wasn't looking for a job as a television newsreader and certainly didn't feel this job was suited to me, with my unruly mane, sallow cheeks and Lennonesque glasses. Have you seen any elegantly wasted poets reading the nightly news on television lately? Exactly.

But I was desperate for work so I'd lobbed myself at the TV station's newsroom looking for a job as a reporter, yet for some reason they insisted on trying me out for this unsought role. What were they thinking?

After the audition I stepped out of the booth into the studio where the news editor, Greg Adermann, and another person were chatting in the corner.

'Never mind,' he said which indicated that, as imagined, I hadn't made the cut to be their new talking head. That was a relief. Even with a makeover I wouldn't have suited the job and my nervous disposition would have been a definite disadvantage. Dodged a bullet there, but another with my name on it was tracking not far behind.

They hired me to do some reporting. So I would be on television after all. That sounded glamorous. Until it wasn't.

I ended up working for the station for a few weeks, which was probably a week longer than I should have. I covered mostly mining-related stories and there were a lot of them in that part of the world in early 1980. One of those stories, the opening of the Gregory open-cut coal mine near Emerald, was a big deal and I was dispatched to cover it. I wouldn't have sent me to cover a barbecue but never mind. Here was the rub: I had to fly, along with the cameraman and a couple of other journos, in a small plane from Rocky to Emerald. As you know, I didn't like flying at the best of times and the prospect of soaring through the sky in a plane not that much bigger than a coffin was not attractive.

It was one of the most terrifying experiences of my life and, from time to time I have flashbacks, like some sort of shell-shocked war veteran. In those flashbacks I am white-knuckling it and trying not to vomit as the plane bounces through the clouds on its way west.

I don't remember speaking during that journey as I was frozen with fear while my fellow travellers laughed and chatted, seeming to delight in the adventure. I shut my eyes and prayed, as I have often done on planes, promising God that if He got me through this ordeal I would be really good forevermore, amen.

I'm assuming it was the same on the way back, although for some reason my mind has blanked out the return trip. It's a kind of traumatic amnesia, I guess.

But we got there and back. Obviously.

On camera, holding the microphone awkwardly in front of me like a lollipop, I was not the greatest TV reporter. I'd love to get hold of that footage, though I think I'd be safe in saying they haven't archived it for any reason. It would be funny to watch, or sad, I'm not sure which.

My television career was mercifully short. It didn't take, and that left me stranded in Rocky, staying with my new friends, the O'Connors.

Rock Vegas – that's what they called the Central Queensland city back then, long before Brisbane got in on the act and dubbed itself Brisvegas.

Rocky was the original Australian Vegas although the name didn't signify a resemblance to Las Vegas, Nevada, because it didn't resemble that city at all. It was dubbed Rock Vegas after *The Flintstones* cartoon series which featured a garish Stone Age city named Bedrock and then, at the turn of the century, the characters in that classic resurfaced in a movie called *The Flintstones in Viva Rock Vegas.*

Long before then Rockhampton had been dubbed Rock Vegas. I don't know that it made any sense to me, especially as I wasn't yet having a yabba-dabba-doo time there.

Prior to my brief and not so brilliant TV career I had been to see the boss at *The Morning Bulletin,* Rocky's daily newspaper. I thought I had a chance because that boss happened to be the father of my friend Sheena Dunn. Despite recommendations from his daughter, Peter Dunn was unconvinced by my résumé and perhaps by the fact that I was a long-haired git.

After getting knocked back by him and having flopped as a news reporter for the telly, I worked briefly in a bookshop and in between times wandered round town like a lost soul. I was into blues music at the time and that suited my situation perfectly.

I was also reading John Donne. My John Donne period had been inspired by a record the O'Connors had of Richard Burton reading the works of this English metaphysical poet. The record was on the Caedmon label, which was famous for its literary fare. It was named after the first known English-language poet, Cædmon, a Northumbrian cowherd who cared for the animals at the monastery of Streonæshalch during the abbacy of Saint Hilda.

Burton's voice was incredible, and I can still hear it echoing through my soul.

Go and catch a falling star, / Get with child a mandrake root, /
Tell me where all past years are, / Or who cleft the devil's foot, /
Teach me to hear mermaids singing, …

Beautiful stuff, and I loved the reference to mermaids singing because I was still very much in thrall to T.S. Eliot's classic poem *The Love Song of J. Alfred Prufrock* ever since studying it under Bruce Dawe. *I have heard the mermaids singing, each to each. / I do not think that they will sing to me.* Poor old Prufrock.

Eliot became religious later in life, like Donne who eschewed the sensual and romantic poetry of his youth when he became a bit more divine. He rather famously slept in his coffin to remind himself of the temporal nature of the world.

In my earlier life I fashioned a few poems on Donne and other English poets including William Blake. I was experimenting with form at the time, unfashionable as that was.

One of my early Rockhampton poems, *The Mango Trees,* was published in the journal *LiNQ* (*Literature in North Queensland* – Vol. 10, No. 2) in 1982.

It was written after observing kids on their way to and from school.

> *Slowly morning wanders in / Past the mango trees, / Gently blessing everything / As the magpies wake and sing / In the early rustling breeze, / Ruffling every leaf and wing.*

The kids are described thus:

> *Chatting, whistling as they walk / Come the children bred on chalk.*

The earliest poem I can find from my time in Rocky is *Butterfly Death*, a paean to a dying lepidopteran found by the roadside.

> *Sadly, I walked on / Mourning those innocent fluttering squadrons / That were rising even now / From the long-shadowed fields / As the setting sun silently claimed the safety / Of its long-lost continent of clouds.*

I guess I was a bit of a romantic.

But I was not about to make a living from writing poems, was I! What I needed was a job.

After a few fallow weeks my host, Gerry O'Connor, came home the bearer of good news. My friend's father had been promoted to the newspaper group's head office in Brisbane and there was a new caretaker GM, Roy Theodore, who was a bit of a legend in Queensland regional journalism.

'He's a great bloke, you should go and see him,' Gerry said.

What did I have to lose? I rang the paper and got a late-afternoon appointment with Mr Theodore. I went to the historic building that housed *The Morning Bulletin* on Quay Street, a colonial heritage precinct overlooking the Fitzroy River, which itself would spawn a few poems.

Directed upstairs to an office overlooking the street, I was welcomed by Theodore himself, a bearded, smiling man. I sat down, clutching my scrapbook and résumé, such as it was. He was drinking a glass of wine (well, I guess it *was* the cocktail hour) and had a tube of toothpaste and a toothbrush on his desk nearby. Was he sleeping in the office? He had come up from Bundaberg to fill in, after all.

He looked over my slim, let's say emaciated, résumé, and smiled.

'So you were born in the Hunter Valley?' he said.

'Yes, Maitland,' I replied. He nodded and flipped through the meagre scrapbook.

'Great wine from the Hunter Valley,' he remarked. A brief awkward silence ensued.

'Yes, I guess so,' I ventured. I didn't know anything about wine apart from drinking it.

'Love the Hunter Valley,' he said with a faraway look in his eyes. 'Well, I think we might have something for you.' I was astonished. Had I just got a job on the strength of coming from a well-known wine region? That seemed to be the case.

He got up and told me to follow him into the newsroom next door, which was still buzzing with the clack of typewriters and chatter in the early evening.

He introduced me to the chief of staff, Martin Simons, I was assigned a desk and told I could start the next day. I shook hands with both men and went back out into the street which was quiet except for a bloke who was obviously down on his luck.

He had been drinking from a bottle wrapped in a brown paper bag but the bottle was now resting against his chest as he slept. His clothes were filthy and, voyeuristic as it seems, the sight of him inspired a new poem that came to me unbidden.

In the streetlight's naked arc / Sits a lonely, ragged man; / Like a moth out of the dark / He came by a garbage can / To his place of present sleep / Near the river running deep.

The poem, *Derelict by the Fitzroy*, ends: *And he wakes, alone, to weep / Near the river running deep.* One never knows when or where a poem is going to occur but when it does a poet must respond. Later that night I wrote out the whole composition in a rough draft.

Rock Vegas would, strangely, be fertile poetic ground for me but first I had to focus on my new career. In Monto I had been a kind of accidental reporter but now I was a real journalist working on a reputable regional paper. *The Morning Bulletin* had an illustrious history and in its early days was a bit of a bolshie rag in a town that had long been a Labor stronghold. The paper was now a lot tamer and a tad subservient to the conservative side of politics.

The editor, Frank Sanderson, a shambolic but kindly character, was very much a Country Party kind of guy.

The paper may have been conservative but its young staff weren't. There were a few younger journos including me, the new chum, and a few old hands still working there in those days, one of them an ancient sub-editor who I think had been there since the 1950s.

I began as a general reporter covering local events. Each day we would arrive at work and check a daily sheet attached to a big Bible-like book that listed our jobs for the day.

I attended to my allotted tasks but also began slowly carving out a niche for myself covering the arts and entertainment. While I still had to do the menial stuff, I was given free rein because nobody else was really doing it. I established a weekly one-page culture section, The Arts on Friday.

With my long hair and Lennonesque eyewear, plus being a poet, I was the obvious candidate to become the arts writer. (Hell, I even shared John Lennon's birthday, and desperately hoped some Beatles fan in HR would notice.) I also covered books and music.

It was 1980 and the year before that Rockhampton had gained a regional cultural hub, the Pilbeam Theatre, named after Rex Pilbeam, its legendary, and at that point still incumbent, mayor. The theatre turned out to be a surprising hotbed of activity and for me a kind of immersion in the performing arts. In my first few months at the paper, the Sydney Dance Company came to town and I got to meet Graeme Murphy. Veteran actors Googie Withers and John McCallum turned up in a show that played Rocky and I interviewed them, along with Australian actor and poetry buff Leonard Teale, and even Spike Milligan and Harry Secombe, two of The Goons, who came on separate tours.

I was very excited one day to be assigned to go out to the airport to meet British comedians Jimmy Edwards and Eric Sykes, who were also doing a show at the Pilbeam. These guys were British comedy icons and on a slow news day the photographer and I waited for their plane to arrive. In those days, you could walk out on the tarmac, so we headed over to greet them.

The place was deserted. It was a sunny, windy afternoon and I wouldn't have been at all surprised to have seen a tumbleweed go past.

Jimmy Edwards, famous for his bushy moustache, came down the stairs first and, seeing me standing there with my notebook and the photographer with his camera at the ready, he shouted: 'Aaaargggh! Mobbed by the media again!'

We were then ushered into the VIP room to conduct the interview. I was surprised that in those days Rockhampton Airport even had a VIP room.

The Pilbeam Theatre's living namesake was then in the final days of his thirty-year mayoralty. He was known, rather famously, as Sexy Rexy after a notorious incident early in his career when a spurned lover shot him for ending their affair. (Details of the adulterous background to the shooting emerged at his assailant's subsequent trial.)

The name Sexy Rexy stuck, although he wasn't that sexy when I came face to face with him for the first time while covering a meeting of the Harbour Board, which he chaired.

I was ushered into the meeting and told, by the mayor, to sit at the far end of a long oval table. After half an hour or so during which I jotted furiously in my notebook it was time for a tea break. In those days, councils had a tea lady with a trolley, and hers came laden with scones and biscuits. She put some of each in front of the mayor and began pouring cuppas all round.

Then I noticed that the mayor appeared to be waving at me.

'Yes sir?' I perked up.

'Do you want a biscuit?' he asked. 'They're Arnott's Assorted Creams.' No expense had been spared.

'I'll have an orange slice,' I said, at which he pulled a face. 'If you say so,' he countered and, placing the biscuit on its side, rolled it the length of the table. I saw the amazed looks on the faces around that table as it went past and was gobsmacked that it actually reached me. I thanked him and dunked it in my tea as the mayor slurped his and then, scoffing a few scones, resumed the meeting.

In my early days at *The Morning Bulletin*, after relieving the O'Connors of my presence, I briefly inhabited the leafy suburb of Frenchville at the foot of the Berserker Range on the northern edge of town. I lived there with a couple of Sheena's friends, Starr and Clare (who ran a dress shop in town), but was kicked out one evening after being accused of using Clare's towel. First of all, I didn't; but secondly, even if I had, was that a sackable offence?

I then moved to the underside of a house on Water Street in North Rockhampton. Two nurses and an ABC journalist, Elspeth, lived upstairs in a kind of bawdy chaos. My basement abode was two small rooms in a kind of Besser-block bunker known as The Cave. I got pretty well set up there with my record and cassette player in one room together with my trusty Remington typewriter on a small table.

It was my garret or, if you like, inverted garret since a garret is usually an upper room. Or it could have been my dungeon – one or the other.

Here I spent many a lonely evening listening to music and writing out my poems in longhand before typing them up and putting them into the burgeoning group of folders that travelled with me, containing my life's work, such as it was.

While dwelling in The Cave I produced the longest poem I had written to date. Inspired, of all things, by covering the Rockhampton Show, it was entitled *An Alien Writes Home to His Love from the 1980 Rockhampton Show*, a title which, I confess, was in turn inspired by the Bruce Dawe poem *A Victorian Hangman Tells His Love.*

There the similarities ended though.

My work was about how confounding it would be for an alien to arrive on Earth, alighting in the midst of an Australian agricultural show. Upon arrival, the alien is mistaken for a child wearing a mask, a grotesque accessory found in a show bag.

It's been a month now, our time / And their cold sun hasn't set: / Still they're walking round and round / And one (the sheer audacity!), / He tried to pull my head right off, / Tugged frantically at both my ears / And, finding that it wouldn't come, he hit me and I cried right out.

Crazy stuff, I know, but I thought I was being clever.
In the end the alien says he's lonely and misses his love.

I miss the pink hills of home, / The five moons, / Our purple dusk / And you, my love, / Your antlers and your toothless smile / And the touch of your paw in mine / When walking on the diamond beach / Into the soft gloom / Of the all-consuming lunar night.

It was a one-off, that poem, for better or for worse. It saw the light of day in *Free Poetry*, a small student-run magazine edited by Andrew Lonsdale, a poet I had befriended. The magazine was produced on the campus of the Capricornia Institute of Advanced Education (CIAE), precursor to CQUniversity, and various of my verses got a run in several issues.

I'm not sure how I met Andrew. Poets seem to find each other somehow, to naturally congregate, as I imagine criminals do in the underworld. They say misery loves company.

After publishing some poems in *Free Poetry* a few of my creations even made their way into *The Morning Bulletin*, including one entitled *The Ibis Come*, a lyrical piece about watching a flock head west at dusk. Ibis seemed romantic in the days before they became 'bin chickens'.

I went out to the campus a bit, sometimes to interview people such as the poet and author Nancy Keesing, a leading figure in Australian letters. I knew her from her introduction to *The Autobiography of John Shaw Neilson,* of which I owned a copy. Back then he was my second favourite Australian poet, after Slessor.

His poem *The Orange Tree* is one of the most wondrously mystical nature poems I know of and *The Crane Is My Neighbour* is utterly beautiful.

> *The bird is my neighbour, a whimsical fellow and dim; / There is in the lake a nobility falling on him. / The bird is a noble, he turns to the sky for a theme, / And the ripples are thoughts coming out to the edge of a dream.*

Nancy Keesing was doing a residency at the campus and, as a desperate young wannabe, I did of course ask if she would look at some of my stuff. She was very gracious and we met on a few occasions. I continued a correspondence with her afterwards and have her letters here in my file at home.

While she was very kind to me, re-reading her letters and a critique of some of my short stories has reminded me that she could also be very blunt. Sometimes you have to be cruel to be kind, they say. I published some of my short fiction in *The Morning Bulletin*'s free weekly supplement, *The Capricorn Community*.

I tended to get all the jobs of an arty or literary nature at the paper. So, when UQP's famous founder, Frank Thompson (who first published Peter Carey), turned up one day with the poet Roger McDonald in tow, I was the one assigned to interview them.

McDonald's mum, Lorna, whom I got to know while living in Rock Vegas, was the official city historian: I still have her history of Rockhampton in my bookcase. I spent oodles of time with Lorna and liked her a lot.

As well as getting the assignments concerning arty or literary types, it had evidently been decided that whenever someone unusual turned up I was also the man for the job. So, when a turbaned Ananda Marga guy named Dadaji arrived one day to spruik an event the sect was holding in town, I did the interview and bizarrely enough this guy, who seemed to have nowhere to stay, ended up dossing at my place for a few days.

By then I was in a share house in the suburb of Wandal with a couple of blokes who worked at the ABC. The house even had a name, The Ripples, God knows why. I was also writing songs and doing a bit of singing at that time and thought that if I ever formed a band I would call it The Ripples. I didn't, and I didn't.

Dadaji insisted on initiating me with a secret mantra in a private meditation session. The secret mantra was … Baba. (Yes, I know, it's not a secret anymore.) As well as gurus and artists I got to interview visiting rock acts such as Australian Crawl and Split Enz when they came to town. I remember sitting in a motel room with Aussie Crawl all squeezed onto a couch for our chat. When Split Enz came out from their hotel into the blazing Rocky sun for our sit-down and pic session they looked positively stunned to be there. I know how they felt.

One day I was entrusted with interviewing a rather famous figure in Australian intellectual life, the esteemed historian Professor Manning Clark, who was in Rockhampton to give a lecture at the CIAE campus. He and his wife, Dymphna, were staying at a riverfront motel not far away along Quay Street and I was dispatched to do the honours.

We had studied Manning Clark in Toowoomba and he was quite the daunting figure in Australian literary and academic circles.

So, I was a bit nervous about the imminent prospect of meeting him. His wife, Dymphna, was very friendly while the professor himself seemed largely unmoved by my arrival.

'I'll leave you to it,' said Dymphna as she excused herself and went outside. I could see her strolling around the swimming pool as we got down to our interview. Although, truth be told, that process took a while. Professor Clark seemed more interested in the mandarin he was peeling than in me. He was meticulously removing the skin and placing it in a pile on the coffee table in front of him.

At one point he squirted a bit of citrus juice in his eye, which bothered him.

When he was done, he popped a piece of the fruit in his mouth and asked me in a rather distracted fashion: 'Do you have a girlfriend?'

I was puzzled. Wasn't I the one supposed to be asking the questions?

'No, I don't,' I said, and he continued eating his mandarin before pausing and looking up.

'Do you like girls?' he said, a little more animated now. I wasn't sure where this was going.

'Yes, I do,' I said warily.

'But you don't have a girlfriend?'

'No. I'm not sure I have ever really had a proper girlfriend, not in the traditional sense.'

'Interesting,' he commented. I then managed to deflect him into chatting about his forthcoming lecture and eventually his wife, choosing her moment, re-entered the room which I construed as a signal that the interview was over.

It was a very odd encounter. I have never been entirely sure what it meant but I suppose it was nice that one of Australia's most famous historians and men of letters had been so interested in my sex life.

I was pretty monastic at the time as I was see-sawing between being of the world … and not. Part of me wanted to retreat from the material world. I still attempted meditation from time to time and attended church. In fact, I attended two churches, Anglican and Catholic, which was handy because the Anglicans thought I was one of them but so did the Catholics and I actually *was* Catholic, having converted, identifying intellectually with its core beliefs.

Around this time I became friendly with an Anglican minister, Godfrey Fryar, and sometimes attended services at his modest church. He did a lot of work with indigenous people which was fairly groundbreaking back then, and I was amazed that one Sunday he had a visiting poet give the sermon, one Kath Walker, whom we now know as Oodgeroo Noonuccal. I remember a small woman in a hat who had us mesmerized.

Wrestling with spirituality was one thing but I was also wrestling with the grog. I avoided tippling altogether if I could – and, when it was inescapable, would drink as little as I could in the situation. When I did succumb it was usually to excess, and the aftermath was never pretty.

I see-sawed between my lighter and darker angels during those two rather intense years in Rockhampton. But I learnt a lot too. Rock Vegas was the crucible of my career as journalist and minor poet.

It's a strange place for a literary genesis story but it was a vital part of my growing up and I was away from home, making my own way in the world and mad as a hatter half the time.

And, though I was aware that back at home nothing much had changed, I wasn't witnessing it myself. I felt a bit guilty leaving my mother and brother and sister to deal with dad.

But I loved my job. *The Morning Bulletin* was one of the first newsrooms in Australia to be computerized, and halfway through my tenure we were working on what we then called VDUs (visual display units). That was a revelation, although no one had personal computers back then and I was still happy with my rickety old Remington, which moved with me from place to place. I wish I still had it so I could show it to my son as a relic from the olden days.

I have never sought glory in the way of awards or public plaudits for my journalism. I have never entered any journalism awards, possibly because I have had quite enough rejection as a poet.

But, strangely, I did win one in Rocky. It was quite circumstantial, really, because I just happened to be working the 2 to 10pm shift the day a big story broke. Well, it was a big story for Rockhampton at least – a mass pensioner food poisoning.

For some reason this sort of stuff tended to happen more on late shifts than on mornings.

You would start your shift ringing round the police stations and hospitals looking for bad news.

One evening, after I had been sent out to get Chinese food for the sub-editors, I remember ringing the senior sergeant at a country station to ask if there was any news and he said there had been a car accident on the infamous Marlborough stretch of the highway north-west of Rocky. Upon hearing this, I put my hand over the phone and shouted, 'Car accident!' to the chief sub.

'Is it a fatal?' he asked, and after I'd queried the sergeant on the other end of the line, and he said no, I shook my head. The chief sub was quite disappointed. Brutal.

Not long after starting my shift one day, I discovered during my ringaround that there had been a mass food poisoning at an elderly residents' lunch and that now, in mid-afternoon, ambulances were rushing senior citizens to what was then known as Rockhampton Base Hospital.

The subs' desk was very excited about this and in case you think I'm making light of a serious incident let me assure you no one died. But some did get very sick.

I rushed to the hospital with one of our photographers and we propped outside the emergency entrance. As they carried people past us, I would try to ask them how they were feeling and not surprisingly most of them didn't answer until one old man, rather kindly, told me he was feeling 'a bit crook' and added: 'Write that down.'

Which I dutifully did. Through an interview with one of the organizers of the fateful lunch I divined that it was the chicken that was the culprit.

'Must have been off,' she said. 'Funny thing, though. The mayor was there and he had the chicken too but he's fine.' Why didn't that surprise me?

The next day I had the splash, a full front page emblazoned with the headline 'Food poisoning hits 109 city pensioners'. There was a sidebar piece headed 'Mayor fears for the elderly' stemming from an interview I'd landed with Mayor Pilbeam who told me he had eaten everything ('Very nice it was, too') but had escaped unscathed. He was a tough old bugger.

For that story I won – without even trying – the Reg Birch Trophy for best story of the year. Reg Birch was an old journo recently retired, a thorough gentleman, and he came back into the office to present me with the award, my one and only gong in journalism. My name was emblazoned on a little shield displayed on the newsroom wall. It's probably covered in dust and languishing in some storage room at the paper's largely deserted offices, or maybe it was binned years ago. (The paper is just a website nowadays.)

But hey, I won an award there and they can't take that away from me.

During my second year in Rocky, I went home for a family visit. That was always a bit fraught. My parents had sold the beautiful home where I had spent my teenage years and moved closer to Broadbeach. Financial troubles prompted the move and now my father was virtually semi-retired. He was quite unwell with type 2 diabetes and other alcohol-associated ailments.

It was during that visit home that my father had a massive heart attack and died, right there, in front of me. Saying it like that seems strange, distant. I remember being by his side as he lay dying in bed, gasping for breath, and the only comfort I can get from this memory is that he once told me he didn't need to go to church because he could just pray in bed. It's so long ago now but it's something you never get over. The shock, the ocean of grief, a sadness that is deeper than any sadness you will ever know, engulfed me afterwards and still lingers.

The days after Dad's death, the funeral, the stunned silence at home … it was all a blur and delayed my return to Rockhampton. We were in shock, of course, as anyone would be.

Eventually I did go back to Rock Vegas. By then we had a new editor, by the name of Barry Bransdon. I didn't like him much and he didn't like me. I was a tad too effete for him, I think.

I had a lot of time for my chief of staff, Marty, though. He was a gentleman and very encouraging. But when I lobbed back into the newsroom this Bransdon bloke summoned me into his office for a shitcanning.

'You were supposed to be back at work last week,' he said.

'Yeah, I know, but my father died,' I responded.

I almost expected him to say, 'Well, that's no excuse.' He might as well have done.

'Well, that's not good enough.'

'Well, is this good enough?' I came back with. 'You can stick your job up your arse.'

And that was that. Farewell, Rock Vegas … Parting was never such sweet sorrow.

CHAPTER 9

DOWN AND OUT IN PARADISE

I KNOW IT SOUNDS COUNTERINTUITIVE but sometimes one of the worst things a journalist can do is read the daily newspaper. Because sometimes the story one has written is not quite the story that appears in print the next day.

After coming home to the Gold Coast from Rockhampton after my dad's untimely death I got a job on the *Gold Coast Bulletin* in 1982 and then worked for the *Sunday Bulletin*, a short-lived experiment with a seven-day operation. Did I help speed the demise of the Sunday edition? Quite possibly.

Let me explain. It all started one sunny weekday. I sat at my typewriter (the paper hadn't quite made the quantum leap to computers yet) staring out of the long window that ran above our bank of desks, waiting for inspiration. It never came. I learned early on in newspapers that one just has to write regardless.

The news editor of the *Sunday Bulletin*, an excitable Sydneysider named Ralph Sharman, came up to me with a look of urgency on his face, a look news editors tend to perfect.

'This tidal wave story of yours is a good yarn,' he said. 'Can you tighten it up a bit, make it a bit newsier?'

'It's bullshit,' I said and, as I said it, I realized that wouldn't matter.

'I know, but we might use it a bit closer to the front of the book.'

The story he was referring to was based on an interview I had done with an author living atop Tamborine Mountain in the Gold Coast hinterland. James Essex, a retired Englishman, was in the process of writing a novel about the Gold Coast being wiped out by a tidal wave, which seemed rather fitting to some people.

A friend had told me about Essex and introduced me to him. I had a penchant for disaster movies at the time (still do) and you could describe my expectations as generally catastrophic. I had spent the early part of 1982 preparing for Doomsday after reading that the alignment of the nine planets later that year (outlier Pluto then still regarded as a paid-up member of the solar system) would cause global destruction. As usual, Doomsday was postponed.

So, the tidal wave idea appealed to me and I'd gone up the mountain to interview James and his wife, Norma, who thought they would be quite safe when the worst happened.

The theory outlined in his never-completed manuscript was, roughly, that any one of three events – an earthquake in the Pacific, California falling into the sea due to a rupture on the San Andreas Fault or a massive volcanic eruption – would cause a tidal wave that would sweep ashore along the South East Queensland coast, inundating the Glitter Strip and funnelling inland via the many canal estates beyond the beaches. James got the notion from a Canadian geologist he had met in Spain who reckoned one day an Hawaiian volcano would blow up and devastate Australia's east coast. Not such a wild theory, it turns out. I read some reports recently that said the Gold Coast is vulnerable, adding in for good measure that, since some people feel that the place is like a modern Sodom and Gomorrah, maybe the joint has it coming …

But in the early 1980s no one was thinking about this and no one wanted to. Except James Essex, a former adman who grew avocados and dabbled in journalism. He was chuffed that I was interested in his book but puzzled at how big a story it would be. Little did he know.

I added spice to the piece by consulting a friend of mine, an astrologer I had met in Surfers Paradise café society. He also predicted that a tidal wave was coming, although the details and timing were sketchy. He may have watched Peter Weir's classic movie *The Last Wave* once or twice too often.

The story I wrote for the paper was just a bit of fun for the features section but Ralph Sharman and the associate editor, Roy Chapman, had other ideas. And when Ralph asked me to make it a bit newsier what he really meant was … attack it with an egg-beater.

So I sensationalized it a bit, not entirely happy with having to do so. I left the office late on the Saturday afternoon and left them to it. Walking out, I saw Ralph and Roy conferring rather conspiratorially in the editor's office, but then again that was nothing unusual.

On the Sunday morning my mother knocked on the door of my downstairs bedroom.

'I think you'd better come and have a look at the paper,' she said.

Upstairs I went and there it was, on the kitchen table, with the blazing front-page headline 'TIDAL WAVE!" By Phil Brown.

I was mortified. We didn't have mobile phones in those days. If we did, I would have been inundated with calls. I mean, it would be news if it had happened but this was just a tabloid fantasy.

Later that day I was due to meet some of my colleagues at a local pub, and when I arrived one of them was holding an open umbrella. Everyone was laughing. An umbrella wouldn't quite be enough to keep a tidal wave at bay but I got the joke.

Back at work that Tuesday the calls came in thick and fast from people either laughing hysterically or outraged. The Gold Coast is, after all, a tourism hub and the local tourism authorities were seriously unimpressed. They denounced me and so did the real estate industry. A tidal wave would not be good for business. But it wasn't all doom and gloom: I did get a call from a born-again Christian agreeing that the wave and Judgment Day were nigh.

James Essex was amused. He didn't ever finish that book. Much later, when Norma was a widow, she confirmed that to me. What a shame. It would have made a great movie.

But it wasn't quite deserving of front-page treatment in 1982.

This story took me a while to live down and by the time I did the Sunday edition had folded and the paper had gone back to publishing six days a week. You're welcome.

I was back at home in Nerang, where my mum had bought a house after selling their previous home following Dad's death. Nerang was not exactly the centre of the Universe. I'm not sure it is even part of the Universe. Once a quaint rural village, it was now a burgeoning and unattractive suburb with a highway running through it. I occasionally travel that highway nowadays and always speed up when I see the NERANG sign to get past it as soon as possible. I never stop.

I lived there with Mum and my younger brother Steve. My sister, Jane, had married and was living elsewhere, starting a family.

My brother was a cop. He had been stationed in Brisbane but after Dad's death he wanted to come home to the Gold Coast. His transfer request had been denied until my mum placed a call to a family friend, Faye Hinze, wife of the then Police Minister, the colourful and expansive Russ Hinze. He and my dad had been mates. Hinze, known as 'the Minister for Everything', had quite a reputation but he kindly accelerated my brother's transfer. On being told by his superior officer in Brisbane that this was impossible, Steve's boss, after a call to *his* superior from Hinze, sheepishly announced that Steve would be transferred to the Gold Coast immediately. Thanks, Russ.

Steve, who was a bodybuilder at the time (he once worked out with Arnold Schwarzenegger in Bob's Gym at Southport) was known as The Hollywood Cop because he looked good but never arrested anyone.

Steve lived upstairs, with me downstairs, in the house at 8 Jerilderie Court, and if the name rings a bell you may recall that Jerilderie is a small New South Wales town that figures in the Ned Kelly story. The bushranger's famous Jerilderie Letter was his manifesto.

My journalistic career on the Gold Coast began on the daily edition of the *Gold Coast Bulletin* where, after the demise of the Sunday edition, I continued to focus on the arts and entertainment and was, to a degree, the celebrity roundsman. I had a couple of brushes with fame, one of them with British comedian John Cleese who we heard was coming to the Gold Coast to indulge his passion for seafood.

When we got wind of this I was dispatched with a photographer to Coolangatta Airport (renamed Gold Coast Airport later in the decade). We spotted the lofty comedian arriving and approached him but were fobbed off by his minders. He was fairly famous at the time, so I guess he warranted minders.

We were told in no uncertain terms there would be no interviews and so to 'piss off' but instead withdrew to a safe distance and hung around just in case. When his minders went to deal with some paperwork Cleese went and sat by himself, so we pounced. The star himself was happy to have a brief chat and pose with a stuffed parrot someone had given him – a dead parrot, no doubt – and when the minders saw this they went ballistic, abused us and pretty well chased us out of the airport. But who cared? We had our story.

The Gold Coast has always been a bit of a celebrity hot spot and the clubs and venues attracted some big names. Eccentric American singer Tiny Tim visited and I was again dispatched to do the honours. I met him downstairs at his hotel in Surfers Paradise and the photographer and I went up to his room in the lift. On the way up he pulled out his wallet to show me some photos of 'Miss Dixie', his latest love, to whom he had dedicated his new album. His wives and girlfriends were all Miss this or Miss that. Oxymoronically, Tiny Tim was surprisingly large and gave off a pungent odour or, should I say, fragrance. He positively stank of lavender.

We had taken along some tulips as props (his big hit was *Tiptoe through the Tulips*) and we got photos of him with the bouquet against a backdrop of the Pacific Ocean with Surfers Paradise beach far below.

That night I went to see him perform at Twain's nightclub in Surfers, one of the dives I would become a regular at. He played his trusty ukulele and performed some Tin Pan Alley tunes but also some rock 'n' roll numbers, and at one stage played lying on his back in the middle of the dance floor with strobe lighting creating the effect of a deranged, long-haired whale of a man in his death throes. I couldn't unsee that.

I enjoyed working at the paper but was still having health problems – namely my tummy – and was popping pills and starting to drink more than was healthy, despite the fact that alcoholism had killed my father.

A girlfriend at the time (like all my relationships until I got married it was fleeting) suggested I attend a health farm in Sydney's west where she had been. In those days I was up for anything and was, in desperation, dabbling with alternative therapies, so I checked into this sanatorium at Dural. Turned out I got the wrong health farm, though, and instead of a pleasant place serving vegetarian food with people sunbathing in deckchairs and playing outdoor table tennis I found myself incarcerated in an institution where they starved me and fed me nothing but fruit juice for a week. I paid thousands for the privilege, making it one of the most expensive mistakes of my life.

I grew weaker and weaker by the day and remember looking in the mirror one time and being convinced I had turned into D.H. Lawrence. Mind you, Lawrence had consumption so he had good reason to look ghostly. I absconded from this joint (you can read all about it in my book *Any Guru Will Do*) and when I made it back to the Gold Coast was so weak from the starvation that I had to quit my job.

I was now a freelance journalist and closet poet. I say 'closet poet' because not many people knew I poetized at all. It wasn't the sort of thing you professed to be doing on the Gold Coast in the 1980s. You could be a con man or a gigolo or a surf bum but not a poet.

I mistakenly confessed to writing poetry to a couple of people who weren't convinced. It was my secret life but mostly it was concealed like a dirty little secret.

Forging a freelance career that actually became quite busy, I wrote for all sorts of publications from *The National Times* to *Australasian Post*, interviewing authors, celebrities and businesspeople. But I also did stories on weirdos and nutters, and there was a proliferation of both on the Gold Coast at the time.

I recall – how could I forget? – an elderly German woman who claimed to have been Hermann Goering's secretary. She was married to a transvestite English bricklayer. There was another story about a man who lived in a hole in the ground, and I also wrote about a couple who ran an Egyptian temple-dancing course, for which they were ideally qualified if you believed their claim to be reincarnated ancient Egyptians.

I interviewed Barry Humphries for the first time back then. He was on the Gold Coast doing shows at the Twin Towns Services Club, which is technically in New South Wales but only by a street or two. I interviewed him as Barry and as Sir Les. There was a big discussion on the Gold Coast at the time about the need for an arts centre, which was on the drawing board, but a segment of the community was against it, arguing that a new sewerage system was more urgent.

Humphries, always on the lookout for local material, weighed in, suggesting the Gold Coast build a sewerage system that could be drained to serve as an art gallery when required. I wrote a piece for *The National Times* headlined 'Art Versus Sewerage: The Great Gold Coast Controversy'.

Being a freelancer, I worked sporadically – by which I mean not very much – which suited my delicate constitution. I had my office set up in the room adjoining my bedroom downstairs. Here I had my dad's Chinese antique desk, atop it my trusty Remington, my bookcase nearby and a record player.

My days were spent ranging around the coast with Paul Riley, the photographer I worked with regularly. My mornings would usually begin, however, in Surfers where I was becoming a fixture in local café society. My field office was Tamari Bistro at the top of Cavill Avenue, a stone's throw from the beach. It was an Italian café and popular in the day with all sorts of people. The Gold Coast was quite multicultural, in a European kind of way. I often had coffee with my Greek friend Robert Gregory (the society may have been multicultural but many people's names were anglicized). Robert's dad (Harry!) owned the top end of Cavill Avenue. There were Serbs and Italians, as well as the Greeks, and I became friends with the Jewish set that hung out there. That led to my meeting a local Jewish doctor, Joe Goldbaum, an orthomolecular practitioner who introduced me to his sister-in-law, Catherine, who was visiting from New York.

I think there was a vague notion that we would hook up but it turned out she was married already so I never discovered what that was all about.

Catherine's parents were Hungarian Jews, Holocaust survivors, and they were on a long visit, staying in a building called Condor Apartments.

I went to see Joe a few times (I was even invited to his house once for *Shabbat* dinner) for assistance with my 'condition', whatever that was. He pumped me full of vitamins and seemed to think I would make a good Jew. He suggested I might like to convert.

I explained that I was a Christian and he outlined his hypothesis that Jesus behaved the way he did due to vitamin deficiencies. Interesting theory.

When I told him that I'd already converted once, to Catholicism, he said: 'That's perfect! You've got the guilt.'

At Tamari Bistro I also met people who were into naturopathy. I consulted a German natural therapist, Dieter Luske. He and his wife, Giselle, had a beautiful property at Canungra where my father had done his army jungle warfare training in 1943. Their place was a bit of a hippie haven and a gathering place for the weird and wonderful folks who made the Gold Coast of that era such an interesting community. It was a lot more countercultural in the 1980s than it is now.

My reading was also a bit countercultural. I was already steeped in Herman Hesse's works but I expanded my reading to a plethora of self-help books which were, by and large, no help at all and only created more confusion. I was undergoing therapy at the time, too: transactional analysis with an intense pipe-smoking bloke who lived on a yacht and was a bit of a New Age guru for the self-indulgent denizens of Surfers.

He switched me on to Sheldon Kopp's *If You Meet the Buddha on the Road, Kill Him!*

That became my bible for a few months at least. I was also reading texts by a guru called Bubba Free John, who had several names in his earthly life. I had an American friend, Jack, whom I had met through the Jewish set (his wife Elaine was a Jew) but he wasn't of their faith, he was a follower of this guru instead, and I used to visit him at his home in Surfers Paradise where we would sit under a tree while I took instruction from him on the meaning of life.

Her put me on to the Bubba Free John book about health, *The Eating Gorilla Comes in Peace*, which used Ayurvedic therapies and philosophies – all of which just goes to show I was ahead of the curve, right?

Sounds nutty but it wasn't completely unhelpful, and I still have it sitting nearby in a bookcase. From time to time I dip into it and re-read all the intensely underlined passages – to remind myself just how mad I once was.

All this was seeping into my subconscious, I guess, and would, of course, express itself in my poems, which were being hammered out in secret on my trusty Remington in that little room in Nerang. How many other people in Nerang were writing poetry in such rooms? Not many, I thought. I may be wrong but I don't think I am. It makes me think of one of my favourite Leonard Cohen poems, *I Wonder How Many People in This City*, in which he sees faces in windows and writes: *and when I turn away / I wonder how many go back to their desks / and write this down.*

In fact, you couldn't come up with a less poetic place than Nerang. Nevertheless …

I was beavering away, still sending poems out and getting the usual rejections but also having the occasional success. The respected author and editor Geoffrey Dutton had expressed an interest in some of my work, and in November 1983 I had what I considered another watershed moment when he published my poem *Flying Fox* in *The Bulletin* Literary Supplement.

I was in good company because there was also a poem by Bruce Dawe in that edition as well as writing by Xavier Herbert, Gabrielle Lord and other notables.

Flying Fox was written after seeing a ranger on television doing a wildlife segment with a flying fox (or fruit bat, as we Australians tend to call them) in the studio.

> *You encumbered fox, / Small dark gentleman / Pulled out of a box / By a woman on the television … On the television the lady / Pulled you out of that box by magic, / Like some magician's rabbit / Dark and tragic. / Half-bat, half-fox, / Half-found, half-lost; / A little pot-pourri of creation, / A sweet little piece of damnation.*

I had sent this poem, among others, to Les Murray, with whom I was still corresponding, and he hadn't liked that last line. in a letter to me he rejected it out of hand, saying flying foxes were beautiful and had nothing with to do with damnation. Of course I begged to differ, even with Les Murray.

I wrote a longish poem around this time entitled *Gold Coast Alliterations*, which finishes like this:

> *After the sun has slipped from sight / And nice new neon has nullified the night / Lilac Lamborghinis do their languid laps / Full of bleached blondes and big burly bruisers, / All totally*

tanned and terrifically tight. / Soon someone seedy is sick on the sidewalk / And Dad finally declares the day a decided disaster.

In another poem – *Notes from Binna Burra* – I write about escaping Tinseltown for a day trip to the mountains of the Gold Coast hinterland where I reflect from on high:

I come here to sit outside myself / And gaze out upon endless plateaus of possibility / As my panacea, a cure for my civility. / I cannot give myself to these forests / But I need them nonetheless … I am no cave man, to be sure / But something's stirring here in me – / Passion or Devonshire tea? Well, I thought it was amusing.

I wasn't reading that much poetry in those days, distracted as I was by esoteric literature, but I was very fond of a book by New York poet Anne Waldman, *Giant Night*. Waldman was associated with a couple of literary movements most notably, to my way of thinking, the Jack Kerouac School of Disembodied Poetics. I wanted to attend that school!

And anything disembodied suited me. Reading Waldman allowed me to free up my style, I think. Her signature poem, *Giant Night*, is still a favourite.

Awake in a giant night / is where I am / There is a river where my soul, / hungry as a horse, drinks beside me. / An hour of immense possibility flies by. / And I do nothing but sit in the present / which keeps changing moment to moment / How can I tell you my mind is a blanket?

I still love that. It was definitely Waldman who influenced what came next. Both Waldman and D.T. Suzuki, that is. I had been reading his book *Essays in Zen Buddhism* and was very attracted by the idea of Zen and Zen poetry, haiku in particular. I had read some haiku but while loving the minimalism I've never been big on following set syllable syncopations. I like rhyming verse but prefer to compose in a freer-flowing style if I can. I'm not always successful of course. But the spirit of haiku I loved.

Orientalism has always been a big influence. Since my teens I had been interested in Chinese culture and literature: Lin Yutang's book *My Country and My People* was a favourite and pointed me in the direction of Chinese poetry.

When I first read Li Po, Tu Fu and Wang Wei in translations by the great Arthur Waley, it resonated because I had thought of myself as a tad oriental. My seven years as a kid in Hong Kong hugely affected my aesthetic sensibilities and in my own imagination in a past life I may have been a Chinese scholar, poet or sage. Dream on, right?

One clairvoyant I went to on the Gold Coast (I saw a few) confirmed that once upon a time I had been a Chinese poet. Of course I had. She knew exactly what I wanted to hear. Did she know aught about Tang verse? I doubt it – but the gleam in her eye told me she was keenly aware there was one born every minute.

After reading Suzuki, and with Waldman and the Chinese and Beat poets echoing in my brain, I was ready to embark on one of the most interesting experiments in my long, and only occasionally successful, literary life.

My brother was in the US on an extended tour that would end up with him staying and settling in Canada. And then my mum decided she would take an extended trip to England to visit my father's homeland. She would also stay with my dad's former Hong Kong secretary, Mavis Cunningham, who lived in the small and remarkably well-named Derbyshire town of Bakewell (famous for its tarts, or puddings, or whatever you want to call them. That's an historical debate I won't go into here).

The memorable Mavis would make a couple of reappearances in the far-off Nineties when my future wife and I visited her in Bakewell. On one visit she took us on a tour of the Peak District in her small car. Hurtling through that Jane Eyre countryside with Mavis at the wheel, I had never been so terrified. Whenever she asked if we'd like to stop somewhere and have a look, I shouted: 'Yes!'

With Steve and Mum both away I had the house to myself. I decided to embark on a little poetic project. I would write one hundred poems and do so as they came … in a kind of stream-of-consciousness style in small batches, several each evening as it turned out.

I was going to describe it as automatic writing, coming from the 'great beyond', from the collective unconscious if you will (I was also a Jungian at that stage) or from the ether.

Automatic writing it was, in a way, but it wasn't altogether so because it was aided by the ingestion of wine and tobacco.

Each night I would sit in the lounge room drinking, smoking and jotting down these bizarre random little poems that paid tribute to Chinese poetry and Zen Buddhism while at the same time lampooning both. I would channel the Beats and other free-flowing poetry movements and take a figurative leaf out of the two previously mentioned books of verse I treasured most at that time …. *The Spice-Box of Earth* by Leonard Cohen (a very accessible and pure book) and *Giant Night* by Anne Waldman.

The result is a poetry collection entitled *Plastic Parables*. That is a title shared with my (also previously mentioned) first published book of verse, which contains a modest sampling of products from the original experiment.

Many of the others remain unpublished and I may ultimately remedy that by putting them out myself in a single volume. Meantime, those that have seen the light of day appear as a smattering across my two books of poetry – *Plastic Parables* and *An Accident in the Evening.*

I have the folder here beside me and under the title *Plastic Parables* I had given it a subtitle, something I'd forgotten: *Poems for the Disgruntled.* So, if you are gruntled they may not be for you but, otherwise, enjoy.

The first product of this nocturnal brainstorming, which came out of thin air, was my *Religious Poem*, although originally the works were simply numbered rather than titled.

> *Jesus, carrying a cardboard box, / slipped into a fun parlour / and came out naked. / He had hollow eyes / and, also, a banjo. / In my top hat / I went gliding by. / 'Bless you,' / he said. / And I hadn't even sneezed.*

Strange. Written, of course, under the influence, and I don't recommend that at all. I have always believed the old adage *in vino veritas* is rubbish. Alcohol does not assist creativity in the long term, it ultimately destroys it. There are so many examples of writers whose lives confirm that.

But those were the circumstances under which these odd poems were born … cheap wine and, no, not a three-day growth but a packet or two of Benson & Hedges cigarettes.

That first poem is a direct result of walking past the Tunza Fun pinball arcade in Surfers Paradise and seeing a mendicant-like character going in and then quickly coming back out. And yes, he did look a bit like Jesus.

Many of these are Surfers Paradise poems. *Traffic* is another one, a vision of driving into Surfers at night on the Gold Coast Highway from Southport.

> *Traffic is pulsing into town. / What else is there? / Sugar gliders don't live here. / Nor do desert skinks.*

It ends with me astral-travelling out of the car.

> *I am in gear / way up above / as traffic / is pulsing / into town.*

As you can tell, I am rather fond of these poems that are full of nonsense and wonder, bewilderment and silliness … signifying nothing? More poetry should be like that.

I would imagine Stevie Smith, whom I studied under Bruce Dawe, might also have had a bit to do with the birth of my *Plastic Parables.* They are nutty and whimsical like her poems. Well, maybe a little bit like hers only. She was, after all, strangely brilliant.

These effusions flowed over a month or so. Often, they aped Zen poetry without adhering to correct formal tradition.

> *The crane is watching for frogs / in the still water. / They hold their breaths, still.*

Or:

> *Hunched among the hills I sit / wishing I was elsewhere. / As if I could be.*

Here are the opening lines of another (No. 71 in the series):

> *An existential expression / of all this / is my blank stare.*

Some have their origins in my Hong Kong childhood, particularly one of my favourites, *The Chinese Princess*:

> *I haunted her garden / Like a memory … / Seeking her scent / Or just a glimpse. / She, the Chinese Princess, / Wafts daily around the shrubbery. / I am an ornament, bewitched.*

This poem is inspired by afternoons in Kowloon Tong where I lived as a boy (and where Bruce Lee was a fellow resident when he died), a gracious if elitist suburb where all the streets have very English names. We lived in Devon Road; nearby was a little park, Kent Road Garden.

Here, in the mornings and afternoons, elderly locals would do their tai chi, grasping invisible birds' tails and chasing non-existent butterflies, flailing in slow motion, which always made us laugh. We had no idea what they were doing. We thought they were mad. After school we would go to play there sometimes … or, more accurately, to lurk. As boys of around 12, we were intrigued by the gaggles of Chinese schoolgirls who went there to buy soy drinks at a stand where we bought Coke and ice-creams. One of these was my Chinese Princess.

All this was a thousand years ago, I wrote, and it does seem like that to me, a scene from an ancient dynasty. *And* (in the end) *I am a stone / Crouched in recollection / By the pool of her forgetfulness.*

Funny how things transmute through the alchemy of the imagination into poems – or remembrances embellished enough to become poetic memories – that may not be written down but can still be savoured. That poem is a remembrance of things past, if you want to be Proustian about it or, in search of lost time, as the modern translation of the title of Proust's novel has it. For Proust it was a madeleine cake that sparked his memory and a flood of literature ensued. Not sure what it was for me … wine and a cigarette, a vague longing and *'letting my mind wander where it will go'*, as Paul McCartney once sang.

My *Plastic Parables* are often nature poems, too, in the Chinese and Japanese fashion, such as *Becoming the Wind.*

I laugh and wonder / What a rock could impart./ Each day I am becoming the wind.

Upon completing *Plastic Parables*, which were written out on a foolscap pad, I typed them all out, numbered them and went on with my normal life, not that it was all that normal.

I began to tire of life on the Gold Coast. I tried to fit in but never quite managed to. There was no cultural life to speak of and I spent my days sipping coffee, writing mostly inane stories to keep financially afloat, then in the evenings I was off nightclubbing at places like Twain's and The Penthouse, everyone's favourite Surfers Paradise nightspot at the time.

It was the disco era and the DJ at The Penthouse was a vertically challenged fellow with an Afro, and all you really saw was the Afro bobbing around behind his console as he put on another Bee Gees or KC and the Sunshine Band tune.

It was a vacuous life and I was trapped in it. Mornings would be spent lamenting over coffee at Tamari Bistro, watching the clouds pass by overhead and smelling the briny Pacific nearby. I had stopped surfing, having just drifted away from it (I would eventually drift back). One of the books I read around then was *Chronicles of Wasted Time* by Malcolm Muggeridge (I had been a Muggeridge fan since devouring *Something Beautiful for God* as a teenager) and I thought this later title of his could have been written with me in mind. I didn't know where my life was going, had no plan for the future, was approaching 30 and still lived at home with my mum.

I wasn't *Down and Out in Paris and London*, I was down and out in Paradise without the penury or ragged clothes. My poverty was an emotional and spiritual bankruptcy.

I had to get out of the joint. There was one moment when this thought became crystallized. One night at The Penthouse I had a vision of hell … and that was it. The disco music, the strobe lights, the mindless blather. I've never used LSD but was having a bad trip without it.

It was then that I ran into a Gold Coast socialite whom I knew and liked. I got chatting to her and outlined my aspiration to make a break for Brisbane and leave Tinseltown behind, start a whole new life.

'Oh Phil,' she said. 'You'll never leave the Gold Coast.' And that was what did it for me. A couple of weeks later I was gone, and in my head was the quote at the beginning of a Thom Gunn poem I had read when studying under Bruce Dawe. The poem was called *On the Move* and underneath it, in quotation marks, was this Beat slogan: 'Man, You Gotta Go'. Exactly.

CHAPTER 10

THE WEATHERBOARD JUNGLE

STANDING ON THE VERANDAH of my new Brisbane home, I watched clouds scudding across the sky in a stiff south-easterly. At one time that breeze would have marked, for me, the building of swells that wrapped around the point breaks of the southern Gold Coast. When those winds blew, I could hardly sleep for the excitement, dreaming of long lines breaking on the points at Kirra and Coolangatta, and of days when the waves had been so good we would surf until dark, exhausted but happy.

Now it was just such a cooling wind that I likewise embraced as I regarded my vision splendid.

The house at 49 Plunkett Street, Paddington, was owned by friends who would become former friends by the time I was done with the joint. Months in arrears on the rent, not answering the phone in case it was them chasing me for the money … that was all ahead of me.

For now, it was peaceful enough and an ideal spot. This old Queenslander cottage on stilts was perched on the side of a steep hill capped by the impressive edifice of St Brigid's Catholic church, a favourite subject of the late great Lloyd Rees during his early days in Brisbane. Southerners like to claim Rees as one of their own but the inconvenient thing is he was from Queensland.

Houses cascade down the hill in front of St Brigid's, some precariously so. My house fronted the street. It had a small, steeply terraced backyard and a high front verandah accessed by a long flight of stairs angling up from the street. The view from here was amazing. I looked out across the historic suburb of Paddington with its lush subtropical greenery, a mosaic of weatherboard houses and a plethora of tin roofs before me.

That view included two Brisbane icons – in the distance the XXXX brewery on Milton Road and, just south-east of me, Lang Park (now Suncorp Stadium), the home of rugby league. The Cauldron, they call it, the spiritual home of State of Origin. On clear nights I could clearly hear the crowds cheering.

For me, this house was a poet's eyrie and for the first months spent holed up there I fancied I was some Tang poet, withdrawn from the world, observing and writing verse about his surroundings. Mine was a poet's backyard if ever there was one, a perfect place for contemplation. The only thing missing was a pond with lotus flowers afloat and goldfish kissing the surface.

The stone-walled terrace on the hillside behind the house seemed ancient but really couldn't have been. There was moss and lush foliage with a mango tree crowning the scene, all quintessentially Queensland. Fruit bats visited when the fruit dangled temptingly, and they cackled through the night as they feasted.

I moved around the house thinking about poetry and penury, often still clad in my Chinese dressing gown well into the afternoon. I didn't have much to do because, romantic as I thought it all was at times, the fact of the matter was that I was actually unemployed.

The job I had been offered in the media unit at World Expo 88 dried up moments after I arrived at the Expo office in South Brisbane expecting to start work. The unit had a new manager who had probably already made up her mind about me before I got there.

When I presented myself to her, she could barely conceal her indifference, which seemed to be mixed with instant loathing. It twisted her visage into an insipid sneer.

'The fact is that we don't have a job for you right now,' she said as I sat there dumbfounded, undergoing a kind of out-of-body experience. In my mind's eye I was looking down and saw myself nodding with a look of hurt and puzzlement on my face. I mean, after all, I had moved to Brisbane for this job. It was my future this total stranger had just demolished.

'But I was promised the job,' I said feebly.

'I'm sorry,' she said. 'There is no job.' She couldn't have said it any plainer than that. I left in a state of shock and, driving home, kept repeating to myself: 'There is no job, there is no job' as If I couldn't quite believe it.

'Well, here's another nice mess you've gotten me into,' I told myself, echoing what Oliver Hardy often said to Stan Laurel.

This left me with no means of visible support besides some patchy remnants of freelance work that included my social reportage for the glamorous fashion magazine *MODE*. I was the Queensland stringer, a most antisocial social columnist.

I had begun working for them on the Gold Coast and continued now in Brisbane where I teamed up with well-known fashion photographer Ian Golding. Not long after moving to Plunkett Street I wrote an autobiographical piece for *MODE* based on my childhood in Hong Kong. It was part of a series of profiles and Ian took a photo of me standing on the front verandah of my new abode wearing a Chinese jacket for effect. I failed to mention in the article, which was autobiographical, that I was verging on destitute and struggling with depression, alcohol and prescription drug dependency.

One doesn't mention such things in polite society, and certainly not in glossy magazine puff pieces.

Golding and I would go out once or twice a week to cover some social event for the mag and I would leave as soon as humanly possible so I could get home and hole up again in my poet's lair.

I had moved a family heirloom, my father's teak desk, made for us before we left Hong Kong, to Brisbane where I set it up in the second bedroom of my lofty cottage. It was here I typed out my poems after writing them in longhand at the dining-room table (luckily the table was there when I arrived) using my father's vintage Parker Gold ink pen, which I had restored to working order for sentimental reasons.

In the mornings, after rising late, often with a hangover, I would go up to nearby Given Terrace to take my elevenses at Le Scoops, a pioneer of Brisbane café society. There wasn't much café society around in 1986. The Gold Coast was way ahead of the game on that score.

At the café-cum-ice-cream parlour, bleary-eyed, I would hide behind my sunglasses, sip coffee and wonder what the hell I was going to do in Brisbane without gainful employment.

Back at Plunkett Street the days passed slowly and I lost track of time as the cooler weather began to blow in from the south.

The house was sparsely furnished – a bachelor pad as I laughingly referred to it – and there was hardly ever anything in the fridge. Besides my antique teak desk, there could be found an old lounge chair, the resident table, a bed I had bought for the house, a tatty old chest of drawers in my bedroom and a rack for hanging my clothes on. All very Zen.

I had a toaster called Linda (that was the brand name) and a poster of a very skinny shirtless Mick Jagger on the wall as a kind of inspiration. If he could be that thin and successful, why couldn't I?

I was very, very slim. Painfully so. I hardly ever ate breakfast and just pecked at food during the day. In the evenings I made forays to nearby takeaway joints, like the Kookaburra Café, where I got my pizzas, and a Chinese takeaway staffed by an inanimate and un-communicative Chinese family.

I was a regular there and occasionally attempted to use my rudimentary Cantonese but there was never a flicker of recognition. The son, who I think was at university, served the food with a look that said: 'So what?'

At times I went to a little Indian takeaway run by a bad-tempered Sikh (I had thought Sikhs were supposed to be even-tempered) who eventually turned his back room into a little restaurant called Singh for Your Supper. No, really!

The sun rose and set, clouds passed overhead, storms blew in and left the suburb cool and its greenery dripping, while I spent my days largely ensconced in my domestic cocoon reading, writing poems and wallowing in that quiet desperation Thoreau talked about.

Bizarrely it was quite a fertile period, poetically speaking, and, quite happy with what I was producing, I was, as usual, sending poems off to various journals and mostly being rejected.

But I had unexpected encouragement from Barry O'Donohue, the bloke behind a journal of Queensland poetry called *The Border Issue*, which was quite influential at the time. Sporadic publication is a kind of sustenance for a poet: it keeps you in the game. I thought I'd scored a hit there but when I turned up at the launch the first thing he did was tell me I hadn't made the cut.

I was with my Monto friend Wayne, now living in Brisbane too. He watched O'Donohue cut me dead. I just nodded and said okay.

'You handled that well,' said Wayne.

'What can you do?' I replied. 'Fucking poets.'

Back at Plunkett Street, every evening I would get through a six-pack of Heineken lager, which was about all my constitution could manage. I convinced myself it was classy to drink imported boutique beer.

In my cups I would read and write before laying my labours aside in the evening to watch television in the darkness, with the screen glowing and the city lights twinkling away in the background, glimpsed through the windows that overlooked my front verandah.

Evenings would end with a benzodiazepine nightcap. By this stage my bad habits were raging. The doctors had helpfully continued to prescribe the pills for my supposed nervous disposition, first diagnosed back in my Toowoomba college days, and that habit had grown steadily. The booze I prescribed myself and I survived on a cocktail of both.

Evenings would also often involve another family heirloom I had brought with me to Brisbane, my father's samurai sword. This is an amazing artifact that has been in my possession since my dad died. He brought it back from Borneo after partaking in the landing at Balikpapan where a huge battle ensued in the last months of World War Two.

The objective for the Aussies (joined by a few Dutch troops) – to dislodge the Japanese from a large oil installation – involved a major amphibious landing followed by intense jungle fighting once they got beyond the beaches. My father, who joined the 2/14th Australian Infantry Battalion at 17, never said much about the action that he'd seen. Like many diggers, he kept it to himself. Consequently, I never discovered the story of the sword and how he had come by it.

Whatever the back story, it's a gorgeous weapon (if a weapon can be gorgeous). Dad used to keep it in his home office and today it sits near me in my study, as it did in those Paddington days. The only difference is that nowadays I do not wave it around my head, in a drunken stupor late at night, cursing while dressed in a silk oriental dressing gown.

This became a bit of a ritual. There was no one to witness the madness, though, because I was a solitary man, as the song goes. Very solitary.

I would wake in a benzodiazepine fog, groggy and alone, then do it all over again. Talk about tragic. But poets are meant to be tragic, are they not?

It's one of those fallacies that have elements of truth about them.

Still, I felt I was writing some good poems, or at least poems that I liked.

One of my favourites from that time is *The Weatherboard Jungle*, which is quite a long piece of work with an expansive view of the world I lived in, my own minor poetic version of *Under Milk Wood* if you like.

Here in the weatherboard jungle / The atmosphere is dense: / Birds seem to swim through the air / Up to a bed of grey clouds: tense, / Taut above the suburb. Saturday afternoon / And only a cat stirs, chewing grass stems …

Having begun in summer, the poem ends in winter.

In the stillness, the deep, chilled stillness / Of a winter evening, only the tap drips. / The TV's epilogue signals the finale / Of the scene. Now the weatherboard jungle slips / Into a deeper peace than it has ever known / As the stars tick by and the bony moon drops.

In another work I wrote, christened *From Inside My Car*, about driving in to the city, I imagined I was a conductor and the city my celestial auditorium, with the pedestrians as the wayward orchestra.

My Garden, Late, After Rain was a kind of oriental piece about my verdant garden after a subtropical storm.

It begins:

My garden is as cool as green jade / In the wet. Now it is bathed / In a dull and distant light / Cast by the city, late at night.

Except in very few cases, writing poems is not a living, and my debts were mounting. Each night I would spread all the bills out in front of me on the table and work out which one I could afford to pay. Most nights that would be none of them.

I had a small calculator to add up how much I owed but was basically calculating a sliding scale towards bankruptcy. I still owed money on a now defunct American Express card and was fielding occasional calls from a debt collector who was threatening to pop in and see me. To break my legs? God only knew.

It was a downward spiral and Gil Jamieson's description of me still rang true. I was, indeed, 'a poet with a liquidity problem'.

But it's funny how the Universe provides for you even in times of desperation. If you can just keep the faith and hang in there somehow.

I had contacted the various news outlets in Brisbane trying to secure some regular work – *The Courier-Mail, The Sunday Mail, The Daily Sun* and *The Australian* – but there was nothing going. No room at the inn, so to speak.

But then I got a call out of the blue from *The Australian* because, all of a sudden, they needed someone. They asked if I could do some casual reporting for them. Well, this was flattering but then again I had a pretty good pedigree of publication from my freelancing days on the Gold Coast, so that doubtless helped.

I pulled myself together as much as I could and started work there the following week.

It was patchy, just casual shifts, but it was something, and the workplace was fun and welcoming.

In those days *The Australian*'s Queensland office was a shabby little building in gritty Fortitude Valley, directly behind the one occupied by *The Daily Sun,* a racy Brisbane tabloid. This was Rupert Murdoch's precinct in Brisbane. *The Australian* shared space with *TV Week*, and the cramped office was a bit tatty.

The Queensland editor was author Hugh Lunn who in 1978 had raised his already high profile as a writer with the book *Joh: The Life and Political Adventures of Johannes Bjelke-Petersen*. This was, after all, Joh Land, the state behind the Banana Curtain at the height of the Hillbilly Dictator's reign over what had become, in cultural terms, a pariah state. A few years before I arrived, Hugh had also published his critically acclaimed *Vietnam: A Reporter's War* and some years later he would publish what some regard as the quintessential Brisbane memoir, *Over the top with Jim*.

He was not in the office when I arrived at *The Australian* in 1986, nor did I see him in the weeks I worked there … and it was only weeks. I was shown the desk where he sat as if it were a museum exhibit, and there was a coat over the back of the chair giving the illusion that he had just stepped out. A neat trick which I have used myself in the years since working there. I thought of the famous poignant last words of Captain Oates, from Scott of the Antarctic's doomed expedition: 'I'm just going outside and may be some time.'

The editor's role was, perhaps, more figurehead than anything anyway. Hugh, I was told, was at home writing another book. Fair enough too, he's a very fine writer.

In charge during his absence was Mike Seccombe whom the news-reading public will know in recent times for his work on *The Saturday Paper*. The others in the Brisbane bureau were: Liz Johnston; Pamela Robson, who covered property; Heather Brown, a famed rural reporter who, as time went on, would occasionally introduce me jokingly as her husband, since we were both Browns; and Kris Houghton, as she was then but who these days is Kristina Olsson, a well-known Brisbane author and creative writing teacher.

It was a jolly enough place. I have absolutely no recollection of the stories I wrote for *The Oz*, as we tended to call it … and still do. They may be mouldering somewhere in the grave of my scrapbooks. Working there was quite enjoyable and got me out of the house. By late afternoon each day a party atmosphere prevailed and antipasti would be procured from Sala's, a local deli just around the corner on grimy old Brunswick Street, the main artery of this disreputable suburb not far from the CBD. A bottle of bubbly was popped for this cocktail hour.

Around this time Mike Seccombe would bring out his guitar and start strumming to add to the festive atmosphere. I quite enjoyed it.

The money I was now earning was just keeping my head above water although I was still in a bad way. But in journalism at that time everybody else was, too, so it went largely unnoticed.

But the work was limited and, being in close proximity to *The Daily Sun*, I'd been in there to put myself forward for work there as well. That soon bore fruit.

I got a call from the news editor, Steve Howard, asking if I was available for some casual reporting shifts. Regular shifts. I couldn't have been more available if I'd tried.

So I didn't have to go far … just around the corner and upstairs (or via a rickety lift) to *The Daily Sun* where I did some rudimentary reporting for the news pages.

I got rather excited by the fact that one story I did, about some Iranian stowaways seeking asylum who were on a ship coming into the Port of Brisbane, actually made the front page.

'You've got the splash tomorrow,' I was told. So excited was I that I couldn't wait to see the paper next day. I drove into Fortitude Valley just after midnight to get a paper literally hot off the presses, which were downstairs in the building chugging away like some giant engine that ran the good ship *The Daily Sun*.

I'm not sure what state I was in to drive but that didn't seem to worry me or anyone else in those days.

Still, it wasn't quite a job, just some casual shifts. I knew a few people who worked there including my Monto mate Wayne who was now the political reporter, having been poached from *The Courier-Mail*, which wasn't yet in the Murdoch stable.

I wanted a full-time job and had asked the editor, Mike Quirk, for one a couple of times, only to be told there were no full-time vacancies.

So there I was, still sitting at my table at home adding up the bills each night trying to work out how I was going to survive. I was starting to make incremental inroads but the rent was still in arrears, which was embarrassing.

Then one evening, after one of my casual shifts, I was walking up the long staircase to the house in Plunkett Street and, as if to add injury to insult, a bird perched on the front of the house crapped on my head.

'Well, that's just perfect,' I said to myself as I went inside, trying to brush it off (in both senses). I had pulled through the bottle department at The Paddo tavern on my way home, as was my custom at the time, and, having cracked open my first drink of the evening, was raising a greenish bottle to my lips when the phone rang.

It was my Greek mate Cratis.

'How's it going?' he asked.

'Well, it's going,' I responded. 'Just. I've just got home from the paper. Still just getting casual shifts.'

'There must be a job there for you,' he said.

'Well, not at the moment apparently,' I countered. 'And coming up the stairs I just got shat on by a bird so that's the sort of day I'm having.'

'Wait a minute!' Cratis sounded excited. 'A bird shat on your head? That's fantastic! In Greece that's good luck.'

'What about in Australia?' I asked.

'Yes, here too,' he assured me. 'No, I mean it. That is good luck. It means things are about to change. Something good is coming.'

Now I'm not saying Cratis is clairvoyant but the story goes that his mum, Fifi, an effusive Greek lady, had the gift.

So perhaps the gift was transferable from mother to son? I certainly hoped so. Cratis was convinced my luck was about to change and he'd seen me go through quite a bit, always remaining optimistic on my behalf even when I wasn't.

But the next day, without a shift, I was at home again with still no prospects of a full-time job in the foreseeable future.

That afternoon, I got the call that changed all that.

It was from my mate Wayne. He was in the newsroom and speaking in a hushed tone so nobody beside him could hear what he was saying (although everyone in the newsroom hears everything).

'Mate, three people have just resigned,' Wayne said. 'The editor is in the office with his head in his hands. Mind you, that's not that unusual. Anyway, the thing is they just resigned this morning and they don't have anybody else yet. I was just talking to the chief of staff and he said they are desperate.'

'Desperate works for me,' I said. 'I'm desperate too.'

'I'll hang up now and you ring Mike Quirk in about half an hour,' he said. 'After news conference.'

So I waited out the allotted period, rang the paper, asked for the editor and was put through straightaway. I told him I was enjoying the casual work but wondered if any full-time jobs had opened up.

'It's funny you should ring right now,' he said. 'Because we actually do have something.'

Mike seemed to like me and had congratulated me on my splash about the Iranian stowaways. He was a genial bloke from Adelaide. If you were from Adelaide, where the Murdoch Empire had started, you were special. They called it the Adelaide mafia and Mike Quirk was part of that. I guess that made Rupert The Godfather.

I rang Cratis and brought him up to date.

'I told you,' he said. 'Birdshit never lies.'

'Is that an old Greek saying?' I wondered aloud.

'It is now.'

CHAPTER 11

I'M BROWN, FROM THE SUN

MEMORY IS a funny thing. Looking back, one's past becomes a kind of personal mythology or, worse, a kind of cartoon. Or perhaps something from an old, half-remembered movie. You recognize yourself in it, to a degree, but was that really you? Well, yes, it was … but it isn't.

I am not now the elegantly wasted dandy who sauntered into the newsroom at *The Daily Sun* in 1986 in a double-breasted Najee suit. Remember when men wore double-breasted suits all the time? I blame Paul Keating.

Back then this was me, just turned 30, with that Mick Jagger or David Bowie build (I wished). That isn't hard to comprehend. However, now that I'm playing back scenes from that time on the projector in my mind, it really does seem like someone else. That person's future was finite under the circumstances, his world fuzzy and confused.

But at least that person now had a regular job and, if asked, or even if not, would tell you with pride that he was a reporter on *The Daily Sun*.

This newspaper was the Murdoch tabloid run out of that old building in Fortitude Valley, also home to the *Sunday Sun* until

Rupert decided to expand the operation. Fortitude Valley was (and to a degree still is) a kind of poor man's Kings Cross, a once popular retail area a kilometre from downtown Brisbane and just north of the storied Story Bridge. It had degenerated into Queensland's capital of sleaze when the state was ruled with an iron first by the devout Lutheran Joh-Bjelke Petersen (Sir Joh to you). The Valley, as it has long been known, was rife with nightclubs, illegal casinos, brothels, dowdy pubs and a place where drugs and alcohol – and coffee – were the main forms of sustenance.

Perched on the edge of this *demi-monde*, our newsroom was a kind of brown indoor swamp three levels up and quite regularly drunks or loonies would find their way into the office. There was no security in those days. I remember a guy who used to shadow-box at the crossing on busy Ann Street nearby, and sometimes he'd step out onto the road to challenge oncoming cars.

There was a bus stop outside the newspaper front door where someone was usually curled up asleep on the bench. Occasionally it was one of the journos.

In the newsroom the windows were constantly fogged over so you couldn't see out because of the grime, but what was there to see anyway? The traffic on McLachlan Street, not much else.

There was a pub next door, the Empire, which is still going strong and now heritage-listed. Traditionally, newspaper offices always seemed to have a pub next door. The Empire fuelled the newsroom and was a virtual field office, although despite my then fondness for the sauce my drinking was done mostly at night in the privacy of my bachelor pad in Paddington rather than in the pub. I never became an habitué of that pub. I have never much liked pubs.

At any rate I didn't drink much during the day. During work hours I lived on coffee, cigarettes and tranquillizers.

I would arrive in the office around 9.30 or maybe 10am looking good (at least I thought I did) but feeling awful.

I sat down the back of the newsroom in a section designated for fashion and features journalists. One of my colleagues from that time recently reminded me that she and the other women used to feed me Panadol upon my arrival to help me transition into the working day.

I was not a well man. I would usually pop a little pill not long after that to settle myself down. I remember one day one of my colleagues saying: 'Please don't take another one of those pills.'

I just looked at her and said, 'I have to.' And I meant it.

There was a bank of computer terminals nearby where one would sit to file stories. I would tap away there with a cigarette in one hand (we had a handful of dinky tinfoil ashtrays for the ash and butts) and disgusting, sludgy coffee beside me in a little plastic cup.

I would usually leave the office for elevenses, taken at the Cosmopolitan (the Cosmo in our parlance), a little Italian café and coffee roastery, across the road in Brunswick Street, which was still a traffic throughfare then although it has long since been turned into a mall. It must be the shabbiest, saddest mall in Australia. They keep trying to tart up The Valley but it has valiantly defied all attempts at gentrification.

The Cosmo was tiny. You sat cheek by jowl with the other habitués and I often shared a table with two regulars – local nightclub owner Gerry Bellino and his associate Vic Conte. Before too long, they would become infamous as figures at the Fitzgerald Inquiry, which laid bare Queensland's rotten core. Uncovering the worm in the bud of Queensland's soul began with journalist Phil Dickie's revelations about crime and corruption, published in *The Courier-Mail.* Gerry Bellino was one of the stars of Dickie's stories, not that he wanted to be.

Gerry and Vic eventually went to jail but at this stage they were not banged up inside. According to them, they were just local businessman. I knew they were alleged to be a kind of local mafia but I found them pleasant enough to chat to. I was a little naïve as to their nefarious activities. Vic had an appropriately gravelly voice like some character from *The Godfather*. Gerry was smooth and affable, and when I ran into him at the café and shook his hand I felt a vice-like grip. He had once been an acrobat and still seemed fit and very strong. You wouldn't want to mess with him.

At the time I didn't consider myself to be fraternizing with criminals, I was just having morning tea (a flat white, a slice of baklava and a cigarette) with a couple of blokes from the block.

A rival newspaper columnist who apparently spotted me there with Vic and Gerry one day mentioned me in his column in *The Courier-Mail*, then our rival paper. The context was that a journalist from that terrible Murdoch tabloid (we were all riff-raff supposedly) was consorting with crims.

At *The Daily Sun* in late 1986 I was put on the general news round and would write the occasional feature but before long, and to my horror, I found myself earmarked to become assistant political correspondent supporting, ironically, my Monto mate Wayne who was the paper's gun political writer. I figured I would be as good at covering politics as I was at cutting railway sleepers.

There was an election looming that November and I was to be his sidekick. What would that entail? Well, travel for a start, some of it to far-flung regions of the state on the campaign trail. I was mortified. I knew nothing about politics and certainly didn't want to go anywhere. I was having enough trouble just getting to the office in the morning. I was a tad agoraphobic at this stage and suffered panic attacks, which I'm sure were caused by my benzodiazepine habit.

The doctors give you those pills to settle you down but they really don't help in the long term. They have a deleterious effect and are, of course, highly addictive. I managed to convince several doctors, though, that I needed them and was using them sparingly, which wasn't true.

I was popping numerous pills during the day and using them to get to sleep at night after drinking for several hours in a bid to attain some kind of equilibrium. Such a regimen could have had fatal consequences, I know that now. But at the time I was oblivious.

I was still at Plunkett Street, Paddington, and in such bad shape at times that I would use taxi dockets from work to travel a few hundred metres to the late-night convenience store where I acquired my meagre supplies. Called Wee Willie Winkie, it was on Waterworks Road not far from Zig Zag Street, all three names made famous by Nick Earls in his classic novel.

In my condition the notion of travelling widely to cover the forthcoming state election was terrifying. I simply couldn't do it, yet I was expected to. Did they know who they were dealing with?

I was supplied with all the phone numbers and other details I would need in my new role and they were sketching out an itinerary for me while I sat trembling in the corner of the office hopped up on Panadol and benzos. Each time they spoke to me about it I would take another pill.

But again the fickle finger of Fate intervened. Perhaps I have a guardian angel? I might. No, correction: I did. The guardian angel in this instance was news editor Steve Howard, a Sydneysider who had been drafted to come to Brisbane to work on *The Daily Sun*.

Steve was a tough bloke in some ways but also a nice guy who seemed to accept me as I was, to a degree. I remember one morning when he approached me and asked if I would go to Caboolture, an hour or so north, to cover a council meeting there.

'I couldn't possibly do that,' I said. 'Not today. I'm sure you'll understand.'

That was grounds for sacking – refusal of duty – but I just remember him shaking his head and walking away. He seemed to accept that I was a bit eccentric. Or just plain nuts.

And he turned out to be my saviour.

With the election looming and my terror mounting, I was on the verge of resigning the day I heard him call my name from the other end of the newsroom. (It sounded unnervingly like the hoot of an owl, considered a harbinger of death by some Native Americans.)

I looked up and saw him gesturing for me to come over. When you see the news editor summoning you like that it's normally bad news. Generally, you would pretend to be on the phone or feign not noticing. I went over to him a tad gingerly.

'Sit down,' he said. I did. He looked me in the eye, smiled and said: 'We're going to make you a star.'

I had no idea what he meant by that.

'How so?' I inquired.

'We're going to make you our daily columnist.' The paper was about to launch a social column, A Place in the Sun (the name of distinguished journalist Keith Dunstan's long-running column in Melbourne's *Sun News-Pictorial),* and apparently I was to be the inaugural columnist. I processed this for a moment.

'Does this mean I am off politics?' He nodded. 'I'm in!' I shot back.

They knew of my work for *MODE* magazine and I faked the sort of urbanity that made them think I might be Brisbane's budding answer to Dorian Wild, their Sydney social columnist.

I went back to my desk elated and took another pill to celebrate.

Meanwhile, I was still writing my poems at night although my evenings would soon become busier, as part of my duties as a man about town entailed attending glittering social functions (or as glittering as they got in Brisbane and on the Gold Coast) and rubbing shoulders with the rich and shameless.

I would still go down to Nerang some weekends to visit my mum and on one visit I had drunk a few stubbies of XXXX before driving back to Brisbane in the sporty two-door coupe I then owned. I think it was a Mazda. It was yellow. Disgusting. Anyway, I took a stubby with me for the journey back to Paddington. What was I thinking? Well, I wasn't.

I was swigging beer while driving my car into Brisbane on the freeway when a police car appeared beside me, an officer inside it gesticulating for me to pull over. There on the freeway? Yep.

Wearing a pair of drawstring hippie pants, blue singlet and sandshoes, I looked quite the part. Surrendering the keys and the vehicle I was taken to the watchhouse where I was booked, processed and released pending my court appearance.

As I left the watchhouse the young policemen who had arrested me gave me some parting advice.

'You want to do something about yourself,' he said. I nodded. Couldn't argue with that.

The following week I left the office for my court appearance, running into a couple of reporters on my way in. They seemed surprised to see the *Daily* columnist there.

'What are you covering?' one of them asked.

'Nothing,' I said. 'I'm appearing.' And with that I went into the court.

I lost my licence for several months and decided to sell my car after that. I really couldn't afford it anyway.

Getting to work became difficult so I decided to move closer to the office. I moved from the weatherboard jungle of Paddington to funky New Farm, an area that is hugely popular now but was still a bit underground then. It was popular with Italians, gays, actors, artists and the like. And journos. As a matter of fact my wife, Sandra McLean, lived there not far from where I moved to. (Sandra was not my wife then, I should point out. But we would become friends and she worked on the paper too.)

I moved to a lovely old Federation building with an ambitious name: Hampton Court. It was on Bowen Terrace, about a 10-minute walk from the paper.

It was perfect. A lovely old building, it's still there although a little dwarfed now by the development around it. It's three storeys high with gorgeous old stained-glass windows (including one featuring a kookaburra). I occupied the top right-hand flat with what was at that stage an uninterrupted view of the Story Bridge. Lit up at night, it was stunning. I had the best view in Brisbane.

As will be no big surprise to you by now, I wrote about my fresh digs in a poem – entitled *Out of My New Window.*

> *The city burns. The dreamers toss. / Sleep – I'll soon be there. / But now, a cigarette's glow / Is comfort – and the sparkling view / Past the stark sill. / Sorrow dissipates over the city … On the bridge buses still run / And the city remains alight. / Sleep – I'll soon be there.*

My abiding memory of that apartment is sitting up late at night, smoking, listening to Blossom Dearie and tapping away on my typewriter at the dining table as I enjoyed that vista.

Not long after losing my licence I met the historian and author Ross Fitzgerald, now emeritus Professor of History and Politics at Griffith University and an enduring friend. At that stage he was Dr Ross Fitzgerald, already an academic at Griffith and famous for having his history of Queensland pulped by UQP after threats of libel litigation from Sir Joh, whom he had lampooned in a series of novels starring Grafton Everest, one of the great satirical characters of Australian literature.

I did a story on one of his books, we got on well and he invited me to visit him. He and his wife, Lyndal Noor, an artist and art academic, and their daughter, Em, lived at Kenmore, which is a little way from the city.

'Well, I don't have a car right now,' I said. 'I lost my licence for drink-driving and I sold my car.'

He looked at me a tad quizzically.

We got chatting some more. I didn't realize at the time that Ross was a stalwart of Alcoholics Anonymous. In our discussion we broached the subject of Barry Humphries, whom I was soon to see in his latest Dame Edna show. Ross told me how he and Barry had got sober together in Sydney. Humphries didn't really talk that much about his drinking, which threatened his life until he got sober, but he was emphatic that giving up the drink had *saved* his life … and his career.

He always made it very clear that putting down the bottle was the best thing he had ever done. Over the years I would get to know Barry better and I was invited to his memorial at the Sydney Opera House after he passed away in 2023. I couldn't go due to a bout of COVID-19 and that's something I'll always regret.

I had met him on the Gold Coast and was soon to attend his show at Jupiter's Casino there, which I mentioned to Ross. Armed with that knowledge he cooked up a scheme to confront my substance abuse (which he had twigged to), but I was blissfully unaware of that until, sitting down the front at Barry's show, I heard Sir Les Patterson refer to 'young people with substance abuse problems, like Phil Brown over here'.

What had just happened? *Did Sir Les Patterson actually refer to me?*

I was with my photographer friend Ian Golding at a small table and he looked across at me dumbfounded.

After the show I met up with Barry, who apologized on behalf of Sir Les and smiled sweetly. His work was done.

On the way back to Brisbane I thought, *If Sir Les Patterson thinks I have a problem maybe I do.*

Ross had, of course, prepped Barry about my situation. It is known as twelve-stepping, and those were the first steps on the road that would lead to my own sobriety.

But I still had a little way to run before chucking the towel in on my life as man about town, gadfly, dandy … sybarite.

Meanwhile I was still turning up as the daily columnist and would often arrive at functions and introduce myself thus: 'I'm Brown, from *The Sun.*' Occasionally some wag would say: 'You don't look it' and I didn't. Because actually my complexion was rather sallow, not brown at all. It was more pallid. My surfing days were far behind me then and I hardly ever saw the light of day. That light certainly didn't penetrate the dull interior of the *Daily Sun* newsroom which was anything but sunny in oh so many ways.

And yes, I was still writing poetry, secretly. Besides Wayne, no one in the newsroom knew that I was a poet. It was the craft that dared not speak its name.

Eventually one of the tougher characters in the office heard I was a poet and so far as he was concerned that was tantamount to being gay. Not that there's anything wrong with that, as Jerry Seinfeld would say.

I also wore red socks at the time as a kind of signature, and this was also construed as proof of effeminacy. The straw that broke the camel's back for him, though, was when he was sauntering past a nearby nail bar one day and saw me sitting near the front having my cuticles done.

My reasoning was straightforward enough: a gentleman owes it to himself to have a regular manicure.

I had to keep myself nice. My hair was attended to at this time by Mona Dubois, sister of the famous Brisbane hairdresser Stefan, at his main city salon. I would generally be given a Scotch while she was tending my coiffure.

One of my poems from that time was ultimately published in *The Australian*, where Geoffrey Dutton had become poetry editor. Entitled *Old Diggers, Brisbane*, it's basically about regarding city tramps as returned servicemen.

> *Sometimes they march around, these old soldiers. / But their own salutes / Mock them as they remember old wars. / Now, even peace is fraught with battles. / Still, they are resolute / As they shuffle past stark, neon corridors / Into the jangled night of the city.*

Getting a poem published nationally is always a treat. Another work from this time that I quite like was *Some Friday Couplets* which evokes a vision of Brisbane city from a taxi on my way back from some swish function.

> *Friday afternoon and the punters / Are oiling their hunches. / Journalists are wandering back / From their late lunches. / Schoolgirls are meandering in the mall / On the verge of puberty / While nearby, someone slim is selling / A newspaper and calling for liberty.*

I was writing my poems in relative isolation and publishing only sporadically.

I guess the poems from that period reflect my dominant emotional state at the time. In *Dialogue* I basically raved about my existential crisis:

Who is listening to me / By lamplight? I wrote. *When will another star / Shine over Bethlehem? / Can you, with your books and computers, / Sing me a song of the sky?*
... Out in the back yard / Squats a darkness / I have never fathomed. /Sometimes, I am driven out / Into it / Where shapeless things live.

Yes, I know. Odd.

But I kept on writing, as I have always done, in between my daily chores as a scribe of the Fourth Estate. Some estate, huh?

My job as columnist at *The Daily Sun* brought me a modicum of public recognition. I was a legend in my own lunchtime, semi-famous, now a minor celebrity in addition to being a minor poet.

My photo appeared in the corner of my page every day as I wrote about social events, morsels of gossip and other titbits, sharing some of the content with Dorian Wild for his column in Sydney.

But I was getting sick of the shtick and it showed. Being highly strung out as one tends to be on a cocktail of coffee, alcohol and benzodiazepines, I began to have some tiffs in the office, including one in which I pushed one of the associate editors into a large garbage bin. He eventually forgave me.

It was a fraught workplace, to say the least, with drunkenness and bad behaviour part of the everyday.

My moodiness ultimately caused me to quit the daily column. Or was I sacked? I can't recall, it's all a bit hazy. Let's just say it was mutually agreed that I cease coming in. I went back to being a feature writer, occasionally dabbling in news, which meant I was once again vulnerable to the vagaries of the newsroom schedule. I'd had my brief shot at fame, I guess.

I tended to be given stories that were up my alley, though, involving the arts and entertainment which was nice. And I was still moonlighting as *MODE's* Queensland representative, which the editor and managing director disapproved of.

At least I was lucky enough to be spared the daily news round, and politics, but only up to a point.

All this was happening in the last days of Joh, and if that sounds a tad Biblical, well, it should.The Hillbilly Dictator, the man Gough Whitlam once called 'a Bible-bashing bastard', well, his tenure was coming to an end during this period, though he seemed to be the only one unaware of it.

Revelations of corruption triggered the establishment of the Fitzgerald Inquiry in July 1987 which ultimately led to the jailing of my café pals.

While I continued to dodge serious news, the inquiry got under way in Brisbane District Court No. 29.

The collusion between the criminal underworld (Gerry, Vic et al.), the police and people in high places rocked the very foundations of the State and the pressure on Sir Joh to resign was mounting.

In November 1987 it looked like his time had run out, though he didn't see the bus coming until he right was under it.

Towards the very end, the embattled Premier went home to Kingaroy to consider his future. In those last days I was sent to stake him out, to get one last interview before the axe fell. It wasn't the sort of work I usually did or the sort of story I wanted to follow, but for some reason the editor thought I was the man for the job. Maybe because nobody would be expecting me? Maybe because I wasn't a political hack? I'm still baffled as to why I got the gig.

So photographer Bob Fenney and I were sent to Kingaroy to wait for Sir Joh to return from Brisbane to his property at nearby Bethany. Then we would doorstop him and get a scoop. I guess it was a good idea but a job that was supposed to take one day turned into several as we cooled our heels waiting. Not much to do in Kingaroy, I can tell you. I did buy some peanuts, I seem to recollect.

We were unprepared for a stay of more than a day and I didn't even have a proper change of clothes with me. We booked into a local motel (the Burke and Wills – how appropriate!) and had money wired for expenses, food and, embarrassingly, to buy a change of underwear.

Sir Joh finally flew himself home by helicopter (yes, really) on the afternoon of Friday November 27, 1987. I know this from checking my own story in an old scrapbook.

We had staked out the entrance to his property, blocked by his bodyguard, a certain Detective Sergeant Tom Lunney. We looked like the loneliest paparazzi in the world waiting on a deserted country road, but we had the field to ourselves. Nobody else had bothered to come to Kingaroy.

So we were counting on that scoop but not too confident about getting it until Sir Joh arrived home and, to our complete surprise, Det. Sgt Lunney waved to us to enter the property.

'Gee, you blokes are lucky,' the sergeant said. Sir Joh, it seemed, couldn't resist feeding his chooks, as he called the journos who he also fed off. He was always good copy, for better *and* for worse. We walked up to the front door of a house that was anything but grand.

'You boys have been very patient,' said Sir Joh, opening the flyscreen door to greet us. 'But I haven't got anything else to tell you.' Just then his wife, Lady Flo, appeared.

'Joh, I thought you weren't doing any more interviews,' she sternly admonished. But Joh couldn't resist a chat with his chooks and though he was all but finished he was unrepentant.

He described his parliamentary colleagues to me as 'babes in the woods'.

'They think I'm a ghost you can just chase away. But I'm still there.' Soon he wouldn't be.

He took us for a walk around his garden and Bob Fenney, ever the wily photographer, asked if he could take a picture of the Premier on the road leading to Bethany. 'Oh no, that would make me look alone,' Sir Joh demurred. He posed instead in a seat on the front porch.

I am looking at that photo as I write. It adorns a yellowing copy of the front page of *The Daily Sun* for Saturday 28 November, 1987. We must have driven back at a pretty fast clip and I would have written the story in white heat to get it in the next day's paper.

'Lone Retreat to Bethany' reads the headline, with my byline underneath and the caption: '*A solitary Sir Joh ponders his future at his Bethany homestead near Kingaroy yesterday.*'

We had spent the whole week getting that story.

Three days later he was gone, resigning on December 1 to be replaced by the rather affable Mike Ahern, whom I had first met in my Rocky days. It was the end of one era and the beginning of a new one.

Gerry Bellino and Vic Conte became less frequent visitors to the Cosmo until they disappeared from the scene altogether and were ultimately on the inside looking out.

But the Cosmo remained my field office.

Then one day I had a final dummy spit, quit the newspaper and started working freelance again.

The following year I covered the opening of World Expo 88 for *MODE* and I've always been rather proud of the fact that I did so without ever leaving my Bowen Terrace apartment. Ian Golding went over to South Bank to snap photos of the Queen doing the official opening but I stayed in, watched it all on TV and wrote my piece on the basis of that. I was told later my report was tantamount to actually being there. Go figure.

Research was a problem, though, what with me not being at the paper anymore. It's always handy to have access to a newspaper library. In those days, before the advent of the internet, we did our own research by going through the newspaper files or looking stuff up in books – yes, actual books. In the newspaper's library fat compendiums of news articles were contained between bland cardboard covers ('the cuts', they were called, as in cuttings) and were recovered for the journos by the people who toiled away in the Dickensian depths of a place where no natural light ever shone.

As an ex-employee I had no access to any of this, but I figured out a way of getting in anyway. A young colleague, who had been a copy boy before rising to the giddy heights of junior reporter, helped me out. He would do research for me for a pittance. I would furnish him with the subject matter I was writing about; he would fish out the cuttings files and photocopy the relevant pages.

Once that was done, he'd secrete the material in a brown manila envelope which he would leave with Eddie, the young Filipino guy who worked behind the counter at the Cosmo. The envelope was unmarked.

When my personal courier made his drop, he would ring me and I would leave my Bowen Terrace eyrie and walk to the Cosmo where I took delivery of the envelope with a nod and a wink. This raised eyebrows. After all, wasn't I the guy known to be friendly with Gerry Bellino? What was I up to now? What was in those brown envelopes? I would often sit with one of them in front on me on the table, sipping coffee and puffing away on my ciggie with a sense of smug satisfaction.

Surely on the basis of that evidence it was worth calling me before the Fitzgerald Inquiry? With my connections was I not, at least, a person of interest? But that call thankfully never came. Ministers of the Crown were jailed, along with the police commissioner. The government eventually fell, and Gerry Bellino was packed off to seven years' jail for official corruption: Vic Conte also went down.

When I walk the streets of The Valley today I can't help noticing it has changed a lot but some things remain the same. It's still scuzzy, the one area to outlast all efforts at gentrification.

The newspaper office is long gone, of course. *The Daily Sun* folded in 1991 to make way for a true monopoly when Rupert Murdoch took over the Herald & Weekly Times and won control of *The Courier-Mail*, a thriving broadsheet back then. As it turned out, years later my wife and I would both serve as Arts Editors on *The Courier*, which never fails to strike us as a strange synchronicity.

The *Sun* building is now Sun Apartments. Working in the joint was bad enough – I shudder to think of what living there would be like. It retains too many conflicted memories for me, from a time that was, in so many ways, ridden with angst.

But I was out of there. I'd stopped drinking though I hadn't quite kicked the 'mother's little helpers' habit yet but that would come. More poetry would come, too, but I was entering a somewhat fallow period.

All things considered, perhaps that was for the best.

CHAPTER 12

KAFKA IN BRISBANE

I STUBBED OUT MY CIGARETTE and entered the Brisbane Administration Centre to my job at Information Services for the city council. I was between gigs in journalism and had, as we say in the business, gone over to the dark side. Public relations, public affairs, call it what you will, it's just the same swill. (*Note to self: this rhymes, could be a poem.*)

I was working for the council administration presided over by Lord Mayor Sallyanne Atkinson, a Liberal and the city's first female Lord Mayor, soon to be pilloried as Salaryanne by the Labor machine seeking to install Jim Soorley, the bloke who wanted, and would ultimately get, her job.

Information Services was run by a genial former journo named Brian Grace who was a very nice man. The gist of the work undertaken by Information Services was however not, as I had assumed, to disseminate information but rather to control it and, ultimately, to stop it getting out. Disinformation Services might have been a better name for it. Like such departments at all levels of government, it was hostage to the politics of the incumbent.

Now I know it's an overused adjective but if I had to choose one word to describe my experience there it would be 'Kafkaesque'. I have also considered 'Orwellian' (Franz Kafka and George Orwell having inspired two of the most overused literary adjectives of the 20th and 21st centuries) but that may be a bit harsh.

To me, 'Kafkaesque' indicates that the experience was reminiscent of the oppressive or nightmarish qualities of Franz's fictional world. I do love Kafka and have to admit that at times, upon waking, I have felt exactly like a giant bug.

I first read Kafka's famous story *Metamorphosis* at the age of 12 and can remember the circumstances to a T: it was a weekend and I was holed up in my bedroom at our grand old house in the Hong Kong neighbourhood of Kowloon Tong. Listening to The Doors while simultaneously reading Kafka, I was living the dream – or the nightmare, in Kafka's case. Something about that story felt very familiar to me then and it has always resonated.

It was the Kafkaesque nature of council bureaucracy that really did my head in working at Information Services where I had a cubicle rather than a desk. We were like battery hens churning out material that might never see the light of day or which, if it did, by the time it was released would bear no resemblance to the original draft. Any pertinent facts and colour would have been drained from it like blood from a victim of Count Dracula. What was left was the textual version of the undead.

The stifling hand of bureaucracy killed originality with countless denuding interventions along the way. As a working journalist I enjoy churning out copy and am used to intervention from sub-editors and ultimately, the editor, but at Brisbane City Council anything I wrote passed through so many hands that by the end of the ordeal – sorry, process – it had been reduced to bland gibberish.

Often there would be meetings to discuss what we were doing – many, many meetings. Interminable meetings. Bureaucracies thrive on meetings which evolve and revolve until the participants finally disappear up their own orifices. Meetings are more important than actually achieving anything in such places.

I was sitting in one of these meetings one day, discussing an issue that I was supposed to be devising a press release about, when I broke the sacred code among bureaucrats and foolishly blurted out, 'How long is this meeting going to take?'

A hush fell over the room and the bloke chairing the meeting looked at me and said quietly: 'How long is a piece of string?'

There's really no right or wrong answer to that question. It has confounded pundits for centuries. Who has ever got to the bottom of that one? Not Jesus or Buddha or Nietzsche or Jean-Paul Sartre. I'm not sure even Einstein ever got around to figuring it out, although his modern predecessors, the exponents and proponents of string theory, may even now be working on the answer. It's the second most perplexing existential question after 'To be, or not to be …'

The fact was, I didn't actually give a shit how long a piece of string was.

Besides, I was grappling with my own philosophical and existential issues.

I wrote about them in a poem that is a direct result of working for Information Services at Brisbane City Council. I guess if I got a poem out of the experience it can't have been all bad.

Here's a small sampling from the poem entitled *A Primal Rave*, aka *A Query at Night Followed by Existential Ruminations from the Third Floor of the Brisbane Administration Centre.*

During the day / I attend to my hair / Breathe fumes, shuffle paper / And ignore cosmic messages.

I was producing this output in the spare room of our old flat in Llewellyn Street, New Farm, which we'd moved to in 1991. I was living there with Sandra, my girlfriend (if I can still use that term). We had been colleagues and friends but were now much more than that and were happily cohabiting in this funky pad. 'Happily' being the operative word because Sandra is the love of my life and was, if the truth be told, my first proper relationship.

We had both lived in the suburb before getting together – me in my bachelor eyrie at Bowen Terrace, Sandra in Foxthorn Court, an old Art Deco building on Moreton Street directly under a flat with a junkie rock band. Sandra was TV Editor for *The Sunday Mail* when I worked for Brisbane City Council.

I had been away for a time in Sydney, six disastrous months of a failed experiment that included a stint as social columnist for the *Sunday Telegraph.* Sydney didn't take. But it did complete my journey to sobriety. While there I was advised to enter The Langton Centre where I would be enabled to withdraw from my bennies habit. I had given up the grog but not yet the pills.

I was in there for a week or so detoxing, sharing a room with two Māori junkies. Oh yes, that was fun. After a few days they were both up and about, bright-eyed and bushy-tailed, while I was still suffering.

'He's doing it tough, Brian,' one Māori said to the other one day. Coming off prescription pills isn't easy and an indicator of how pernicious prescription drug addiction can be. But I managed it and am thankful I did.

When I eventually came back to Brisbane there weren't any jobs going on the papers but I managed to get that position with Brisbane City Council and, unsuitable as it was the job did come with a pay packet, which made it bearable.

I continued to have literary aspirations and set up that room in our flat as a study with a computer that in the 2020s would seem like something Fred Flintstone might have used. I had to paint that room because the handyman who serviced this small block of flats hadn't, even though he was supposed to. He was dubbed Ted Shabby (his name was actually Garth) by a mate of his who had even dreamt up a fictional business name for him: The Ted Shabby Group of Companies. Its motto was 'If a job is half worth doing' …

I spent a weekend painting the room he was supposed to paint but never got round to, listening to the radio and smoking cigarettes as I daubed away. I was still smoking then, getting through half a pack of Benson & Hedges a day. I was now clean and sober and attending my twelve-step meetings but couldn't manage to give away the smokes. I was concerned about this but one of my friends passed on advice that he had once been given in early sobriety: 'If it gives you any comfort, smoke two at a time.' It never came to that. but I got the point.

On the Brisbane poetry scene there was an evolving group of verse creators centred on the Metro Arts building down Edward Street in Brisbane's CBD. Metro Arts was Brizzie's beating bohemian heart with a theatre, café, cinema, art studios and galleries.

It was a heritage building that was a kind of rabbit warren for creatives. My friend the artist Stephen Nothling lived in his studio there, which was not quite legal. Metro Arts was run at the time by a poet, Robert Hughes (no, not the *Fatal Shore* guy). I joined Rob in forming Queensland Poets Society, a small outfit of desperadoes intent on bringing our lyric lines to the masses. Our ranks included, among others, the respected bard Brett Dionysius, who in a few years would go on to become founding director of the Queensland Poetry Festival.

The problem was that the masses weren't that interested, and at our poetry readings the audience could only be described as sparse.

I was giving a reading in the theatrette downstairs at Metro Arts one evening and could swear I saw a tumbleweed go by.

Sandra was amused by the vagaries of Poetworld and I would often come back from meetings cussing and complaining. We poets can be a tad fractious at times.

That brief period in 1991 and 1992 when we lived in premarital bliss in that spacious flat in New Farm was a kind of idyll really. It was also significant for me because around this time I started surfing again. That happened one day at Fingal Head just across the NSW border.

We had gone to the beach for the day and I'd decided, on a whim, to take out an old twin fin of my brother's which was still in the garage at my mum's place.

We were with friends and they were amazed to see me paddle out and catch a wave in the shore break. Almost instinctively, I stood up and did a few turns and hey, I was back, baby! After a ten-year layoff my surfing life was suddenly rebooted: I would keep at it for decades.

I retired from the waves a few years ago now but am still surfing between the ears, which at my age may be the safest option. Although given the right conditions, a perfect four-foot swell (we still use imperial measures in the surfing world) wrapping in to Tea Tree Bay at Noosa, I might get back out there. Never say never …

I had a bizarre routine for keeping myself surfing-fit in that old New Farm flat, a little regimen with dumbbells and running on the spot that lasted around 30 minutes and was performed to the tune of Handel's *Messiah* which is, I can report, great music to exercise by.

In the evenings I was jotting at my desk in a room that never quite lost its fresh paint smell.

I wasn't prolific but did write quite a few poems in New Farm after that fallow period. I was fairly settled and I guess that helped.

Sending a few poems out again was generating the usual influx of rejections although I was placing a few pieces. One I wrote then, entitled *Out in the Suburbs*, was published the following year by *Imago,* which was a fine but short-lived local literary journal back in the day.

> *Out in the suburbs / Time is measured by / The shadows of clouds / Sailing in silhouette / Across the rooftops … / And the city is a distant forest / Of glittering hourglasses / Sifting people like sand.*

Imago was published out of QUT (Queensland University of Technology) and was quite a force for some years with one of the state's finest poets, Philip Neilsen, as editor.

It was during this time – what I fondly recall as my later New Farm period – that my duck-shooting poem *Hunting with Gil on Three Moon Flat*, from which I quoted in Chapter 7, was itself declared a dead duck on grounds I've mostly consigned to oblivion, but that didn't make a lot of sense to me at the time. Some complicated explanation as to why it didn't work and was all wrong. You wonder why you put yourself through this stuff when, frankly, the piece is fine as it is. Poetry is so subjective, and poetry editors are usually just other poets with personal biases. Or grudges. They go mad with their little bit of power and laud it over their peers, rewarding those who agree with them and ignoring or discounting those who don't. I have always been proud of that poem because it memorializes a dear departed friend.

A few years ago, after writing an article about a book by the renowned Australian poet and author John Kinsella, I began corresponding with him (we share a love of cricket) and sent him a few poems from across my *oeuvre*. The one he liked best was that one about hunting with Gil. I was chuffed.

It was published in my first book, the painfully slim *Plastic Parables*. Much to my delight, Robert Hughes had offered to put it out through Metro Community Press, the publishing arm of Metro Arts. I used the title of that zany collection I had written in my cups on the Gold Coast and used some poems from that experiment, as well as others from my more mainstream body of work.

I asked Bruce Dawe if he would write a little introduction to the book, which he agreed to do, and that was quite an honour.

'Here is poetry which is naturally, and not artificially, engaging,' Bruce wrote. 'To be genuinely engaging necessitates good humour, and Phil Brown's poetry is poetry of good humour, the sort of humour enlisted on behalf of the central human interests such as love and the persistence of memory (*The Chinese Princess*), the lonely aged (*The Hermit*; *In a Thousand Gardens*), the surreal creatures of our dreams (*Ichthys*), as well as the flip send-ups of potentially destructive stances of the self as in *My Little Black Joke*. Also, here you will find effective evocations of those moods when the natural world draws us away from any particular awareness of ourselves as separate entities so that we may return to a more primal relationship with it (*Becoming the Wind*).'

That little book was a watershed. People seemed to like it. I know the serious poetry world may not have entirely approved but what has it ever entirely approved of? I have never felt completely part of that world and don't imagine I ever will. Poetically speaking, I'm more of a boundary rider.

I can't recall how many copies were produced – a few hundred, I think. I remember at the time a bloke I knew was boasting that his recent book had 'sold into double figures'. I thought *I can go one better because mine sold into triple figures*! And it sold out pretty quickly. As far as slim volumes go, they don't come much slimmer. Emaciated as I've joked it was back then, I fear it has managed to lose more weight over the years. These days I think of it more as a pamphlet.

But there it was, it existed, in print. *In print, therefore I am.*

The launch for the book was held at Metro Arts and I think it even made the social pages in one of the local papers. Fame at last! Well, again, but as if for the first time.

Being a poet while working in a mind-numbingly boring job does situate me in a great literary tradition. Lots of famous writers have had boring jobs. Stephen King was once a janitor.

Kurt Vonnegut worked at a car dealership, William Faulkner was a mailman (as was Bruce Dawe once), T.S. Eliot was a banker. And, of course, Philip Larkin was a librarian.

I was working in a job that gave me no satisfaction at all. One highlight, however, was that I was called upon to write a booklet celebrating the fiftieth anniversary of the Story Bridge. I enjoyed that.

The other highlight, in retrospect, occurred when for some reason I was given the task of booking entertainment for the Queen Street Mall. This was some time in 1991. I had to find an entertainer who would appeal to the locals and my darling Sandra suggested a young bloke she had interviewed for *The Sunday Mail.* Sandra thought he might go places. His name was Keith Urban.

I had never heard of him and neither had most people back then. Anyhow, I got hold of his management and booked him to sing in the upper part of the mall near George Street. I remember going down to check how he was faring and there were half a dozen people listening to him. For me it was job done. And, yes, he did kick on after that when his first album brought him to everyone's attention. Glad I could be of assistance!

I made friends with some of the folks I worked with at Brisbane City Council, friends who stayed friends. A few of us get together now and then like a gathering of diprotodons, and they still refer to me as the one that 'got away', like the colt from old Regret.

I gave it a go but my heart wasn't in it. Which may have been why I usually got to the office as late as I could, sauntering in around 9.15am after a final cigarette in the plaza downstairs before heading to the elevators for my little trip into *Nineteen Eighty-Four*. Orwellian, Kafkaesque, call it what you will. It was futile whichever way you looked at it.

I arrived one morning and was immediately called in to see Brian Grace, who was smiling as bosses do when preparing to impart bad news or give a dressing down. Brian asked me to sit down, exchanged a few pleasantries and then got to the point.

'Phil, I've had a couple of complaints about you arriving late for work,' he said, looking uncomfortable. I glanced back into the office wondering who had done the complaining.

'What's the problem?' I asked.

'Well, under our flexible guidelines the latest possible starting time is 8.45am,' Brian informed me. I nodded. Seeing that would be insufficient, I forced out the words 'I see' in a tone of mild insouciance.

'Yes,' he continued. 'So, what I'm wondering is if you could possibly see your way clear to following those guidelines and getting here a bit earlier. By 8.45am at the latest.'

I mused on this for a few seconds and then said: 'No, I don't think that will be possible.'

He just looked at me with a mixture of befuddlement and defeat. Kafka had won this one.

'I see,' he said. He wasn't expecting to be rejected.

'Is that all?' I asked.

'Yes, I suppose it is.'

Brian looked deflated and confused so I left him to it and went back to my cubicle. Then I looked around to see which of my colleagues were avoiding my gaze, before I got busy doing as little as possible once more.

At this time I was also involved in helping develop text for Lord Mayor Sallyanne Atkinson's bold plan to advance the city. It was called the Brisbane Plan (which sounded like something out of World War Two, but never mind). It was a good enough idea but was struggling to get airborne politically.

There was an election looming and the Labor Party machine was running Jim Soorley, a former Catholic priest nobody had ever heard of. He was promising to take a pay cut as Lord Mayor and Labor was running ads showing Sallyanne (who is a friend now, as is Jim) as Salaryanne, a party girl who was all about having a good time and being in the spotlight rather than attending to the nitty-gritty of people's everyday concerns. This wasn't actually true but that's politics, right?

Sallyanne had been a groundbreaking Lord Mayor who had presided over the city during an era of rapid evolution. She was Lord Mayor when I came to Brisbane and Lord Mayor when I was the columnist at *The Daily Sun*; and as Lord Mayor during the momentous World Expo 88 she had done a terrific job. In what was quite a shock to most of us she was ousted by Jim who, as I say, came out of nowhere and won narrowly thanks to preferences from Greens candidate Drew Hutton.

When Jim's administration came in and set about ridding itself of apparatchiks he, or his people, wrongly assumed that the denizens of Information Services were all Liberal Party stooges. I certainly wasn't a Liberal stooge; I felt more like one of The Three Stooges.

It was obvious Jim and his team wanted to divest themselves of, well, us … so when an offer was forthcoming for voluntary redundancies my hand shot up almost automatically, like Dr Strangelove's. I don't think anyone else wanted to leave but I was ready to shoot through like a Bondi tram. People all around me were worrying about their futures, their super and mortgages. I didn't think about such things – I just wanted out.

And I could now see the light at the end of the brown-carpeted tunnel!

Soon the paperwork for my redundancy was in the pipeline but not signed off on when I heard a whisper that the administration had decided to rescind the offer. I was mortified. Anticipating we would soon no longer be desk-bound, Sandra and I had already booked ourselves a six-week overseas holiday. We were heading for Thailand and Nepal (where we would trek in the Himalayas) and would come home via Hong Kong, all care of Brisbane City Council.

But if the paperwork wasn't ratified I would be getting nothing. Nada. Bupkis. Sweet FA.

I was told the documents were awaiting the Town Clerk's signature so I made an appointment to see him. Phil Berthold was one of Nature's gentlemen and seemed to think this request to get my paperwork signed off pronto was reasonable enough. And I just happened to have the said paperwork with me.

I felt like an insurance salesman as I guided him ever so solicitously: 'Mr Berthold, if you could just sign here … and here … and here.'

He was happy to do this and I left his office buzzing. It's my understanding that the redundancy offer was ultimately reversed, but my paperwork now bore that all-important autograph and I was good to go.

Free at last, free at last, thank God …

My life in civil admin had only lasted eighteen months or so. My Kafka experience was over. I was out.

Soon after my escape we were on a flight bound for Bangkok where we stayed at the shabby and now defunct Federal Hotel.

We spent a few days mooching around the *sois* off Sukhumvit Road. I hadn't been to Bangkok since I was a boy. My father had a business there in our Hong Kong days and I remember a family holiday at Pattaya which was more of a family resort in the 1960s. What I recall most about that holiday is that one of my father's accountant Harry King's sons, Gregory, was bitten by a monkey at the resort we were staying at and had to have rabies shots. I don't trust monkeys, besides being one (I was born in a Monkey year of the Chinese zodiac).

Flying from Bangkok up to Kathmandu was an otherworldly experience made even more so by the fact that for many years I had barely travelled, being in no fit state to do so.

But I was now unencumbered by the substances that had previously kept me earthbound and now here we were flying to the most exotic city on the planet.

Sandra had visited Nepal before and had talked me into this holiday with her enchanting description of trekking in the Himalayas as 'walking from one little hotel to another'. 'Hotel' is not the word I would have chosen to describe the little wooden hovels that served as the sole accommodation option in the High Himalayas back in 1991, but there you have it

We spent the first week in Kathmandu staying with Sandra's friends Jayce and Dale, followers of Tibetan Buddhism who were part of the Western dharma crew that called Nepal home. They lived in an old colonial-style mansion which suited me down to the ground, being an old colonial myself. I know that's not fashionable to admit but I can't help being an old colonial, I just am.

I wrote about the experience of visiting Nepal in A Trek Too Far, one of the tales in my book of road adventures, *Travels with My Angst*, which was published by UQP.

I didn't get many poems out of the experience although a couple popped out of my long-term memory, fully formed, just recently. In one, called *Arrival in Kathmandu,* I describe the city at first sight:

> *It is bathed in morning light. / It looks like somewhere / Alexander might have conquered … / And later, on the flat roof / Of the old mansion in Maharajgunj / Gazing out across the fields / Skirting the city / We see buffaloes grazing / And children fly kites / As dusk softens the scenery / That first evening / In Kathmandu.*

Its sights and smells are still vivid three decades later.

The trek itself began after a horrendous six-hour journey north from Kathmandu to the little town of Dhunche where the trekking began. That also resurfaced in a recent poem, maybe a better one … *A View of the Hills* (with apologies to Kazuo Ishiguro) which recounts our time in Dhunche.

> *Next morning we set out on a rocky path / And walked all day – crossed rushing rivers, / Traversed aromatic woods, / I thought of Shangri-La / And fixed in my mind was that image / Of a mountain where the sky should have been.*

I found trekking challenging, to say the least. I swore a lot and had to stop and spend an entire day resting at a place called Lama Hotel, convinced I couldn't go on. But I rallied and when we got into the upper alpine reaches of the Langtang Valley it was easier going and the scenery was mind-boggling, the mountains towering around us. Our destination was Kyanjin Gompa, at an elevation of around 4000 metres. '*Gompa*' indicates that the area is a Buddhist compound, and a Tibetan Buddhist lama lived nearby in a kind of mini-stupa at the foot of a mountain and beneath a nearby glacier.

The valley here was awe-inspiring. We spent my 35th birthday, October 9, 1991, here and celebrated with a can of Coke. Luxury.

Sandra and I were granted an audience with the lama in the nearby *gompa* and upon departing I asked if there was anything he needed and he said, through a translator: a pair of sunglasses. When we got back to Brisbane, I bought a pair and posted them to him but was never sure if he actually got them. So if you were in the vicinity back in the Nineties and saw a Tibetan Buddhist lama wearing shades I'd be pleased to hear from you.

We flew on to Hong Kong after Nepal, my old hometown and spiritual home, and I proposed to Sandra while we were there. Marriage, that is.

I have recounted the story before so I will spare you the whole tale but just mention that I bought an engagement ring on her credit card, which is perfectly normal, I guess, for a poet with a liquidity problem.

On our return to Brisbane, I was without a job but very soon heard that *The Australian* needed a correspondent for its then expansive higher education supplement. I managed to get the gig so I hadn't really missed a beat after my redundancy. I had enough money left to buy a new computer, pay off my debts and head off on honeymoon.

I was grateful to Brisbane City Council for the little lottery win but nervous too. All the way up those Himalayan valleys I was half expecting to look over my shoulder and see Jim Soorley chasing after me, shouting: 'Phil! We've changed our minds; you need to give the money back!'

Working in the higher education sphere was new to me but I quickly got across it. I had to. I was working for Helen Trinca, who edited the section, and she was a hard taskmaster. Hard but fair. Helen drove me relentlessly and that was rather good for me. I learnt a lot in that job.

I found it interesting interviewing academics and writing about the politics of the sector. And it was fascinating to get an insight into the world of vice chancellors, those Grand Pooh-Bahs of unis who are like demigods and are now paid accordingly. They are a little like state premiers, ambassadors, CEOs and archbishops all rolled into one.

I fondly remember Roy Webb, who was Vice Chancellor of Griffith University at the time. He was a friendly, genial man and I know he was well liked. A gentleman of the old school, as they say.

I also got to meet Philip Lader, VC of privately run Bond University on the Gold Coast. Lader was a mate of Bill Clinton, who would become US President in 1993. I was asked to grill him about Clinton, who had the White House in his sights at the time and was being mocked by some political commentators who had first branded him Slick Willie back in his early days as Arkansas Governor. But Lader assured me there was more to Clinton and the story we published on August 19, 1992, suggested that. It was headed 'Clinton: he's no "Slick Willie"'. Another line above the heading announced: 'Presidential mission has Bond chief's blessing'.

Lader eventually went back to America and ended up being appointed US Ambassador to the United Kingdom in 1997. Quite the gig.

I worked out of *The Australian's* office within an office in the *Courier-Mail* building at Bowen Hills, which was fairly 'industrial' back then. So appalling, it was referred to as 'the brown swamp'.

But we soon moved into rooms at Newspaper House, an historic building beside the GPO in Queen Street, Brisbane, which was like being upgraded to the business-class lounge after Bowen Hills.

In June 1992 Sandra and I got married at historic St Patrick's Catholic church in Fortitude Valley, with Fr Peter Dillon presiding. We honeymooned in Singapore and Malaysia, where we stayed on

Tioman island, a rather exotic beauty spot in the South China Sea off the east coast where I managed to get seasickness, sunstroke and food poisoning. Some honeymoon. Although they do advise you to start as you mean to go on …

Back in Brisbane, Sandra was still TV Editor at *The Sunday Mail* while I was beavering away for Helen Trinca – and enjoying that. Then out of the blue Sandra received a job offer from *TV Week* magazine in Melbourne. An offer she accepted. I'd just settled back into Brisbane when it was time to pack up our Pulsar and get out of Dodge.

The Sunday Mail produced a mock cover of its *TV Scene* magazine featuring the two of us – promising a story about how we were absconding south. I packed up my home office and folders of poems and quit Queensland Poets. I still have the resignation letter in my files. That sounds a bit formal, really. I mean, I wasn't resigning from a major corporation or anything, and why did I even need to send a letter? The group disintegrated not long afterwards, as poetry groups tend to. Quite organically. Organizing poets is like herding cats. Or echidnas. Or something like that.

Authorwise, I had my slim volume behind me and, economywise, some money in the bank thanks to Brisbane City Council, which never did ask for any of it back. Phew.

CHAPTER 13

THE CITY AT THE END OF THE WORLD

AS WE APPROACHED MELBOURNE I was thinking about Ava Gardner. In a purely platonic sense, of course. It's part of the pop culture mythology of the Victorian capital that the Hollywood actress once described the city as the perfect place to make a movie about the end of the world.

She was in the city starring in the 1959 film *On the Beach*, based on the post-apocalyptic novel by Nevil Shute. It turns out the purported quote regarding her feelings about Melbourne was invented by journalist Neil Jillett, who was writing for *The Age* at the time.

But it stuck and was uppermost in my mind as we passed the notorious Pentridge prison (one of Melbourne's most historic structures reminding us we were nearly there) on a cold, grey, rainy October afternoon in 1992. The prison looked as grim as its reputation as we crawled past in increasingly heavy traffic along Sydney Road – our entry route and, nearly three years later, our escape route.

But on this day we were moving to Melbourne indefinitely and it wasn't looking good so far. The traffic was bad enough but then things got complicated because we were sharing the road with trams. We would have to get used to that.

The sky darkened, the rain beat down and I wondered if we might have made a terrible mistake.

Ava Gardner didn't say what she was purported to have said but I was ready to concur anyway.

Sandra and I had been married for just a few months when Sandra got a job offer to work at *TV Week* magazine in Melbourne. It was a hugely successful publication back then. I had no job offers but was used to winging it so off we went on our grand adventure. There were tearful goodbyes and incredulity in some quarters, as in 'You're moving to Melbourne? Why?' I mean, Queensland was on the up and up after the Fitzgerald Inquiry and with Wayne Goss as the new Labor Premier it was quite an exciting time of change. Too bad. The Sunshine State may not have been heading south, but we were. Way south.

We took several days to drive to the Victorian capital. Our goods and chattels had gone on ahead in a van paid for by *TV Week*. They would be stored and waiting for us so we took our time, stopping along the way to visit friends and family in Maitland and Sydney.

We didn't have anywhere to live in Melbourne on our arrival that grim spring day, so my friends Ivor Ries and Diny Slamet, both former *Age* journos, offered us a room at their Hampton home until we got settled.

They were still in shock. We Queenslanders had elected a progressive Labor premier while Victoria, after some difficult years, had gone the other way. Jeff Kennett, the *Bloody Jeff* of that song by Scared Weird Little Guys, had been elected just before we arrived. I guess it was a time of change all round: it certainly was for us

Sandra started work right away while I went looking for a house. My target area was Albert Park, which I had visited on a previous trip to Melbourne. I decided if I ever lived in Melbourne, which seemed unlikely then, Albert Park would be the place for me.

We were staying with Ivor and Diny until the right place came up. Not long after Sandra started work at *TV Week* she announced that we had been invited to the Melbourne Cup by Channel Ten. Perks of the job, I suppose.

Now I'm not even faintly interested in horse racing and, as a non-drinker, I shied away from such events, but I guess it was nice to be asked, and we would be in the salubrious surrounds of the Channel Ten marquee, rubbing shoulders with Kerri-Anne Kennerley and other Ten celebrities.

Be still, my beating heart.

It was November 3, the beginning of what would become one of Victoria's wettest Novembers. In Brisbane it would have been superbly balmy, in Melbourne the temperature struggled to get into double digits and it rained all day, including throughout the race itself which was won, appropriately enough, by a horse called Subzero.

We all went into the stands to watch and I had never been so cold. I was wearing a sports jacket but, really, I needed thermals. By the time we got back to Ivor and Diny's place I was pale and shivering, had a bath, went straight to bed and tried to get my core temperature up. It's called hypothermia. What a lovely day at the races that was! The first and last time I attended the Melbourne Cup.

Not long after that outing, we found a little terrace in Little Page Street, Albert Park, near the Hare Krishna Melbourne Temple and on the cusp of Middle Park. It was a tiny house with a kind of toy courtyard where you could stand and soak in the rain. It seemed to be raining every day that spring. Welcome to Melbourne: awful one day, horrible the next.

Sandra was finding her feet at *TV Week* and I would drop her at the office each morning. Southdown Press was in Walsh Street, West Melbourne, close to the famous Queen Victoria Market. Southdown Press, part of the Murdoch Empire, was ruled over by the formidable Dulcie Boling, known in the business as The Ice Queen. *TV Week* shared the offices with *New Idea* (very much Boling's fiefdom), *Australasian Post* and other titles.

With an introduction from Ivor and Diny I managed to get some casual work at *The Sunday Age*. That was quite something. I mean, *The Age* was a Holy Grail of journalism in those days. I had studied journalism with Ivor in Toowoomba, and upon graduating he had won a cadetship at *The Age*, which amazed us all since Queenslanders were still thought to be a tad Neanderthal back then. If you worked at *The Age*, you'd kind of made it. So I had kind of made it working at *The Sunday Age* too, I guess looking back. Maybe I should have been more impressed than I was at the time.

I worked under Peter Fray, who was editor (or news editor: I can't recall his exact title) under Steve Harris, the big boss. We worked in a small room on our own and then on Saturday moved into the main newsroom where Steve Harris presided. To me he seemed serious, remote, unapproachable: such was the culture of the place.

The atmosphere was as dour inside the building as the weather outside. It was a serious place full of serious people. I struggled to feel at home there and was, to a degree, suspect, having come down from Queensland, which was tantamount to having just come down from the trees. I was walking upright – amazing! I think they were shocked that I could even write. They fancied we were still scratching our names in the dirt with sticks.

I remember one day I was asked to write a shortish feature and I finished it pretty quickly. Working for *The Daily Sun* and for

Helen Trinca at *The Australian* I'd been trained to work quickly and intensively.

But apparently I finished it *too* quickly. This was disturbing to people who would spend days labouring over their masterpieces.

'You're finished already?' said the bloke sitting next to me.

'Yeaaah, mate,' I said, bunging on a Queensland drawl. 'I'm a banana bender. We don't muck around up there.'

I felt like the proverbial stranger in a strange land and, admittedly, we weren't in Kansas anymore, so to speak.

We loved living at Albert Park, though, close to the waterfront of Port Phillip Bay. Of an afternoon, Sandra and I would walk to nearby Kerferd Pier and stand there blasted by the freezing breeze, which usually felt like it was coming straight off the Antarctic, which it probably was. I kind of liked it. It was different. It felt like living in another country altogether.

My first poem after moving to Melbourne – entitled, rather obviously, *On Moving to Melbourne* – begins:

> *They said the weather was cranky / and it is / here on the rim of the bay.*

Later, the poem refers to our life there as:

> *a kind of internal exile – / We sit and count the clouds as they rush past / resigned to our banishment.*

That poem appeared in an anthology called *Queensland: Words and All*, edited by Manfred Jurgensen, the following year. Flicking back through its pages now, I can see I was in good company, alongside Janette Turner Hospital, Hugh Lunn, my friend Ross Fitzgerald, David Malouf and Judith Wright, among others.

Meanwhile, I was acclimatizing. As it happens, I don't mind a bit of weather, and there was an upside to living in Melbourne. I could wear my black merino turtlenecks all year round.

I was getting used to the city and to the weather but not quite to *The Sunday Age*. It felt temporary because, well, it was. I remember toiling over a piece one day and Peter Fray asking me to rewrite it. He was being helpful, or so he thought. 'Don't worry, I'm sure you'll get the hang of our style eventually.' That was like the kiss of death. I didn't want to get used to their fucking style!

However, my guardian angel was, as usual, lurking somewhere nearby in the ether, looking after me in the form of one of my colleagues, Peter Lalor, now an acclaimed sportswriter and commentator with *The Australian*. Peter had jumped ship from our little band of casuals at *The Sunday Age* and gone to work with the hated Murdoch mob over at the *Sunday Herald Sun* in Flinders Lane behind the Paris End of Collins Street. Peter phoned me one day and suggested I jump ship: there might be a place for me over there, he indicated. *That's awfully nice of him*, I thought. He was basically giving me the journalistic version of: 'Come on in, the water's fine!'

So, I rocked over there the following week to see Steve O'Baugh, the news editor, a lovely American guy I had actually done some freelance work for when he was with the *Sunday Press*, one of those lively tabloids that used to exist back in the good old days of newspapering.

Steve hired me to work three days a week, which suited me down to the ground, so I informed the folks at *The Sunday Age* that I wouldn't be coming in anymore. I'm sure they were devastated.

The *Sunday Herald Sun* was, for all its sins, a fun place to work.

For Sandra, however, 'fun' was not the operative word at *TV Week*. She liked most of the people she worked with, including the editor, Lawrie Masterson, who was a terrific bloke. But she was finding it a bit inane reporting on things like *Neighbours* nuptials, treated as tantamount to a royal wedding even though it was just a fictional telly affair. Silly.

Because I was just three days a week at the paper, I had to rustle up some other freelance work and I managed to get quite a bit with *Australasian Post*, which was located on the same floor at Southdown Press as *TV Week*.

Australasian Post was full of hokey or zany Aussie fare and not as downmarket as you could get but it was close. I used to write nutty stories for them when I was freelancing on the Gold Coast. Once I did a story for them about a man who lived in a hole in the ground. Riveting stuff.

The news editor was a bloke named Graham Holdstock who, because he already knew and presumably trusted me, commissioned some pieces from yours truly. And one day, when I was visiting the office, he asked if I would write a regular weekly showbiz column for him. I jumped at the chance.

'Okay, here's the thing,' he said. 'I want to call it The Dirt Pit with Filthy Phil.'

'You're serious?' I asked.

'Deadly,' he said. 'And I want it to feature a photo of you at the top of the page. I'm thinking of something like having you sticking your head out of a garbage skip wearing a sou'wester.'

He wasn't joking. But since he would be paying me I was up for it. From poet to rubbish bin correspondent in one fell (or should that be foul?) swoop.

So I was sent off with a photographer to find a location for my column head shot. The snapper assigned to take the shot was a young bloke named James Calvert-Jones who happened to be the son of Janet Calvert-Jones, who in turn just happened to be Rupert Murdoch's sister.

So, there I was in a car with C.J., as he was known, scouting for a bin I could jump in for my photo shoot. Graham Holdstock had purchased a yellow sou'wester cap for me from some fishing shop, so I was set.

C.J., who lived at South Yarra, suggested his neighbourhood had better-quality rubbish skips and a higher grade of rubbish than lesser suburbs, and we managed to find one relatively quickly. So there I was climbing into a skip in a South Yarra lane to be photographed by Rupert Murdoch's nephew. You couldn't make this stuff up. Graham had asked me to hold my nose in the pose (he had thought it all out quite meticulously) for effect.

Afterwards C.J. suggested we drop by his place for a coffee. It was a rather smart residence in a rather prestigious neighbourhood.

'You're renting?' I asked. 'No, I own it,' he said. It figured.

That column's name was relatively short-lived, for obvious reasons. Someone must have complained, maybe even Dulcie Boling, who knows? It was soon renamed Showbitz and I had a new head shot taken, this time not in a skip. I would just rewrite gossip from the British and American press, which was cheating really, but nobody seemed to care and it was a steady income stream.

So, there I was in my study at Little Page Street composing poetry one minute and hammering out tawdry showbiz gossip the next.

The poetry was intermittent, but it was still coming and I was getting a few poems published.

While in Melbourne I had one in *The Courier-Mail* back home when Bruce Dawe was, briefly, the paper's poetry editor.

That particular creation was entitled *The Serial Killer.*

Naturally the neighbours never guessed / that deep beneath his ordinary lawn / lay umpteen stiffs: the total's not yet known. /

When they flushed the killer from his nest / he seemed quite chuffed by his immediate renown.

God knows where that came to me from. l had also made contact with a Melbourne literary journal called *Bystander* and was invited to read at Readings bookshop in the suburb of Hawthorn, an event organized by the folks behind the magazine. *Bystander* published a couple of my poems, including one that had sparked some amusement at the Hawthorn Readings.

It's entitled *A Poem in Response to the Alarming Proliferation of Poets & Poetry Readings.*

My compatriots roar around me / but I have been struck dumb: / I have nothing to say / out of a sense of decency / not wanting to speak / for the sake of speaking / you understand.

Bystander published my contributions in an edition that included work by, among others, Ouyang Yu, Mal Morgan, Laurie Clancy and Anthony Lawrence.

In Chapter 4 I showed you a poem called *A Little Idyll*, which ended up being published in *Queensland: Words and All.* I sent it along with a few others to Mal Morgan, who had his own contribution run alongside mine in that issue of *Bystander*.

Here, by way of a refresher, are the last three lines of the work:

The air was cool as a wet towel. / I felt the magic deep in my bowels / and was happy as a Greek.

Now Morgan was a Melbourne poet whom I had met in Brisbane, a friend of Rob Hughes. I'll never forget his response. He rang me after reading this and other works from my latest output and told me that I had it all wrong in that particular poem.

He laid it on the line. 'I know a lot of Greeks and they are not happy.'

'Well, it's kind of a throwaway funny line just to rhyme,' I offered. 'It's a joke, if you like.'

This apparently wasn't a good enough explanation.

'No, you just can't use a line like that,' he said. 'Everything in a poem has to be true.'

Really? Tell that to Dante. This was one of the most ludicrous statements about poetry I have ever heard. And that's the problem with the poetry scene: it's so random, subjective and factional, with everyone entertaining different ideas about what poetry is or isn't.

If you listened to even half the criticism or opinions you got – solicited or otherwise – you'd never write another word.

I was getting some appreciation of my efforts at this time from the poetry editor of *The Age*, R.A. (Ron) Simpson, a significant poet in his own right with whom I'd corresponded before coming to Melbourne. I had sent him a few poems and he hadn't actually published one yet but had liked a few and suggested that, with some reworking, they might be acceptable.

I made contact with Ron and we met up on a couple of occasions. We went to the National Gallery of Victoria one day together with his wife, which was nice.

Much to my delight, Ron had finally agreed to publish one of the poems I had sent in – I can't for the life of me remember exactly which one it was. I was elated. To have a poem in *The Age* would be quite something.

But then he rang me and said that, despite having accepted it, he had now reconsidered and decided not to publish it after all because having met me (and liked me) he might have become biased in the process. So his yes turned to a no. This reaction, all too prevalent in the poetry world, left me disappointed and confused. Such backflips, inflicted repeatedly, tend to do your head in.

Luckily, I have always had my career as a journalist for instant gratification. Poetry is a torturous business and you might have to wait years to get something published, forced to put up with interminable rejections along the way.

In journalism you write a story and – wham bam, thank you, ma'am – it's published, if not the next day then very shortly thereafter. And there are those three little words, the most wonderful three little words to my ears … By Phil Brown. I admit it, I'm a byline junkie. I've been mainlining bylines for decades. Seeing my name in print or online has kept me sustained.

I've got used to it. But whenever that byline is attached to a literary endeavour it's just a little more special.

I have always juggled my life as a poet with that of a journalist.

In Melbourne that meant delving into the world of celebrity. Both Sandra and I did a lot of celebrity stories due to the simple fact that there were a lot more celebrities in Melbourne. I mean, in Brisbane there were a few and one would get to interview visiting celebrities but in 1992 most celebrities, in particular people we knew of from the big and small screens, lived in Sydney and Melbourne.

We were always coming across them in Melbourne – Sandra is better than I am at this and can spot one 200m away. Quite a few were living around Albert Park and South Melbourne. After spending our first year and a half living in Little Page Street, we moved to Park Street, South Melbourne, just across the road from the historic Montague Hotel.

This was a great location close to Albert Park's heart, Bridport Street and Dundas Place, with shops and cafés and served by the excellent Avenue bookshop. Here we saw celebrities drifting by, in their natural habitat.

I recall one morning they had a sausage sizzle out front of the local butcher's shop and there larger than life (or at least as large) was famous comedian and TV star Maurie Fields, a legend since he'd first appeared on the ABC series *Bellbird*. He was also a regular on Channel 9's *Hey Hey It's Saturday*. (I went to a taping of the show once while living in Melbourne and don't want to disillusion you but it wasn't on a Saturday.) Anyway, there was Maurie Fields in a safari suit chomping on a snag sandwich with tomato sauce dripping down the front of his clothes.

One day we spotted Claudia Karvan walking across the road holding hands with the Canadian-born Australian actor Aden Young. They got together in 1993 when both were filming a movie called *Exile*.

The studios of Mushroom Records were nearby so you would occasionally see musos in the precinct. We did our washing at a local laundrette called The Soap Opera, and one day as I was walking out James Reyne of Australian Crawl was walking in. He didn't appear to recognize me as the bloke who'd interviewed him in Rockhampton a few years back, but seemed preoccupied. I said nothing to disturb his furrowed brow. I guess rock stars have to do their laundry too.

Our friend Debbie Withers, a well-known TV publicist at the time (Sandra had met her when she was doing publicity for the ABC's *Countdown*), would occasionally invite us to dinner at her place where we would meet interesting people such as Greg Macainsh, songwriter and guitarist for Skyhooks. He's the one who used to wear the cowboy outfit. Lovely bloke, very thoughtful, well read, quite the intellect really, and didn't he write some great songs.

I could never visit Carlton without thinking of the sun setting over the joint *à la* his song *Carlton (Lygon Street Limbo).*

I also met quite a few celebrities through working for the *Sunday Herald Sun*, and it was fascinating to be up close and personal with people you usually see only on TV. The editor asked me to do a column called My Secret Passion. I had to interview people on the subject: the likes of comedians Jean Kittson, Judith Lucy and Nick Giannopoulos, the writer Carmel Bird and others. The exchange that really sticks out in my mind, though, was an encounter with Eric Bana. Eric was already well known then but really just as a comedian on TV. This was well before he morphed into a Hollywood star.

I had to travel to the outskirts of Melbourne to meet up with him on a bleak, windswept piece of scrub. When we arrived, there was Eric wearing a pair of grey overalls. It sounds weird, I know, but there was a reason for this. Because his secret passion was racing go-karts and we were meeting at a shabby little go-kart track. We were there to get some photos of him driving his go-kart and, of course, for me to interview him. Funny where you have these brushes with fame, not always in the most predictable locations.

I became a bit famous myself at one stage. Or perhaps infamous. Mainly because I was assaulted by a colleague one day and that made me a legend, fleetingly.

On my usual shift one day at the *Sunday Herald Sun* I got into an argument with one of the older journos, a bloke who happened to have once boxed professionally.

Anyway, we were having a discussion about a story I was doing and he had a view counter to what I was proposing in my story. For some reason he took offence to me calling him 'a silly old bastard'. So he punched me. In the jaw. I went down like a sack of spuds. Sitting on the newsroom floor I shook my head and then clambered to my feet, by which time a small crowd had gathered. My assailant and colleague had been whisked away and everyone was standing around, shocked.

Steve O'Baugh apologized and asked if I wanted to press charges or take it to management or anything. I rubbed my jaw, which was feeling okay now, so I said no. This automatically elevated me to the status of magnanimous hero. The Walkley Awards were being held in Melbourne that week and apparently the incident was the talk of the night. It was just like the good old days.

Later I was told that the last bloke he'd decked had been a tough-as-nails detective he'd knocked out cold. The fact that I bounced back so quickly was in my favour. I certainly didn't have a glass jaw. The gentleman who biffed me apologized later that day. I accepted the apology and put it behind me.

These things don't happen in the sanitized newsrooms of today, which is probably just as well.

Life at the bottom of the continent was pretty good. Weekends were spent surfing down around Torquay, at Bells Beach or on the Mornington Peninsula, around Point Leo on Western Port Bay. My surfing career had kicked back in so I bought myself a new board from Trigger Brothers surf shop at Point Leo and, importantly, got myself a 5-mm-thick wetsuit, boots and gloves. And – did I mention I'd acclimatized? – I surfed all year round.

Sandra, meanwhile, got sick of sitting in the car waiting for me so she decided to start surfing too, in the middle of a Victorian winter, no less. We got her kitted out with a wetsuit and a bodyboard (a shark biscuit, I called it) and we surfed together in the bracing waters of the Southern Ocean.

I would sometimes go surfing in the mornings on my days off too. I could be at Point Leo or at Bells Beach in around an hour. I would come home around lunchtime and write in the afternoons.

When I was in town and not working at the paper, I would have coffee at the University Café in Carlton or at Marios (or one of the other cafés) in Fitzroy along with Red Symons (another Skyhooks legend) and other denizens of Melbourne's bohemian café society. I loved that about Melbourne and would wander from café to café in my now perennial black turtleneck. I was gradually beginning to feel like a Melburnian.

After moving to Park Street, I started writing a novel. Its working title was *The High Life*, derivative of the column in *The Spectator:* High Life by Taki.

My book was about my life as a social columnist for *MODE*, *The Daily Sun* and *Sunday Telegraph*. I still have what I wrote in a folder in my bottom drawer. I never finished it. I don't think it's any good.

Still, it was impressive, I felt, to excuse myself from some café conversation in Fitzroy, claiming I had to go home to work on my novel. Pretentious? *Moi*?

While Sandra and I were in Melbourne we went home to Queensland a couple of times a year, and travelled overseas from there too. At one stage we jetted off to Hong Kong and from there across the Pacific to visit my brother in Vancouver, stopping in Hong Kong again on the return leg. The Cathay Pacific route between Hong Kong and Vancouver was a busy one.

I remember exactly what it was like when we left – a typical Melbourne morning. The cab arrived at around 5 am in the darkness and driving rain, and as he came down the lane I could see his vehicle had a flat tyre. I'm usually pretty stressed at the best of times when I'm going to the airport but that took it to a new level. We waited while he swapped in the spare and then he couldn't get the bung one into the boot so we rode to the airport with a punctured tyre between us.

In Hong Kong we met up with a friend of Sandra's, a journalist by the name of Sue Green who worked for the *South China Morning Post*, and she asked me to do some pieces for them from Melbourne. That fulfilled a lifelong ambition to write for the paper that had been such an influence in my childhood. We had it delivered daily to our house in Kowloon Tong back in the 1960s and I would always pore over it after my dad was finished with it.

One of the stories I did for her was an interview with the legendary travel writer Eric Newby, author of *A Short Walk in the Hindu Kush* and other classics. Newby was in Melbourne for the Lonely Planet travel summit. He was 75 at the time and to meet this venerable master of his genre was a treat.

'Why do people travel?' he mused in our interview. 'To escape their creditors? In the case of the English, I suspect it's to escape the weather. In my case, I travelled because for many years I was stuck selling large-sized ladies' dresses in Leeds.' One of the best parts of being a journalist is getting to spend time one on one with people such as Newby.

For that and other reasons I loved Melbourne. People complain about the four seasons in one day but that's one of the things I loved it for. I enjoyed the cold, inclement days wandering around in my turtlenecks and corduroy trousers, pretending to be a writer.

And it was a great experience for us early in our marriage, to be away from friends and family, making our own way in another city. As I often said, Melbourne is far enough from Brisbane to feel like it's overseas. And our jobs in journalism got us entrée to the southern capital in a way you wouldn't otherwise get.

So yes, we were *in* Melbourne … but not of it. It's a funny place for an outsider, particularly if you are an outsider who knows nothing (and cares less) about Australian Rules football. It really is a religion in Melbourne and people were amazed and shocked that we just weren't interested.

When I arrived at the *Sunday Herald Sun*, I was asked who I supported. I just shook my head and shrugged. 'Nobody.' Then I was told that there were only three teams in the league that started with an F – Fitzroy, Footscray and Fucking Collingwood. The editor at the end of my time at the paper was Alan Howe, who I happened to know was a Collingwood fan. I didn't get it then though I do now.

When I explained again and again that we were rugby league fans, that was usually met with a room falling silent.

'Cross-country wrestling!' someone once responded.

The only time we went to the MCG was to see a State of Origin match. I should have gone to a Boxing Day Test but we were home in Queensland for each of the Christmases we were living in Melbourne. Our friend Debbie Withers became convinced that we were now Melbourne people. We both wore black turtlenecks, she argued, so we had to be.

There came a point when we would either settle in for good at the arse-end of Australia or go back to God's own country. Then came the job offer that ruled a line under our Melbourne experiment.

Sandra was offered a job at *The Courier-Mail* back in Brisbane. She tended to get more job offers than me, for obvious reasons. Des Houghton, one of Rupert's favourites, was editor at the time. Sandra had worked with him at *The Sunday Mail* before leaving Brisbane and now he wanted her back as TV Editor. We decided that maybe it was the right time to move. Home.

We'd had a fine time in Melbourne, our own little Australian version of London. Over nearly three years I had worn my black turtlenecks thin. We had mingled with the rich and famous, surfed the frigid waters, revelled in the bohemian café society of the place and shunned the AFL.

Now it was time to leave.

I remember taking our last walk along the bay and onto Kerferd Pier with the wind strong enough to blow a dog off its lead. Standing and staring at the grey, choppy waters of Port Phillip Bay I thought again of Ava Gardner and her mythical denunciation of the joint.

'Melbourne's not really the end of the world,' I mused. 'But you can see it from here.'

CHAPTER 14

MAN SWALLOWS PANADOL

'THAT'S A GREAT INTRO.'

'Thanks, Trent.'

It was a passing compliment but one I obviously stored away for some reason. It was two decades ago or so but I do remember it quite clearly and it seems more pertinent now than it did then. I had written a story for *Brisbane News* about wildlife photographer Steve Parish and had described him coming out of his office like an animal blinking in the sunlight after emerging from its lair.

The young bloke sitting opposite me in our Bowen Hills office thought that was a good one. His name was Trent Dalton. He was keen to learn and obviously paying attention. I wish I had paid him more attention. I mean, if I had known he was going to go on to become a literary superstar maybe I would have invested more time, so I could have taken more credit. Oh well …

Brisbane News was a popular lifestyle magazine in Brisbane for a couple of decades. It was in the same News Corp stable as *The Courier-Mail* and gave Trent his first taste of journalism long before that boy swallowed the Universe. I recall Trent being as keen as mustard. To be honest, his enthusiasm was a little confronting for a world-weary middle-aged man with a headache. I'd had a headache since 1974 and was still popping Panadols every morning when I got to work. Panadol was all I was popping nowadays though, thankfully.

I worked with Trent (or did he work with me?) for a few years before he moved across Mayne Road into the main building where Sandra worked. Trent joined *The Courier-Mail* as a writer on the Saturday magazine, *QWEEKEND*. Sandra wrote the first cover story for that magazine. Trent then went on to work at *The Australian*. He went national. Boy, did he go national. I was never sure I'd had any influence although looking back I may have had some, however slight. He was certainly receptive where others weren't. Once he acknowledged me very publicly at the Byron Writers Festival, and I nearly missed that.

Sandra and I had gone to a session featuring Trent. The marquee was overflowing and we sat 'in the outer', on an extra row of chairs that had been set up just beyond the rope anchors. Luckily the weather was fine. As usual I found it hard to concentrate, plus it was a bit of a love-in, which made me a tad uncomfortable. It just so happens that I don't hold with mass expressions of emotion. I'd sat quietly for 20 minutes or so and felt I'd given it a red-hot go.

'Can we leave now?' I turned to Sandra, feeling that I'd done my duty.

'Just a few more minutes,' she said. I crossed my arms and made like Grumpy Cat. Five minutes later Trent spots me down the back. You couldn't miss me really: I was wearing my bright red adidas Originals tracksuit top, so despite the dark sunglasses I was hardly incognito. *Au contraire*, I looked like a mafioso in leisurewear. Blow me down if five minutes later Trent doesn't give me a shout-out and the whole marquee turns round to take a squiz. Sandra smiled and I gave a kind of little royal wave and felt pretty good about myself, for a few minutes at least. That's how Trent Dalton rolls. He makes people feel good. I cannot deny it.

That moment planted in my brain the idea of working with Trent. With Trent and his now wife Fiona Franzmann, who was our chief sub-editor at *Brisbane News* when he arrived. I sat next to Fiona every day at work and was sitting next to her when their love affair blossomed, although I completely missed that too. I missed a lot of things. Still do.

Their relationship fuelled his runaway bestselling debut novel *Boy Swallows Universe* and in it Eli Bell's love interest, journalist Caitlyn Spies, was modelled on Fiona. Their relationship was also the foundation and inspiration for his 2021 book *Love Stories*, which Trent and Fiona worked on together with playwright and theatre director Tim McGarry to adapt for the stage. *Love Stories*, the play, debuted at Brisbane Festival in 2024.

So, I was there at ground zero of Trent's writing career and the relationship that underpinned it. And guess what. I missed the whole thing. Blind to the fact they were having a relationship – and me a trained observer! – I was the last person in the office to twig, which was nothing new. And while I knew Trent was a good writer I couldn't see where it was all heading.

I was sitting there next to them completely oblivious. How? Well, let's just say that I was fairly self-involved at the time and nothing has really changed there. I'm not talking full-blown Trumpian narcissism – more common-or-garden-variety navel gazing.

I'm happy for Trent, though, in a way that writers often aren't. It was Gore Vidal who said: 'Every time a friend succeeds, I die a little.' I can't feel that about Trent despite pangs of professional jealousy because he is such a genuine bloke, who has worked so hard and so honestly in everything he has done, and I know he did it tough as a kid. *Boy Swallows Universe* is quite autobiographical, it laid bare his family trauma and that went global with the Netflix series *Boy Swallows Universe*. But in a literary sense it all began for him at *Brisbane News* and I was there to witness it even though, as yours truly this minor poet has already confessed, I didn't.

Brisbane News sustained me for a couple of decades after we returned to Brisbane from Melbourne.

Sandra had been tapped on the shoulder for the job as TV Editor at *The Courier-Mail* and the company paid for our move back to Brisbane where they put us up until we found our own digs. We arrived at our accommodation to find it less than satisfactory, though. They had put us in a period-era motel which seemed to be populated entirely by old men in shorts and singlets chain-smoking. It was so depressing we got out of the car, looked around, got back in and drove away.

After a week there we managed to find a worker's cottage in Spring Hill, the inner-city suburb where Charles Blackman had once lived. We were at 63 Union Street, a street capped with an historic church just across St Paul's Terrace. That church was the titular St Paul's, a heritage-listed Presbyterian edifice dating back to 1889. Local bagpipers obviously practised there because some of the sounds they were producing drifted down the road to us, haunting and evocative as the skirling of bagpipes always is.

So Sandra went to work in the main building at Bowen Hills on the corner of Campbell Street and Mayne Road, Bowen Hills, just near the train station. Not the most salubrious address if you know Brisbane. I went to work on a casual basis at *Brisbane News* across the road but was soon hired as its Senior Writer. I was 39 which wasn't really that senior. The bloke who hired me, David Crossen, was from Northern Ireland, but he soon moved on and Judithann Guerassimoff, whom I had worked with at *The Daily Sun*, was appointed his successor. It was her job I took over as Senior

Writer. (In case you're thinking you recognize that surname, you probably do: her ex-husband Jules had been a notable Australian rugby international).

That was the beginning of a long and prosperous stint of employment for me, my longest ever. *Brisbane News* was probably the most popular publication in Brisbane until COVID-19 killed it. It was a lifestyle magazine for the city's AB demographic, with a huge real estate section and glossy pages. Everyone loved it and, even better, it was free … if you lived in the right suburb.

Brisbane was divided into those people who got *Brisbane News* delivered to their homes and those who wished they did.

It had been going for around a year when I joined the staff, among whom was a friend of ours, Alison Walsh. (Sandra and I have both worked closely with Alison over the years.)

I became something of a fixture there. Which suited me. I had found a rut and furnished it. Off centre in the overall corporate scheme of things, the new role at *Brisbane News* was probably better for me than working at the paper with all the pressure and office politics that went on there. I heard about all that from Sandra as she moved through being TV Editor and on to become Arts Editor.

Across the road at *Brisbane News* things were a lot mellower. That suited me just fine.

Settling into Brisbane again didn't take long. I had a small study set up in Spring Hill (you couldn't swing a cat in there even if you'd wanted to) and I did produce a few poems there including one entitled *The Dinner Party*, which was *almost* accepted for publication. I say *almost* because I recently found the rejection slip suggesting that with some reworking *The Dinner Party* could be a good poem. I don't think I ever tweaked it but I can see what they mean now, looking at it in one of my folders of unpublished verse. It wasn't all that good, although I did like the premise.

It was about a dinner party up the street at a house from which emanated a smell of something cooking – but a foul smell rather than an inviting one. I watched people arriving for the party *when I went out / for my customary early evening toke on the smog: / it was then that I first smelt it.*

After the party is over, the poem describes the end of the evening:

The people were leaving in / small groups and couples in a rather strange silence. / The hosts stood hopelessly at the door watching their guests / depart, en masse.

That was written in July 1995 which must have been a month or two after we arrived home, and being back in these long-familiar environs had confirmed for me that Brisbane was indeed home.

Spring Hill did yield a few other verses. One in particular went on to lend its title to my second slim – well, slightly bulked up but still slender – poetry volume, *An Accident in the Evening.*

The poem in it of the same name was about an accident involving a cyclist. I'd driven by the accident site on Water Street, one of Spring Hill's central arteries. The cyclist was still lying on the road.

The blow had knocked the wind right out of him / and left a man doing yoga on the bitumen / surrounded by a small, curious and concerned crowd.

I should add a small note, dear reader, in case you too are curious and concerned, that he seemed okay.

Anyhow, the title was probably better than the actual poem.

That book was published in 2001 and by then we'd moved to Wilston where we bought our first house. I took to calling it 'the

Premier suburb' because Peter Beattie lived around the corner. The Labor leader had become Premier in 1998 around the time we arrived in Wilston.

My new book's publisher was Interactive Press, run by Brisbane author and poet David Reiter and the cover featured an element of a painting by Christopher McVinish, whose illustration had graced the cover of Peter Carey's celebrated *Illywhacker*. The painting, entitled *The Watcher,* depicted an atmospheric scene flanked by an inner-city flyover.

The first poem in the book was *Satori at seven-thirty.* One day I got a call from someone at Radio National asking if I would grant permission for it to be read on air. I consented, of course. It was bizarre to be sitting in the lounge room of our house at Wilston listening to someone else reading it aloud on the radio. National fame again!

I tend to write a lot about the joys of ordinary life and that poem was about the beauty of going out to get takeaway food, not the loftiest of poetic subjects:

I had just gone out / to get some Thai food / freshly showered / talc dappled / thong-slapping my way / up the street / when I saw / the full moon / a celestial button / caught on chiffon clouds /amazing, I thought / holy shit / look at that thing / big as the Hindenburg.

It was just a little vignette but it seemed to work and it opened the book. A friend, art dealer Philip Bacon, lent me his self-named gallery for the launch, which was nice of him. There to do the honours was the Arts Minister in the Beattie government, Matt Foley, himself a barrister and creator of verse who became known as the Minister for Poetry because he insisted on reading poems at arts events. What can I say? Matt was ahead of his time.

Many years later, during one of my many fallow periods in the matter of versification, Matt asked me: 'How's the poetry going?'

'I'm in remission,' I said. After a bemused pause he shot back: 'But you know there is no cure.'

Bruce Dawe once said to me that there would be such fallow times for any poet. And just because you're not writing poetry that doesn't mean you're not a poet. You can identify as a poet even during dry periods.

After the launch of *An Accident in the Evening* I entered a very long poetic drought. Because I was, well, busy living my life. That's allowed, isn't it? By the time my book was launched I was a dad. Our son, Hamish, had been born the year before and like all good fathers I was there for the birth, after a fashion. I was there – but looking out the window. I've always been a bit squeamish.

There's a lovely photo that was unearthed recently of the book launch showing Sandra and me with Philip Bacon and Matt Foley, and I'm wrangling a year-old wriggly worm named Hamish.

Working at *Brisbane News* I focused on the arts, although I veered into other subject areas as well. The literary scene was a major preoccupation of my time there.

Publishers loved the magazine with its glossy pages and during my years there I interviewed a cavalcade of literary stars: Geraldine Brooks, Peter Carey, Frederick Forsyth, Ken Follett, Jeffrey Archer, Tim Winton (I had lunch with him at a Japanese restaurant), Michael Cunningham, Tom Keneally, Kathy Lette, Michael Palin … the list goes on. I have forgotten most of those interviews, although I have them all on old analog tapes which I may get digitized one day.

My position at *Brisbane News* also made me attractive (apparently) as a presenter at literary events of which there were far more in the Nineties and early Noughties than there are now.

One of the venues for literary events in Brisbane was the now defunct Irish Club in a building on Elizabeth Street in Brisbane's CBD. I did a number of events there, including one with Geraldine Brooks, who was typically delightful, although the most memorable was a conversation with the actor and author William McInnes. Interviewing McInnes is like herding cats. He was drinking Guinness throughout the session and seemed unable to distract his attention from my black skivvy, which he lampooned mercilessly.

I also had the pleasure of interviewing film director Philip Noyce at Brisbane Writers Festival during my *Brisbane News* years. He had written an autobiography and I spoke to him in a packed marquee at South Bank. He was lovely and never said a word about my black skivvy.

It's interesting what you remember about such encounters.

For example, I also interviewed the author and philosopher Alain de Botton one time at a bookshop café not far from the office. We hit it off at once, two fastidious men of a certain age … although he's a decade and a bit younger.

We were chatting about his 2011 book *Religion for Atheists* which I enjoyed despite being a theist. It was a lovely hardback but I'd managed to get a coffee stain on the cover of my copy. It was just a small spot in the top right-hand corner.

I hadn't realized this until I put it on the table between us. Alain looked at it, I looked at it, we both shook our heads.

'You can't have that,' he said.

'No, I can't,' I agreed. He turned to his publicist sitting nearby and said: 'Can you please send Phil another one?'

She looked like she wanted to point out that it was only a spot but he was insistent.

'I'm glad you said that,' I offered. He smiled. We were OCD-*simpatico*.

I feel privileged to have met so many literary figures including, on a couple of occasions, David Malouf, one of Queensland's living treasures (and a member in good standing on the official list of Australia's National Living Treasures). One day I interviewed him at Riverbend Books in Bulimba, Brisbane; and at the end of the interview he asked me where I was going.

I explained that I was heading back to the north side of the city, which is where he was going. Could I give him a lift? He was visiting family. Of course, I agreed, and 10 minutes later I was driving across the Story Bridge with one of Australia's greatest writers in the front seat and the only thing I could think was: *What if we have an accident*?

Brisbane News also gave me entrée to interview some big stars, instantly recognizable 'household names': Paul Hogan, Kylie Minogue, Daniel Craig, among others. Willem Dafoe was a highlight because he is one of my favourite actors. That's the beauty of the job sometimes. Arriving at Brisbane's Treasury Hotel one day and going to a room where Dafoe is sitting at a small table waiting for you is one of those pinch-me moments.

Mind you, not everyone lives up to expectations. For example, I once interviewed Richard E. Grant for his 2006 book *The Wah-Wah Diaries*, a rather revealing memoir recounting some childhood traumas that I felt I could relate to. So I thought we might click. I recollect sitting with him at a table on the terrace at the Stamford Plaza Hotel. We were by the river, although as the interview proceeded I found myself wishing I were in the river. He was at the end of his tour and for some reason we didn't gel at all. It was excruciating. One of those interviews where you feel relief as soon as it's over.

One of the attractions of working at *Brisbane News* was that it was the perfect publication for my travel-writing career, which was burgeoning exponentially. In our first few years back in Brisbane I managed to secure two trips to England with British Airways. Business class. In the Nineties there was still a certain amount of largesse afforded to travel writers and I made the most of it.

We simply couldn't face long-haul flights with a baby … or a toddler.

In our home-centred world I wasn't writing much poetry at all after the publication of *An Accident in the Evening*, although I did begin work on a more expansive literary career with the publication of two humorous memoirs put out by UQP – *Travels with My Angst* (with apologies to Graham Greene), which was published in 2004, and *Any Guru Will Do*, which followed two years later. The first was a book of travel stories, the second focused on my continuing search for the meaning of life.

I can credit filmmaker and sometime literary agent Trish Lake with giving me the idea for the first book. We were having dinner with her on North Stradbroke Island (Minjerribah to the Quandamooka) and I was recounting some of my travel disasters. Being a neurotic hypochondriac with a fear of flying did make overseas trips a bit challenging at times. Still, I persevered, always with the advice of Susan Jeffers ringing in my ears. I had interviewed this American author on her visit to Brisbane in the late 1980s when I was at *The Daily Sun*. She'd written a book entitled *Feel the Fear and Do It Anyway*. Many blurbs tell you a mere book will change your life. This one did.

Anyway, I must have sounded amusing when we had dinner with Trish because she suggested my travel war stories would make a good book, and my friend Carol Davidson, who was publisher at UQP at the time, agreed but she left before it became a reality. Thankfully the new publisher at UQP, Madonna Duffy, took it on and signed me up making *Travels with My Angst* my debut. So I set to, writing the bulk of it in my Wilston study, although some of it had first seen daylight after hours at the *Brisbane News* office.

It was published in 2004 and my editor was Craig Munro, the bloke who had virtually discovered Peter Carey. I was now an author! As well as a minor poet. The book was reasonably well received; I did the interview rounds and appeared at Brisbane Writers Festival on the strength of it. It did get one stinking review, though, from fellow author and journalist Bruce Elder, whom I had interviewed once when living in Melbourne.

I can't recall who wrote the positive ones – I can look that up – but that negative one is imprinted on my memory. The thing is, I had Elder's phone number in my contact book and it was all I could do not to ring him up and ask him pleadingly, plaintively: 'Why?!'

But, as with all such reviews, no correspondence should be entered into. As Confucius said, but no doubt more eloquently, if you set out for revenge you'd better dig two graves.

I was on a roll so pretty soon I pressed on with another book about the soul searching of my twenties. *Any Guru Will Do* was also shepherded into publication by Madonna Duffy (a good friend and supporter over the years) who had taken over as publisher at UQP when Carol Davidson moved to a big job with Random House in Sydney.

I had various other book projects on the boil over the following decade but nothing quite came to fruition. One manuscript, about junior cricket, I sent to super literary agent Selwa Anthony after a phone conversation with her about something else entirely. She asked if I was writing anything and when I told her about my little cricket book she was quite interested. She wanted to see it so I sent her the manuscript.

Selwa seemed to like what she read but after shopping it to a couple of publishers with no bites she threw in the towel. That manuscript still sits in a red folder on the Chinese camphorwood box in my study. I may try again with it at some stage.

Publishing is a funny business, although – correction – sometimes it's not funny at all. I laboured over a few ideas after those two books. They were generally well received although I'm not sure if they sold all that well. Actually, I *am* sure they didn't because I received a stream of rather sad royalty letters in the ensuing years. Thankfully I'd got advances on them. How can I explain what became of them?

I will borrow a phrase from director Bruce Beresford. I've interviewed him a few times, and on one occasion – it may have been an interview regarding his memoir *Josh Hartnett Definitely Wants To Do This … True Stories From a Life in the Screen Trade* – we were chatting about his achievements and I brought up his film *Driving Miss Daisy*, which is a bit of a classic. 'Yes,' he said. 'It rose without a trace.' (Malcolm Muggeridge's missus apparently coined the great putdown, aiming her barb at David Frost, but I'm not sure Beresford knew that.) Seems *Travels with My Angst* and *Any Guru Will Do* can be bracketed with them. Maybe they will be reissued when I become famous?

Anyway, never mind about my literary career … I was fully preoccupied with being a journalist and dad. When Hamish was around seven we started travelling again, with a major trip to Canada to see my brother, and we followed that up with a trip to Hong Kong to introduce Hamish to the family's spiritual home. Thus started a decade of travel as a threesome.

I don't know how people cope with more than one child but we were busy enough with Hamish. School activities during the week and junior cricket on Saturdays filled our calendar for almost a decade. I often equate composing poetry with playing junior cricket. Both are lessons in resilience. Not that *we* were the ones playing but, for Sandra and me, it frequently felt like we were. We lived every ball for better and, often, for worse.

When Hamish was around ten Sandra left newspapering and went to work with the Queensland government, at first in Arts Queensland and, later, for other departments. I soldiered on at *Brisbane News* until eventually we moved into the main building at Bowen Hills, which had been refurbished at a cost of around $25 million. The newspaper business was still looking healthy at that stage so I guess Rupert signed off on it with confidence that *The Courier-Mail, The Sunday Mail* and *The Australian* all had rosy futures.

Of course, after that things would ultimately go pear-shaped as the digital revolution struck, the 'rivers of gold' classified-ad sections dried up and newspapers had to go online to survive.

After moving into the main building at Bowen Hills I began writing more for the paper. I had always done some writing for *The Courier-Mail* while Senior Writer with *Brisbane News* but now I was in the newsroom they seemed to take more notice of me. I was ultimately installed (without seeking the job) as Arts Editor in a bloodless coup. This was strange since Sandra had previously held the position. The weird thing is that I was still getting letters addressed to her.

I had risen to the position after a couple of abortive attempts to get the gig while still working at *Brisbane News*. So, when I stopped wanting it, I finally got it. There's surely some sort of Zen principle at work there.

As my star rose at *The Courier-Mail*, my mother's health started to decline. We regularly visited her at Nerang on the Gold Coast where she still lived.

She seemed to be getting frail and forgetful but was obsessively worried for Australia. And me. When I rang her every Sunday night the call would always begin the same way. 'Hi Mum, it's me.' To which she would invariably reply: 'Are you alright?'

My mum was always very supportive of my writing career and my poetry, and I regret that I became a bit impatient with her as she entered her eighties. In early May 2016 she had a stroke from which she never recovered. I had a dream at the time in which Mum was on the distant shore of some mysterious river waving across the water.

Shortly after that dream, when she had been transferred from hospital to aged care, where she remained barely conscious, I got that call in the middle of the night, the sort you dread. It was my sister Jane telling me our mother had died.

A week later, going through her things, Jane found a little note addressed to us, her three children, telling us how much she loved us and how proud she was of us. We wept buckets then, for her, for my dad, for all of us. For everything that we'd been through and for everything that was lost.

I'm fighting back the tears even as I write this. Maybe I shouldn't.

The daily grind seemed less of a grind after that.

As people left through redundancy or natural attrition, my star continued its ascent as others' fell away. I came into my own, must I say inadvertently? My friend Kath Rose, publicist extraordinaire, took to describing me as 'the Steven Bradbury of News Corp'. I had to laugh. There he was, skating on as the others lay sprawled over the ice at the Winter Olympics in 2002. It was the perfect metaphor for my rise to a position of note at *The Courier-Mail*. I was still writing for *Brisbane News*, too, until COVID hit and some bean counter in Sydney decided that little number would be the first thing to go.

Nothing lasts forever.

Being in the main building at Bowen Hills was certainly more sociable, though it slowly drained of people as the industry changed irrevocably.

From time to time I ran into Trent Dalton, usually at the coffee bar. He was working at *The Australian* and by now was a bit famous thanks to *Boy Swallows Universe*, which I must confess I didn't actually read until much later in the piece.

If you have ever met Trent or seen him in interviews or on stage at some literary festival, you'll know him as an incredibly friendly, enthusiastic, passionate, engaging guy. Bugger him.

Everyone in the building seemed to wish him well, which is unusual in a newspaper office full of jostling egos. But everyone seemed to be enjoying Trent's success.

I eventually got around to reading *Boy Swallows Universe* when preparing a story on the stage version. It was put on by Queensland Theatre under the direction of Sam Strong during Brisbane Festival in 2021. And I got it, finally … late as usual.

And I marvelled that I had been there alongside Trent and Fiona back in those early days of *Brisbane News* when he was just starting out. Who would have guessed where it would lead? Certainly not me. I don't pick up on this stuff at all.

But now I feel chuffed to have been part of it in my very small way.

Next thing you know, Netflix has picked up this hot property, turning it into a series starring Bryan Brown, Travis Fimmel and Simon Baker, among others. I never realized Trent had such a traumatic childhood back in our *Brisbane News* days. Did he talk about it back then? Not to me, he didn't.

How could anyone have guessed what he had been through? It was quite surreal. And how had he survived this world of drugs and crime? Well, the answer lies at the heart of everything he writes, I guess. Love. Because despite the rigours of growing up in Brisbane's *demi-monde* his mum and dad, for all their imperfections, loved their kids, and Trent survived because of that and went on to become one of Australia's most widely read writers.

I had joked with him and Fiona about writing my own book in a similar vein. I was thinking about that the night we attended the Netflix series' world première at New Farm Cinemas in late 2023. It was a scene out of Hollywood … part of the street had been blocked off, adoring fans were sequestered behind big plastic orange barriers, the stars mingling in the VIP enclosure. There was Bryan Brown in an Hawaiian shirt and Simon Baker looking cool along with the rest of the cast as they posed with the lucky ones who had made it into the VIP enclosure as invitees to what was the most glittering Brisvegas evening I can recall.

Sandra and I were happy to be part of it all.

Before we were finally ushered into the cinema we mingled in the foyer. Then we noticed Netflix had set up a small picture op, a little lounge-room scene from the teleseries with attendant retro furniture, some books and, most strikingly, a red telephone. If you know the book, the play or the series you'll know that red telephone (which was kind of like the Bat-phone) is crucial, a central motif.

The true meaning of that red telephone is never fully explained but Trent has said it's Eli Bell's subconscious or perhaps his brother Gus calling him from the future.

'It's his trauma ringing him and warning him, telling him things aren't right, and he should watch out. In my head, it's a reflection of Eli, his thoughts and internal process,' Trent once said.

And that red telephone sitting on a table next to a lounge chair in the foyer at New Farm furnished an Instagram moment for those of us attending the première that night. We loitered, waiting our turn. We had to get a photo here. This was a special moment.

Then we were on. Sandra sat in the armchair with me on the edge of it. I picked that red phone up and spoke into the receiver: 'Hello, is that Netflix? Are you interested in my new book … *Man Swallows Panadol*?'

CHAPTER 15

THE OTHER GENTLEMAN IN MOSCOW

He was a tall man in a dark suit holding a placard bearing my name in large print.

I went over and introduced myself.

'I'm Mr Brown,' I said.

'I am Sergei,' he replied, and that was all he said. I followed him out to the airport car park and he led me to a large gleaming black Mercedes. He opened the rear door standing like an automaton. I climbed in. I had only been out in the fresh air for a minute or two but that was long enough to tell that it was freezing. Any longer and I wouldn't have been able to feel my extremities. I had felt a bit silly leaving Brisbane wearing a three-quarter-length down jacket but now I was glad I had it on.

I sat back and checked my phone which had picked up a local telco as we began gliding towards downtown Moscow. I couldn't quite believe that I was in Russia but soon there was proof positive – the Kremlin. The bloody Kremlin! Sergei, who might have been a cyborg or a member of the Federal Security Service (FSB), pulled up in front of the Hotel Metropol Moscow and, as I got out, he delivered my bag to a bellhop who had rushed out to the car.

I thanked Sergei – I think he nodded an acknowledgment but it was hard to tell – and went through the doors into the warm glow of the interior of this historic guest accommodation.

It was February 2019 and I had been sent to Moscow for work. Russia's famous Bolshoi Ballet was coming to Brisbane in June that year as part of the Queensland Performing Arts Centre's International Series, the brainchild of John Kotzas, QPAC's enterprising boss, who retired at the end of 2024. The paper and QPAC teamed up to send me, in my capacity as *Courier-Mail* Arts Editor, to interview the Bolshoi's key dancers and preview the two ballets they were bringing Down Under – the epic *Spartacus* by Aram Khachaturian and George Balanchine's *Jewels*, a gorgeous three-act work he had created for the New York City Ballet.

I remember the day I was invited over to QPAC for a coffee, with no idea of the agenda for the meeting. It was a bit of an ambush really – I found out, to my surprise (even horror) that they wanted me to go to Moscow to do some stories on the Bolshoi. I was the sole Australian journalist being given this privilege. The head of marketing for QPAC, Angela Slater, seemed surprised when I looked more shocked than pleased. But I'm a nervous traveller at the best of times, Russia had never been on my radar as a tourist and I don't do a very good poker face. They might as well have told me I was going to the bloody moon.

A normal person back in 2019 would probably be excited at the prospect of a trip to Russia – although nobody would probably be too excited about that prospect nowadays – but I was mortified. I tried to crack hardy.

'Really?' I said, adding in an unconvincing tone: 'That's amazing.' Which was code for, 'Why the hell would I want to go to Moscow?'

I had a vision of myself being arrested on charges of espionage (being a journalist is always a good cover) and sent to a Gulag camp somewhere in Siberia for the term of my natural life. Alexander Solzhenitsyn had kind of ruined Russia for me, I'm afraid. What a killjoy.

When it was clear that, professionally, there was no way out of it, I became resigned to its inevitability.

The folks at QPAC went ahead and booked a hotel for me and looked befuddled when I asked them if it had a bath.

When I told them I couldn't possibly stay anywhere that didn't have a bath I think they thought I was joking but I was deadly serious. I need full daily immersion to achieve the sense of equilibrium I require when travelling. A hot bath it has to be, too.

They couldn't actually confirm this so I rang the hotel in question, which is quite handy to the Bolshoi Theatre, situated on Teatralnaya Square (Theatre Square) in the historic heart of the Russian capital.

A woman answered in Russian but switched to rudimentary English when I explained I was an Australian coming to stay at her hotel and required some information.

'So, what I want to know is … does the room have a bath?' I asked.

'You need a car?' she said.

'No, a bath.'

'Yes, we have car, can pick you up from airport.'

'No, I'm asking if you have a bath in the room or just a shower?'

'Yes, you can have a shower,' she said. Something was getting lost in translation.

The conversation went on like this for a while as I was standing on the back deck of our Brisbane home. My wife was looking at me the way she sometimes does, listening to my side of the conversation and mouthing 'What is going on?'

Eventually I managed to extract from the Russian the vital information that the hotel did not have baths, only showers. I informed

QPAC and they moved me. In the best possible way. To the Hotel Metropol Moscow. I happened to find out that this was where John Kotzas had stayed when he visited Moscow and that made me feel better. If that's where the boss stayed, that's where I wanted to be.

Now those of you who have read *A Gentleman in Moscow* by Amor Towles will know this hotel. It is now world-famous thanks to Towles and his book about a Russian aristocrat who is sentenced to a kind of internal exile there. Ewan McGregor plays Count Alexander Rostov in the Netflix series based on the book (which is terrific but it wasn't filmed at the Hotel Metropol, for obvious reasons). Things have gone a bit pear-shaped since my trip to Russia.

So they filmed it in a vast studio somewhere in Brexitania, using a few North-of-England locations for the shoot as well. I had to suspend disbelief, having stayed at the actual hotel.

The thing is that when my Moscow trip was organized I wasn't familiar with the book. I probably should have been but I don't read a lot of contemporary fiction. In recent years I have spent a lot of time catching up on the canon, so I miss things.

When I told a colleague, a Towles fan, that I was going to Moscow and would be staying at the Metropol she was amazed. 'That is the hotel featured in *A Gentleman in Moscow*,' she said.

'It is?' I was clueless about that but after some Googling realized the significance, and I do love a nice luxury heritage hotel. I finally bought a copy of the book just before embarking. I planned to read it at the hotel which would be, I figured, appropriate. I mean, I could have started it on the plane but I'm usually too anxious on planes to read. I just watch back-to-back documentaries to distract myself. I have watched way too much *Top Gear* on international flights.

A couple of years later I interviewed Towles for his follow-up novel *The Lincoln Highway*. It was a phone interview – me in Brisbane, him in New York – and I told him about my trip to Moscow.

'So, I was the other gentleman in Moscow,' I told him. He was amazed. I don't think he comes across that many people who have actually stayed at the Metropol.

I arrived there with two books: his … and mine. I was in the throes of proofreading the manuscript of my memoir *The Kowloon Kid*, which was published by Transit Lounge in August 2019.

I was very happy indeed to be in the final stages of a book that had taken a decade to come to fruition. I had been wanting to do a memoir about my Hong Kong childhood for years and had undergone many false starts and some excruciating experiences trying to birth it.

The publishing industry is so frustrating and random. The manuscript's original publisher (or supposed publisher) had knocked it back and then tried to get an agent to help me shop the idea around. I had a synopsis and several chapters down but not a full book's worth.

I pitched it to a Brisbane agent. She rejected it and then I sent it to a national agent whom I knew from his work in publishing. He had the material for about six months and, when I pressed him for a decision one way or the other, he sent me a confusing email about how many units (not books, mind you) would have to be sold for him to make a profit. It was more a spreadsheet than a letter of rejection, but the rejection was clearly implied.

So I rang him and said: 'Regardless of all that, what did you think of the material?'

'I haven't read it,' he said. This is what you're dealing with.

I became so frustrated that I decided to shelve the whole idea. But not long after that, having reviewed some books and done stories on others published by Melbourne outfit Transit Lounge, I decided to pitch it to them. What did I have to lose? Besides my mind?

I loved what they did and noted that travel and Asia were areas of special interest to them. Suddenly it dawned on me that my story might work in that context.

I rang Barry Scott, the publisher, and not only did he respond with unfeigned interest: he actually read the material I sent him! Go figure.

So I got to work on it in mid-2018, finished it before the end of that year and was thrilled to have advanced it to the final stages with a hard copy of the manuscript to read while I was in Moscow, as well as Towles' engaging novel.

Whether I would actually go turned out to be problematic, initially because QPAC sent my passport to the Russian embassy in Canberra for a visa and it didn't arrive back until the day before I was due to board my Singapore Airlines flight to Moscow. Now I was faced with the inevitable. I had to go.

I got to Singapore first and had to spend a few hours in transit. While waiting there, I got a text message from Roxanne Hopkins who was QPAC's one-person advance party on the ground in Moscow. Rox had gone ahead to shore up interviews and the visit's fine-grained logistics.

That made it all seem a tad presidential although the upshot was that they would be working me hard as soon as I hit the ground. Rox informed me that upon arrival I would have a full day at the Bolshoi, which is only a couple of hundred metres from the Metropol.

I checked in and signed the obligatory declaration for the security services which all visitors have to do. So they knew I had arrived and where I was staying. Gulp.

Then, famished, I went to the restaurant for breakfast. I don't eat much on planes due to my disposition (as a nervous wreck). I walked into the restaurant to the sounds of a harp being played by a woman on a small stage at the front of that sumptuously elegant dining room, which I had the most uncanny feeling I'd been in before – until the rouble dropped that, of course, I had. It was in the premonition I'd had as I packed Towles' masterwork, of my sitting in this very room turning the leaves. A feat of imagination that would soon be my reality.

Already I felt as if I were on a movie set. The restaurant is vast and ornate, with an incredible coloured-glass ceiling. Who has that?

The hotel is a work of art in itself. It overlooks Revolution and Theatre squares. Since it opened in 1905, like other grand hotels of the era such as the Waldorf Astoria in New York, Claridge's in London and the Ritz in Paris, the Metropol has met the highest of standards for luxury and service in the Russian capital.

Amor Towles gives a handy potted history of it online, which he would. The man behind the hotel was a celebrated Russian merchant and patron of the arts, Savva Mamontov, whose original vision included a theatre but that part of the design plan didn't quite come off.

The hotel did become regarded as an Art Nouveau treasure-house, its walls adorned with bas-reliefs by famous sculptor Nikolay Andreev and interiors decorated by other Russian artists of the era. Nikolay Malinin's book *Metropol: The Moscow Legend* describes it as 'a masterpiece of Art Nouveau' and elaborates on the collaborative effort involved.

'The project, started by Leo Kekushev, one of two trendsetters of Moscow Art Nouveau architecture, was continued by a Scotsman, William Walcot, and finally finished by a team of other architects.'

I stayed in what is known as 'the historic wing' which remains largely as it was, unlike some other wings that have been refurbished. The interior is gobsmackingly beautiful, with artistic touches everywhere you look and the most magnificent antique elevator. The hotel is beyond grand and has a chequered history, having played a central role in the story of the Russian Revolution, which began in 1917, and this is where Amor Towles got the inspiration for his wonderful book.

For its first decade the hotel was an icon for the upper crust but then, as the author explains, 'the Metropol found itself serving as a bastion in a pitched battle with forces loyal to the Tsar defending the eastern flank of the Kremlin from the hotel's suites while the Bolsheviks returned fire from the streets below.

'In the ensuing battle nearby every window in the hotel was shattered. In fact, when American journalist John Reed arrived in the city (shortly after witnessing the fall of the Hermitage), he was assured by the Metropol's unflappable front desk captain: "We have some very comfortable rooms, if the gentleman does not mind a little fresh air".'

The Bolsheviks eventually seized the hotel, threw out the guests, renamed it the Second House of the Soviets and used it to billet officials and house various departments of the fledgling state. Apparently, the new Constitution was composed in Suite 217.

This is where Towles comes in because in this tumult his fictional protagonist, Count Rostov, is caught up in the drama of the October Revolution and spared death by the Bolsheviks because of the pro-revolutionary sentiments contained in a poem he published nine years earlier – *Where Is It Now?*

The Count is moved into tiny quarters, on a floor once reserved for servants, but after that he is left largely alone. And his life in the ensuing years is the subject of Towles' tremendously engaging novel. Life imprisonment at the Metropol – I can think of worse fates.

This historic and, thanks to Amor Towles, now much more famous hotel was the perfect place for me to stay just across the road from the Bolshoi Theatre which also played a role in the founding of the Soviet Union. Lenin delivered his last-ever public address at the

Bolshoi, and Joseph Stalin announced the founding of the Soviet Union on stage in its domed auditorium.

Tumultuous as Russia's history is, it is every bit as fascinating and here I was in the city's most historic hotel, across the road from the Bolshoi, a short walk from Red Square and the Kremlin. Bizarre.

After a breakfast of blinis and salmon caviar washed down by some flavoursome Russian tea (Russians are big on tea), I retired to my room and quickly got ready for a full day at the Bolshoi.

My room had a window looking onto Revolution Square, with Theatre Square next door. There was light snowfall outside and the temperature was around –5°C. I had taken off my down jacket as soon as I entered the hotel but put it back on now and went downstairs and out through the doors that Count Rostov would not have been allowed to go through, crossing the square to the Bolshoi and entering the building beside the theatre, where the administration and studios were.

I was met by Rox, who was accompanied by the Bolshoi's public relations lady, Katya, and we had an interpreter along for the ride too, which was just as well. I knew only two words of Russian – *Da* (Yes) and *Nyet* (No) – and after ten days there managed to pick up only one more: *Spasibo* (Thank you).

Sometimes when you're in the middle of something you lose perspective. Now I realize what an amazing experience this was, to be backstage at the world's most famous ballet company with entrée to stars such as Denis Rodkin, who was a superstar.

I chatted to him, through the interpreter, as well as to other dancers in the troupe, even as I was still battling jet lag and forgetting what an incredible experience I was having. I just wanted to be back in my room having tea and watching *BBC World News*.

I like ballet but am no aficionado so maybe some of it was lost on me, but still it was amazing to have gained entrée to this incredible world. It was like some sort of reality TV show. All day I was struggling to stay awake but I just plugged into the extraordinary stamina and energy levels on display all around me and pushed on through.

I was due to see *Spartacus* that evening with Rox, and though I had never seen that ballet performed I was aware of a most beautiful musical passage from it as many of us do who remember the television series *The Onedin Line*, which uses Khachaturian's *Adagio of Spartacus and Phrygia* as its theme music. It is one of the most haunting, poignant pieces of music you will ever hear.

There was a matinée of *Spartacus* during my visit behind the scenes that day at the Bolshoi and it was fascinating to watch the dancers running on and off stage from the wings. The boys had swords and would be duelling like kids offstage and then run onstage for some dramatic scene. It seemed like fun.

After the performance, when the audience had emptied from that vast, gilt-edged auditorium, we walked out onto the stage and I stood there taking in the vision splendid. This was where Lenin and Stalin had done their thing, where some of the world's greatest dancers had strutted their stuff. As I stood there the theatre looked familiar for some reason and after a few moments I twigged.

'This reminds me of the Muppet Theatre,' I said. That wasn't what everyone was expecting to hear and the translator looked baffled.

I joined an official tour of the Bolshoi Theatre a couple of days later and our tour guide pointed out that Putin, when he came to the ballet, sat in the imperial box where the Tsar and Tsarina had. The guide explained that Stalin preferred to keep a lower profile at the back of a less conspicuous box, more or less out of sight. He was paranoid about being assassinated. Sadly, he never was.

After my day at the Bolshoi interviewing dancers and staff I was shattered. The jet lag had turned me into a virtual zombie.

When I got back to the hotel, I had to have a bath (a wonderful nice hot bath!) and get ready for that night's performance of *Spartacus*. Three hours of ballet to round out the day. Blimey.

I went across Theatre Square dodging little drifts of snow (I had on my suede Italian loafers which was silly of me) and lingered in front of the theatre – which was beautifully lit and looked like a temple – on the lookout for my date for the night, Rox. As I loitered, some shady Russian dude approached me and patted his pocket. 'Tickets?' he asked.

'No, thanks, mate, I have tickets,' I said, and he moved on to someone else.

Once inside the Bolshoi in midwinter, the first stop is the cloakroom where everyone unloads their furs and where I checked in my down jacket. I had my suit on underneath and it was pretty toasty indoors despite the frigid conditions outside, down to around −13°C on that particular night.

The production was spectacular, the music exquisite, and the surrounds of the splendid Bolshoi Theatre are amazing. '*Bolshoi*' means 'big' in Russian and it *is* big. Everything in central Moscow seems big. The scale of things is rather impressive.

I had dinner with Rox nearby before she went back to Brisbane. She had shepherded me through my arrival and big day out at the Bolshoi, organized a couple more interviews for me during the week and now her work was done. We dined at a restaurant on the other side of Revolution Square that seemed to be full of Russians smoking hookahs. It's a thing in Moscow, I guess.

QPAC's production manager, Chris Philippi, was the next emissary from the organization due in Moscow. He was the guy who would be gauging what Brisbane needed to do to stage the productions in the Lyric Theatre and he would be my date the following Saturday night when we went to *Jewels*, Balanchine's stunning classic. This ballet was inspired by the precious gem collection belonging to jeweller Claude Arpels. Coincidentally I had noticed a Van Cleef & Arpels boutique on nearby Petrovka Ulitsa, the thoroughfare flanking the Bolshoi that I walked along most days in Moscow.

With the performance of *Jewels* taking place a week after *Spartacus*, I had quite a lot of time at my disposal.

So here I was, the other gentleman in Moscow, holed up in the Metropol in the middle of a Russian winter. I wasn't at work – that was a plus. I had a work laptop with me but barely touched it. I did file a story about the Bolshoi preparing for Brisbane and we had a Russian snapper shooting for us, so we had photos.

And I had a couple more interviews to do back at the Bolshoi but the rest of the time I was at my leisure, as they say. One of the first things I did was go to Okhotny Ryad, a split-level underground shopping mall at Manezhnaya Square across the road from the Four Seasons Hotel Moscow and just a stone's throw from Red Square, not that I imagine such hooliganism would be tolerated, let alone encouraged, what with the forbidding Lubyanka just up the road.

Here I bought myself a Russian fur hat with flaps that folded down to keep my ears warm, and that was most welcome, considering how cold it was outside.

Then I was free to just potter around. Moscow's historic precinct, which was my patch, is quite high-end and very impressive. Maybachs (top-of-the-line Mercedes) seemed to be purring outside most ritzy shops, lingering by the kerb waiting for oligarchs' wives or, for all I knew, oligarchs themselves.

I did a bit of *flaneur*-ing but also had a list of places to go. One of which was the famous Café Pushkin, an antique-filled dining room evoking a nobleman's house with formal service and a typically Russian menu. Fully focused as I was on my impending order of borscht, I was on my way out the hotel door when the concierge stopped me. 'You are going out?' he asked. Why was he asking? Was he working for the FSB?

'Yes, I am going to catch a taxi to Café Pushkin for lunch,' I said.

'This is not a good idea,' he said. 'I will get you taxi.' There was obviously some sort of dodgy taxi mafia going on and I guessed he was trying to protect me (if he wasn't actually in on the racket). He suggested that I should see him any time I wanted a taxi. As seeing him would be unavoidable in the circumstances, I nodded assent and assured him: 'That is the least I can do.'

Café Pushkin was impressive, if a bit touristy. (The borscht was everything I expected.) There seemed to be quite a few Chinese people there.

The following day I organized a guide to take me on a tour of the famous Moscow Metro, which opened in 1935. It was conceived by Stalin as part of his first Five-Year Plan to rapidly industrialize the Soviet Union. The spectacular stations were meant to show the world the power and possibilities the Communist Party presented, and they are stunning.

One features chandeliers hanging from the ceiling and others are decorated with frescoes, sculptures and other artworks. We rode the Metro hopping on and off at notable stations while my guide, Olga, explained the history behind the various platform decorations.

The following day I caught a taxi (this time organized by the concierge) to The Pushkin State Museum of Fine Arts, the largest collection of European art in Moscow, located in Volkhonka Street, just opposite the stunning Cathedral of Christ the Saviour.

The museum has an extraordinary holding of some 700,000 works including some stunning early-20th-century art and impressive antiquities. It doesn't actually have any connection to

Pushkin other than the name. He's unarguably one of Russia's favourite writers.

One of the things I enjoyed was how Russian writers and poets, novelists and artists have lent their names to places around the city. A Gogol Café can be found near the hotel, for example, and inside there's a Dostoevsky Hall.

I also undertook a self-guided tour of the Kremlin on a particularly freezing day. I didn't run into Putin. Funny, that. Again, the scale and grandeur were amazing. The monumental Tsar Cannon that sits outside dusted with snow is one of the most amazing things I have ever seen and then there's the Diamond Fund, an incredible collection of gems and jewellery exhibited in the Kremlin Armoury. All this must have belonged to dead aristocrats, I presume.

The perimeter is patrolled by soldiers who have something of a lean and hungry look.

I also spent a bit of time mooching around Red Square and the Cathedral of Vasily the Blessed, known in English as St Basil's Cathedral, that incredibly colourful Orthodox church.

I had an idea that I might visit Lenin's Tomb (or his Mausoleum, whichever you prefer) situated on Red Square just below the Kremlin walls. I walked from the hotel and, approaching the square saw a long queue. I went to the end of the line and stood behind a young guy and his daughter. 'Lenin?' I asked. He nodded.

After about an hour I managed to get to the front of the queue and then went down into the little darkened room where Lenin's embalmed body is guarded by soldiers who enforce a strict rule of silence. One shuffles in and out without talking. It's like visiting the Soup Nazi in *Seinfeld*.

The funny thing is that once outside I walked to the edge of the Red Square and was then approached by none other than Joseph Stalin himself. Well, he said he was Stalin. This bloke was dressed as the notorious dictator, accompanied by an enforcer who demanded money after taking a photo of us together. I piled rouble notes into his hand until he was satisfied and off they walked looking for another victim.

That incident gave me the only poem that resulted from that trip. It's called *Meeting Stalin.*

> *... the face was familiar – that brush moustache, the presidential hair. / He sidled up to me, an accomplice nearby. 'I am Joseph,' he said. 'Photo.' / It wasn't a question ... I smiled and tried to joke: / 'I have just visited Lenin,' I said. 'He doesn't look at all well.'*

After my meeting with Stalin, I took myself to lunch at the historic department store that looks out over Red Square. It's called GUM (pronounced Gee You Em) and was built in the 1890s during Tsar Alexander III's reign but became a State Department Store when the Bolsheviks took over. It is quite swish: I went inside and found a flash bistro with a view of Red Square and the skating rink they had set up in the middle of it.

The place seemed to be full of ladies who lunch. Oligarchs' wives? It looked like that. They were all rather glamorous, dripping with jewellery. I felt a bit odd sitting by myself. Ah, but the borscht was good. Who knew I liked borscht?

After lunch I wandered around the mall, purchased a pair of track pants at a sports shop upstairs and visited the Historical Toilet Rooms – yes, they really exist: re-creations of the Tsar's dunny, I guess. For a few roubles you can take a piss then sit on a couch and soak up the history. In case you ever get there. Although it's unlikely any of us will be visiting any time soon, I suppose. Which is a shame because Moscow is spectacular, historically speaking.

And the Metropol is an icon that takes up nearly a block in the heart of the city.

They were promoting Amor Towles' book when I was there and offering *A Gentleman in Moscow* Tours of the hotel, which included a nice hardback copy of the book.

I was taken on a bit of a general tour by the hotel's resident historian and it was fascinating. She wasn't that keen on the Soviets, though, because they didn't really respect the place.

Showing me through the restaurant, she stopped and said: 'They spit on floor here.' I think she was referring to the Bolsheviks.

We passed a large taxidermized bear at one stage and came to a landing where there were photos of famous people who had stayed at the hotel over the years. It is an impressive cast that includes Bertolt Brecht, John Steinbeck, George Bernard Shaw, Mao Zedong, Sergei Prokofiev, David Bowie, Sophia Loren, Elton John, Gerard Depardieu. I mean, who hasn't stayed there!

Michael Jackson had a sojourn at the hotel in 1993 and I was shown his suite.

And now I was here too. I'm not sure they'll put my photo up on the wall to complete the set, but never mind.

For a week in February 2019, I was the other gentleman in Moscow. Despite forays beyond the lobby that Count Rostov was never allowed, I did spend an awful lot of time just wandering around the hotel … reading Towles' novel and then looking for the features he mentions in it, be it an Art Nouveau stained-glass window or the famous Chaliapin Bar. It's one of the most beautiful bars in Moscow thanks to its original Art Nouveau fittings and décor.

The hotel hosted me to a Russian high tea in the Chaliapin one afternoon despite my protestations that it really wasn't necessary.

I felt a bit self-conscious having high tea by myself but they insisted so I relented and feasted on more blinis and caviar, pastries and tiny cut sandwiches washed down by tea – plenty of tea – heated on a samovar at my table.

I hadn't realised that Russians were so into their tea. They first encountered the brew when a Mongolian ruler gifted it to the founder of the Romanov dynasty, Tsar Michael I (Mikhail Fyodorovich Romanov) in the 1630s.

A few years later, this luxury beverage was gifted by a Chinese ambassador to Alexis I (Aleksei Mikhailovich) during trade negotiations with Russia. Tea culture became part of Russian life and is still important today. I noticed some nice little tea shops on my strolls near the hotel.

There was so much food on offer for my high tea at the bar, named after the famous opera singer Feodor Chaliapin, that I squirrelled some of it away in a napkin and took it back to my room for dinner.

When I wasn't lounging by the Chaliapin Bar drinking tea and reading *A Gentleman in Moscow*, I was in the comfy executive lounge sipping more tea and poring over the manuscript of my own book.

Having the whole week to myself was a luxury. I called Sandra every day but didn't bother calling work. They had no idea what I was doing, and the reality was I wasn't doing much. I was just lounging around the Metropol, eating borscht in local restaurants or wandering around Red Square in my down jacket and Russian fur hat wondering what the hell I was doing in Moscow.

On my last day I went to Red Square for a final visit (it's so close to the Metropol) and heard choral singing and music so exquisite I thought it must have been piped in just for the tourists.

But there was a little chapel nearby and I realized the music was emanating from there so I went inside to find a Russian Orthodox Church service in full swing. Priests with long beards and ornate cassocks were swinging censers while a church choir sang in heavenly fashion and, again, I felt like I had stepped into a scene from a movie. Maybe I had stumbled onto an old *Doctor Zhivago* set?

I stayed awhile and bought a couple of icons on my way out (plus a babushka doll for Sandra) and they now decorate my dresser as mementoes of that otherworldly experience.

The second ballet, *Jewels*, was on the Saturday night before my departure and I attended with Chris from QPAC – two dudes from Brisbane in a rather unlikely setting. Chris was on the same plane home. Singapore Airlines again.

It takes 24 hours to get from Brisbane to Moscow and vice versa, via Singapore, so it's relatively straightforward with just a few hours in transit either way. All of a sudden I was back in balmy Brisbane. It was like travelling from one planet to another.

Thinking about the trip while watching Ewan McGregor in the Netflix series *A Gentleman in Moscow* was hard for me because I knew that it wasn't actually the Metropol and that the gentleman wasn't actually in Moscow but somewhere in the North of England.

The book is faithful to the hotel, though, and Amor Towles knows the Metropol well enough to write about it and seems as fascinated by its troubled history as I was when I was … the other gentleman in Moscow.

CHAPTER 16

LATE FLOWERING

I AWOKE WONDERING WHERE I WAS and in that befuddled moment, half asleep, I also wondered who I was. It was one of those blank moments one experiences in hotel rooms far from home. Soon it clicked, with the usual disappointment.

Then I noticed that the room was aglow. We were thirty-four floors up at the Novotel London Canary Wharf in a room facing the city and there, approaching the western horizon, was a full moon in all its splendour, about to drop off the edge of the world.

The moon's setting was accompanied by the sun's rise glinting off the windows of the tower opposite. It was a visually symphonic moment; the music of the spheres incarnate.

The first words that came to me in this moment were T.S. Eliot's. *Unreal City*. I had a slim Faber & Faber volume of *The Waste Land* on my bedside table, a lovely little hardback purchased at the London Review Bookshop (LRB to local bibliophiles) in Bloomsbury. We had stayed in Bloomsbury upon our first arrival in London, before a diversion to Scotland. Now back in Londinium we were ending our stay at Canary Wharf where I'd wangled a deal on a room … or two rooms, actually. Hamish had his own next door to us.

The hotel was fairly new and though it wasn't central there was a rather swish Tube station nearby (this is a financial hub, after all) and the Docklands Light Railway. Staying here appealed to me because of another Eliot connection: it's situated in the Isle of Dogs, which gets a mention in *The Waste Land*.

The river sweats / Oil and tar / The barges drift / With the turning tide / Red sails / Wide / To leeward, swing on the heavy spar. / The barges wash / Drifting logs / Down Greenwich reach / Past the Isle of Dogs.

Here we were on that Greenwich reach of the Thames in the city that Eliot made his own by words alone.

Waking in that hotel room to see the moon setting and sun rising over Eliot's Unreal City awakened something in me. I also thought of his *Preludes* again:

You had such a vision of the street / As the street hardly understands;

And that's the vision of the city that I had, and nor am I sure if the city understood or not.

I believe I can trace my 'late flowering' (my own pretentious description of a poetry revival after many fallow years) to our Canary Wharf hotel room on that early December day in 2017.

The poems would come a few years later after a longish gestation but that vision of London, the sun lighting up The Shard as the moon bowed out, started something.

We had gone to London at the insistence of our son, Hamish. After finishing high school, he eschewed the idea of attending Schoolies on the Gold Coast. This pleased us. He asked, instead, that we take him to London and Paris. An eminently sane request to which we happily acquiesced.

After our arrival on November 21, with the air beginning to chill, we spent our first few days at The Academy, a cute little hotel in Gower Street, Bloomsbury. The literary connections here and proximity to the British Museum were attractive.

Gower Street is just a block away from Russell Square, and it was at 26 Russell Square that T.S. Eliot worked for some time. There's a plaque in memory of him there on a building that used to be Faber & Faber's office. In 1925 Eliot began his time there, having been hired as a literary adviser by Oxford don Godfrey Faber, later to become his publisher and champion.

And, of course, this was the area where the famous Bloomsbury set hung out – Virginia Woolf, John Maynard Keynes, E.M. Forster and Lytton Strachey, among others.

We checked into our Gower Street hotel early in the morning and went directly to a nearby Waterstones bookshop for coffee and a browse.

That day, still jet-lagged, we had an invitation to attend a 4pm dress rehearsal of the Royal Ballet's production of *Sylvia* at Covent Garden. I had met the PR lady for the company when it visited Brisbane and she had said to tell her if we were ever in London. Well, we were … and were almost nodding off thanks to jet lag as we enjoyed the ballet with a select group of media and VIPs.

The next day we went to the British Museum (I'm not going to say anything about the Elgin Marbles) and then across the road to charming LRB where, as mentioned, I'd bought my prized copy of *The Waste Land*. I had first studied it under Bruce Dawe in Toowoomba all those years ago. I had it in various collections, but it deserves its own volume and this one I carried around London throughout our visit as a kind of touchstone.

Hamish browsed, too, and came up with a book by Sartre and another by Kierkegaard which left us both suitably impressed. He hadn't been a reader until relatively late in his schooling. That hadn't worried us but it was curious considering his parents: journalists who read voraciously. But then, something seemed to click and he dived straight in at the deep end, attacking the canon with gusto and with a special interest in French literature.

For lunch that day we went to the Dinner by Heston Blumenthal London restaurant at the Mandarin Oriental in Knightsbridge. Blame that on hours spent watching Blumenthal on *MasterChef Australia*. We had hoped to get a glimpse of Heston himself but if he was there he was keeping a low profile.

We were only in London for a few days before heading to Scotland.

That was a pilgrimage, heading back to stay at Culloden House Hotel outside Inverness where Sandra and I had lodged twenty years earlier. On that previous trip we had visited Plockton, the town where they made the TV series *Hamish Macbeth*, which they were shooting while we were there. It was one of our favourite shows and it's no secret that our Hamish is named after the Highlands policeman played by Robert Carlyle in the series.

I had rung Culloden House Hotel to book, mindful that it was late in the year.

'How's the weather in late November?' I asked.

'Autumnal,' the lady said. Autumnal alright. Very fucking autumnal.

We took the *Highland Chieftain* train north from King's Cross to Inverness, capital of the Scottish Highlands, rattling into snowy darkness beyond Edinburgh. The sun goes down before 4pm in Scotland at that time of year.

We were very happy to be back at Culloden House, which is not far from the grim moor where the Battle of Culloden was fought and lost by the Scots under Bonnie Prince Charlie in 1746. If you know your history – or you're a fan of *Outlander* – you'll know about Culloden. It's a grim and tragic marker in Scottish history and walking on the bleak moor where the battle occurred after a dusting of snow in the bitter cold is bracing. Luckily there's a nice toasty visitor centre to return to afterwards.

Culloden House, just outside Inverness, is a Palladian mansion and it's here, in a previous iteration of the house (it has been modified over the centuries), that Bonnie Prince Charlie and his officers stayed the night before the battle.

Upon arrival Stephen Davies, the general manager of this luxury house hotel, presented me with a fascinating book entitled *The Course of History: Ten Meals That Changed the World*. The first chapter, entitled *Bonnie Prince Charlie on the Eve of Culloden*, recounts the story of the battle and what the prince and his retinue, which included French officers, ate that night.

They feasted as the Highlanders mounted a futile night march to Nairn to attack the Sassenachs. They were turned back by fog and had to march all the way back to Culloden, then, exhausted, face off with the English on Drumossie Moor. While the Highlanders were marching to Nairn in the dark, the Prince and his officers dined on rack of lamb with neeps and tatties, cheese and a Scottish dessert of cream-crowdie washed down with champagne and French claret.

It seemed obscene. After the battle the triumphant Duke of Cumberland (his troops were fresh and better armed than the Scots) took over and occupied Culloden House once they'd finished off wounded Highlanders who had retreated to the grounds. I had been told there were, therefore, ghosts here – as there would have to be. We didn't see any but that doesn't mean they weren't there!

Hamish and I ate haggis here, which seemed appropriate, and I thought of Bonnie Prince Charlie feasting, possibly in the same dining room, before that tragic battle, the last land engagement fought on British soil.

Altogether we spent five days at Culloden House Hotel and on one of them we drove over to Plockton. It's a gorgeous drive on the A890 past lochs, flanked by snowclad mountains and one of Scotland's most picturesque castles, at Eilean Donan, shortly before you turn off for Plockton. This lovely wee town, on the shores of Loch Carron, is dubbed Lochdubh in *Hamish Macbeth*.

Sandra and I thought Hamish should see Plockton but when we arrived the town appeared to be largely closed. It was a bit late in the season, admittedly. Thankfully, there was one pub open for lunch. I had the fish pie, in case you're interested (and even if you're not).

Before leaving Culloden House, we took a boat tour of Loch Ness, hurrying through sleet to make the tour boat in time. The tour includes a visit to Urquhart Castle on the shores of the loch and walking round this stone edifice on an overlooking promontory I scanned the waters for Nessie but there was no sign of the beastie. I don't remember ever being colder than I was that day.

After our Caledonian sojourn we caught the train back to London and took a taxi to the Novotel at Canary Wharf where we would spend a week before finishing off our trip in Paris.

In London I continued indulging my T.S. Eliot fantasy. We were out on the river shuttling between the two Tate museums when a few lines from *Four Quartets* surfaced – the opening of *The Dry Salvages*, the third of the work's four parts.

I do not know much about gods; but I think that the river / Is a strong brown god – and as we churned across the river I muttered, under my breath: *Sweet Thames, run softly till I end my song,* a refrain from *The Fire Sermon* section of *The Waste Land* which Eliot, in his turn, borrows from the Tudor poet Edmund Spenser.

There is so much of London in Eliot; and one day, when we went to London Bridge Station to catch a train for a visit to friends in Brighton, more lines from *The Burial of the Dead*, the opening section of Eliot's epic, floated up from my unconscious:

> *Unreal city / Under the brown fog of a winter dawn / A crowd flowed over London Bridge, so many / I had not thought death had undone so many.*

The first morning in that hotel at Canary Wharf, waking, unsure of who or where I was, with Eliot's 'unreal city' spread before me, a seed was sown. But it would take time to germinate and by the time we got to Paris, where we spent a few days before flying home, that process had begun.

Back at my desk at *The Courier-Mail* I thought of Eliot again. He had written *On Margate Sands. / I can connect / Nothing with nothing.* I substituted *Bowen Hills* (Brisbane's News Corp headquarters) for *Margate Sands* and recited this to myself from time to time. For some bizarre reason it made me feel better …

My job was Arts Editor. This was the job Sandra had before she went over to the dark side to work for the Queensland government.

Its responsibilities kept me busy and I was out several nights each week, often reviewing shows that were of varying interest and quality. Musicals are bread and butter for the major venues but I seem to lack the gene required to appreciate them fully. I had to sit through a lot of musicals as Arts Editor, looking at my watch and wishing I were somewhere else … anywhere else. There is no moment so sweet as when that final song winds up and I stand with everyone else to applaud, not the performance but the fact that the damn thing is over at long last.

Life got busy again and the post-holiday glow quickly faded.

Hamish began his studies at the University of Queensland, Sandra was occupied helping to run the state and I was swanning around town with occasional junkets south for major arts events. The perks of the job were fun even if the money was never enough. Journalism has never paid that well, but it sure beats the alternative … work.

Sitting at my desk with a view out over the car park I watched the days pass, and many of my colleagues ditto. The Battle of Culloden had sparked the tragedy of the clearances in Scotland with Highlanders hounded off their land and into exile. People just disappeared from the landscape.

So, too, was it in the newsroom at *The Courier-Mail* as the repercussions of the digital revolution began to bite.

Redundancies became part of daily life as the newspaper continued to downsize and pivot online. The 'rivers of gold' had dried up long since and the business was feeling the pinch as colleagues departed with alarming regularity, some smiling at the size of their payouts, others peremptorily jumping ship.

The atmosphere was still abuzz, in a subdued way, as I was writing for the daily paper; online; the Saturday magazine, *QWEEKEND*, which was quite satisfying; and still for *Brisbane News* into the bargain, until it was canned. I did tend to churn out the copy. I've always been pretty prolific in my daily journalism – which may be a bad thing, I've never been quite sure.

I remember one day my chief of staff described me as 'a machine' due to my ability at times to produce copy like an automaton.

But, as they say, it's a living.

Our Bowen Hills building, which had been a particularly bustling one, was starting to become much less so. There were all too regular farewells held to usher people out the door with some sort of ceremony, but eventually too many people were leaving to bother with that.

I put my head down and waited. But I seemed to survive each cut.

Only one poem emanated from this period, *Continuum*, and it relates directly to my situation at that time.

… the tedium here is unrelenting / one day bleeds into another / clouds hover like an impending joke / I have a lovely view of the car park.

That was it. One poem. Oh well …

And then came COVID.

I remember one day sitting in the car outside Bent Books in Boundary Street, West End, listening to the radio and the then Health Minister talking about the possibility of 30,000 deaths in Queensland as the pandemic started. *Take the brace position*, I thought to myself … *put your hands on your knees, your head between your legs and kiss your arse goodbye.*

It was frightening and confusing. One of the first things that happened with the advent of COVID was that News Corp decided to shut down *Brisbane News*. There was no income from real estate advertising, everything was shutting down and someone at head office in Sydney decided this should be the trigger for closing down the most popular publication in Brisbane. Go figure. It lightened my workload but the evident shift in management priorities was alarming.

Things were shutting down left, right and centre with rolling lockdowns. The whole world seemed to be going into hibernation. Remember?

We worked in and out of the office in 2020, sometimes for extended stretches due to the lockdowns.

I had never worked from home much until COVID hit. In fact, whenever anyone said they were working from home I would repeat the words 'working from home' aloud, adding air quotes like the *Austin Powers* movie character Dr Evil when he talked about having 'a laser'.

To my mind, 'working from home' was code for not working at all and I would soon discover and come to appreciate the beauty of this euphemism.

Magazines were smaller so there were fewer pages and 'working from home' out of sight also meant being out of mind as it turned out. There wasn't much happening in the arts anyhow as all shows were mothballed too. At the newspaper it was all about news, and the news wasn't very good for a while there. It was scary stuff.

It was during this period that we started turning the news off after watching the 6pm headlines, finding it all a tad unbearable. And so I instituted what I dubbed 'Dub Hour' – an hour preparatory to dinner when we bathe and cook to the mellow tunes of dub reggae.

We still have Dub Hour, though it has also morphed into 'Jazz Hour' and sometimes 'Classical Hour'.

Bad as COVID was, there were some good things to come out of that difficult period.

Being at home so much was actually relaxing. Sandra would be working online upstairs, and downstairs Hamish would be studying, while I was in a Brown study listening to the radio and feigning work. I'm not saying I didn't do any work, but I certainly wasn't overextending myself.

COVID lockdowns did give us the chance to stop and smell the roses. Days at home passed with so much less drama than days in the office. There were mid-morning walks to get takeaway coffee, noticing flowers in bloom along the way, lingering to look at birds in the trees, watching clouds scud across the sky above. There were no interruptions, no traffic, no nights out. I was in my tartan dressing gown by six o'clock each evening. Bliss.

Not being in the newsroom was a blessing in disguise. The newsroom (any office, really) can be a stressful place and, frankly, I was like a wild animal in there before the coming of COVID, which seemed to change everything. It was a watershed of sorts, a time to recalibrate.

I found that I could happily 'work from home' and I had my study downstairs to 'work' in with my old-dude analog radio on the desk tuned to ABC Classic, which got me through the days and still does. Listening to Russell, Greta and the others helped get me through COVID.

The main beneficiary of this period of enforced domesticity was Sarge, our beloved Maltese shih-tzu, who left us at the age of 14½ in mid-2024. We are still missing him as terribly as he used to miss us when we were at work.

During COVID he was confused at first as to what we were all doing at home all day, but delighted to have the company and the walks and the cuddles with us on the bed while we watched movies to help pass the time.

We watched a lot of movies while I was 'working from home' during COVID, including the entire Bond franchise, and worked our way through a schedule of classics that Hamish hadn't seen before.

Then a funny thing happened. A poem appeared, unbidden. The seed planted in London began to push through the soil.

I was thinking about a train journey I had once taken to Sydney as a student. It came back to me in a cinematic flashback as fresh as yesterday even though it was many yesterdays ago, sometime in the mid-to late 1970s. I pulled out a foolscap pad and began writing. The poem emerged from my subconscious fully formed, as they do sometimes, if a little bedraggled in that first scrawled draft. My late flowering had apparently begun.

Entitled *Long ago on a train,* I penned the verses in October 2020, so it is very much a COVID creation. It was published in the online literary journal *StylusLit* in September 2022 by fellow poet Rosanna Licari.

It begins like this:

Long ago on a train / I said to the girl with the feather in her hair / 'Do you never shut up?' / 'Let's talk all night,' she said / As the bush rushed past outside / And the waitress in the soiled uniform / Poured more strong tea / And my new friend Angelo, sitting nearby, / Pored over his tatty copy of The Horse's Mouth / And he smiled as I raised my eyebrows.

And finishes with our arrival in Sydney.

Long ago on a train / On a journey between two lives / I thought of Kerouac and dreamt of riding the rattlers / And living in the hobo jungle of his mind / And the girl with the feather in her hair slept on, muttering still. / When I woke, we were near old Sydney town / And the train was passing through red brick suburbs / And you could smell the city / And it smelt like cars and grit and looked like hell. / All this was long ago / Long ago on a train.

Long ago in a book – this book, in Chapter 6 – I observed that it was a bit of a Beat poem, but it did seem to flow. However, I wasn't sure if it was any good so I sent it to my friend Ross Fitzgerald who has a very good eye for poetry. He said he loved it. And that stirred a thought in me: *Maybe I'm back*? I had left poetry behind, or aside, for so many years but now, with time on my hands, it had returned, albeit with its tail between its legs.

I guess the poetry has always been there, lying dormant, and I have tended to think lyrically even through the lean years when I was 'in remission'. But barrister-politician Matt Foley's words still resonate … when it comes to the making of poetry, there is no cure.

What I did during those COVID days – meandering around the suburb on slow walks, watching the clouds pass by, taking long baths, listening to music – seemed to finally allow space for the return of poetry.

The poems were there all the time, on the perimeter of my consciousness, like the fox in Ted Hughes's poem *The Thought Fox*, poised at a given moment to spring into full consciousness and onto the page.

I'm not saying what followed is brilliant poetry but many of the poems I have written since then have been published and, if you count quantity as significant, I'm now past the fifty mark of poetic blooms in this late-flowering phase (never mind the quality, feel the width).

A typical poem from this period is *Trying To Imagine Eternity*, written in January 2021, a meditation on spending time at home during COVID.

> *Confined to the premises I pace the place / Like a disgraced aristocrat under house arrest. / I've been home for months. / I try to keep busy reading, taking tea and biscuits. / I even cleaned out a cupboard … / The wind whispers in the trees, bats shriek / And possums wobble along the fence line / As I watch, the sound of a bath being run / In the background, lulling me as evening falls.*

In a verse from the following month, *A Tang Gentleman*, I imagine myself back in the Tang Dynasty, that golden age of Chinese poetry. One of the things I did during COVID was study ancient China, and among the volumes I collected was the *Book of Songs* (*Shijing*) featuring antique poetry that seems as fresh today as it obviously must have been 3000 years ago. Love and longing seem to be perennial.

In my poem *I find myself in a courtyard in old Chang'an. / Standing there, I stroke the whiskers on my chin / And listen to a beautiful girl playing the pipa – / A courtesan? A Princess? / A figure from a scroll.*

And so it goes. The late flowering continued with Nepal-inspired *A View of the Hills* which appeared in *Quadrant* in 2022 and a portion of which I quoted to you in Chapter 12.

I fiddled with form, including that of the sonnet. My special affinity for Shakespeare's is because his rhyme and rhythm schemes are easy to follow and iambic pentameter seems a natural cadence for me. One of the non-Shakespearean variety, *Becoming Dorian*, was inspired by Oscar Wilde, whose grave at Père Lachaise Cemetery in Paris we visited in 2017. Also published by *Quadrant*, in 2023, it explores the subject of ageing.

> *This is me, in a certain light; / In a certain light I look alright. / Not when the sun is far too high / But possibly under a mackerel sky. / I really prefer it overcast, / the dullness hides my ravaged past.*

I set aside an hour after dinner each night to work on these poems, leaving pad and pen and notes on the table on our back deck from where they beckon me each evening. I generally write my poems out in longhand first (that seems to reflect the natural flow of thought), then type them later on my desktop computer and work on them again until they feel right. I don't work on them too much. I find it amusing and frankly unbelievable when I read interviews with some writers who talk of doing twenty drafts. That's called masochism.

I was happy to be writing poetry again. My lust for prose publication had been well and truly satisfied by the publication of *The Kowloon Kid* just before COVID struck and now I felt unfettered to engage in the lyric art again.

With *Hemingway in Brisbane* (another piece published in *StylusLit*), I imagined the great man in Brizzy on a humid day:

> *Summer here is fine until it isn't / you tell yourself you love the heat / but that's not God's honest truth / you watch the sunlight blanch the day / and it reminds you of a summer in Spain / but then you recall you don't want to remember that.*

Most of these compositions tend to reflect a greater appreciation of place and ordinary domestic life, a gift of COVID. Even going out shopping seemed romantic at that time as celebrated in *At the Supermarket.*

> *At the supermarket / The surface of the empty car park / reflects the moon as clouds part … / The people are gone / But the lights are still on: / I wander lonely without a crowd / Pushing a trolley with a wonky wheel …*

Sometimes it's the simple pleasures …

Of course, getting back on the poetry horse one wonders if one should get involved in the ever-present scene again. I've never been entirely able to embrace that scene, though, and it has never entirely been able to embrace me. In fact, there are times when it has actively rejected me. I've nearly had punch-ups at a couple of poetry events. I remember once being shirtfronted by an organizer of the Queensland Poetry Festival. He wasn't happy that I'd complained about being excluded from that year's program.

That could have easily turned to fisticuffs.

I think of Slessor's poem *Sleep*.

Do you give yourself to me utterly, / Body and no-body, flesh and no-flesh … / Yes, utterly.

Well, no, not utterly at all. I have reservations about giving myself over utterly to poetry. It's like a cult. And, as with any cult, if you don't follow it slavishly you're dead to the other members of the cult. Excommunicated.

In spite of this I'm dipping my toes back into the poet-infested waters again – a bit gingerly, it must be admitted, but I have been welcomed. Poets can also be generous and congenial. Did I mention that?

A lot has happened since COVID.

Eventually we all went back to the office and by then there were even fewer of us. One of the first things the editor did after our return was to move us down the back of the newsroom as far away from him as possible. Nothing personal, apparently.

The nice sunlit area (overlooking the car park) where we had previously dwelt was deemed too nice for us members of the magazine staff, it appears, and news journos now sit there. Reporters are always more important than writers, as far as editors are concerned. And maybe that's fair enough but you will never get the best out of your hired staff by marginalizing them.

So there we were in our own little Siberia. *Out here on the perimeter*, as Jim Morrison from The Doors says in that poetic song *The WASP (Texas Radio and the Big Beat)*. He talks about being stoned and immaculate. Well, we were neither, but we were definitely out there on the perimeter and there were no stars, just fluorescent lights and an awful lot of empty desks beyond our little island of writers. Here a feeling of impending doom pervaded the atmosphere.

I took to referring to it as 'the newspaper at the end of the world', with apologies to Douglas Adams for the paraphrase. Looking back on the approaching end of days spent at Bowen Hills also puts me in mind of words from the gospels (Matthew 24:6): 'You will hear of wars and rumours of wars, but see to it that you are not alarmed. Such things must happen, but the end is still to come.'

Indeed, it was.

In my early days at *Brisbane News* the editor, my friend Judithann Guerassimoff, used to encourage me to get my copy in early. When I asked why one day, she replied: 'In case you get hit by a bus.'

'If I get hit by a bus, I'll be dead and I won't give a shit,' I countered.

I thought that was a reasonable response. I never did get hit by a bus back then. But that metaphorical bus was still out there and finally collected me one day in May 2023 when a number of writers on the magazine, myself included, were called into a meeting and told there were changes afoot and, basically, some jobs were surplus to requirements. Most likely ours.

Thus far I had been like one of those cockroaches that will supposedly survive the Apocalypse.

Everyone always assured me that, being so productive and prolific, I would be safe despite the constant rumours of redundancy. I had certainly never put my hand up for a redundancy as many others did, because I liked my job. I loved working at the newspaper. Crazy, huh?

But then that metaphorical bus finally turned into Mayne Road, Bowen Hills, with me in its headlights. I was called in and told my job would no longer exist and that, in fact, there was no need for an

Arts Editor at all. It was golden handshake time and that came as a shock. Features editor Laura Chalmers, in charge of the Saturday magazines nationally (at the time of writing she's the federal Treasurer's wife, in case you're wondering), was as devastated as we were – she was losing a small, some might say vital, component of her staff. We were like family, really. Laura took us all out for a commiserating yum cha to mark our passing.

And then, just like that, I was at home, unemployed, cleaning blinds, listening to Chopin and reggae, wondering what the hell to do with the rest of my life.

Thankfully, it wasn't too long before I was approached to edit the arts website *InReview Queensland,* allied with Solstice Media, which champions independent journalism. I work three days a week using all my arts contacts and am still getting invited to those bloody musicals. Although, with a small group of contributors, I can now send someone else to review them. Thank Christ for that.

COVID taught me how to 'work from home'. So here I am, in my study, surrounded by chinoiserie, my books and my old-fart radio – still tuned to ABC Classic, lulling me through the days.

And I'm writing poetry again. I should have my head read, never mind my poems …

Acknowledgements

First and foremost, thank you to my wife, Sandra McLean and son Hamish Brown for love and support.

I'm very grateful to my first reader, Professor Ross Fitzgerald, who cast his eye over some early chapters and gave excellent advice. Thanks to my publisher Barry Scott for his honesty and support. Working with Barry is always such a pleasure. Thanks to my editor Ken Haley for his forensic attention to the manuscript and his erudition, masterly editing skills and shared sense of humour.

Thanks to Griffith Review. Elements of *In the last days of Joh*, which was published online in *Griffith Review 45*, in July, 2014 appear in the chapter *I'm Brown, From The Sun*.

Thanks also to Gillian Cumming for casting her expert eye over the manuscript.

I am indebted to Nathan Hollier for his tribute *John McLaren Remembered* which appeared in *Overland* in December 2015.

Thanks to the late Bruce Dawe for being a friend and mentor and to the late great Les Murray for supporting my poetry early in the piece. Thanks to Paul Hamra, Founder/Managing Director/ Publisher at Solstice Media for giving me a gig after my life in newspapers and to my colleague Peter Atkinson for introducing us.

And I want to pay tribute to my little writing companion, Sarge, our Maltese Shih-Tzu, who checked on me constantly as I wrote. We miss him terribly.

Acknowledgements

Author's Note

I am indebted to the following publications:

Sometimes Gladness: Collected Poems, 1954-1978 by Bruce Dawe, Longman Cheshire, 1978

Condolences of the Season: Selected Poems by Bruce Dawe, Longman Cheshire, 1978

Giant Night by Anne Waldman, Corinth Books, 1970

The Spice-Box of Earth by Leonard Cohen, Jonathan Cape, 1973

Poetry 1900 to 1965, Editor George MacBeth, Longman with Faber and Faber, 1975

The Intellectual Life by P.G.Hamerton, MacMillan and Co., 1907

The Course of History: Ten Meals That Changed the World by Struan Stevenson. Recipes by Tony Singh MBE, Birlinn, 2017

Selected Poems: Kenneth Slessor, A&R Australian Classics, 2014

Li Po and Tu Fu: Poems selected and translated with an introduction and notes by Arthur Cooper, Penguin Books, 1974

Lunch & Counter Lunch: Poems by Les A. Murray, Angus and Robertson Publishers, 1974

Michael Dransfield: A Retrospective, selected by John Kinsella, University of Queensland Press, 2002.

Collected Verse of John Shaw Neilson, edited and introduced by Margaret Roberts, UWA Publishing, 2012.

Hotel Metropol: A Moscow Legend, by Nikolay Malinin, English Text – Natasha Volpina, Hotel Metropol Moscow, 2015

Phil Brown is a journalist, poet, author, and editor of the independent arts website *InReview Queensland* which features on the website indailyqld.com.au. He was formerly Arts Editor of *The Courier-Mail* and over a four-decade career has written for a range of national and international newspapers and magazines. He has published his poetry widely in the mainstream press and literary journals. He is the author of two books of verse, *Plastic Parables* and *An Accident in the Evening*. His book of humorous travel stories, *Travels with My Angst* was shortlisted for the Arts Queensland Steele Rudd Award at the 2005 Queensland Premier's Literary Awards. *Any Guru Will Do* was the second in his memoir series and the third, *The Kowloon Kid* was shortlisted for *The Courier-Mail* People's Choice Queensland Book of the Year Award in 2020. He lives in Brisbane's inner-north with his wife Sandra McLean.